Praise for *Leaving on Top*

"*Leaving on Top* explores how to deal with the trauma of quitting when you're ahead and stepping up to the challenges of the next stage of life. A must read!"

—Michael O'Neill, Chairman of Citigroup

"*Leaving on Top* shows how bidding farewell is not the end of the line, but, instead, how one can use it to open doors to a rich, new life. This book is a practical and usable road map to dealing with a timely and important subject."

—Tom Leppert, former mayor of Dallas and CEO of Turner Corp.

"Dave Heenan's persuasive message of how and when to call it quits makes *Leaving on Top* both a great and timely read."

—Laurent L. Jacque, Walter B. Wriston Professor of International Finance and Banking, The Fletcher School, Tufts University

"Why do some senior leaders 'get out while they're on top' while others 'overstay their welcome'? Dave Heenan thoughtfully probes this question and comes up with some great ideas that will help all of us gracefully face that inevitable moment."

—Jerry Porras, Lane Professor of Organizational Behavior and Change Emeritus, Stanford Business School and coauthor of *Built to Last*.

Also by David Heenan

Bright Triumphs From Dark Hours

Flight Capital

Double Lives

Co-Leaders
with Warren Bennis

The New Corporate Frontier

The Re-United States of America

Multinational Organization Development
with Howard Perlmutter

LEAVING ON TOP

GRACEFUL EXITS FOR LEADERS

DAVID HEENAN

Foreword by
WARREN BENNIS

NICHOLAS BREALEY
PUBLISHING

BOSTON • LONDON

This edition first published by Nicholas Brealey Publishing, in 2012.

20 Park Plaza   3-5 Spafield Street, Clerkenwell
Boston, MA 02116 USA   London, EC1R4QB, UK
Tel: + 617-523-3801   Tel: +44-(0)-207-239-0360
Fax: + 617-523-3708   Fax: +44-(0)-207-239-0370
                   www.nicholasbrealey.com

Printed in the United States of America

15 14 13 12   1 2 3 4 5

ISBN: 978-1-85788-591-0
E-ISBN: 978-185788-938-3

Library of Congress Cataloging-in-Publication Data

Heenan, David A.
    Leaving on top : graceful exits for leaders / by David Heenan.
      p. cm.
    Includes bibliographical references and index.
      1. Career changes—Case studies. 2. Retirement—Case studies.
3. Leadership—Psychological aspects—Case studies. 4. Career
development—Case studies. 5. Executives—Resignation—Case studies.
6. Executives—Retirement—Case studies. I. Title.

    HF5384.H43 2012
    658.4'09—dc23

                                        2012013322

ABOUT THE AUTHOR

Dᴀᴠɪᴅ Hᴇᴇɴᴀɴ is a trustee of the Estate of James Campbell, one of the nation's largest landowners, as well as a visiting professor at Georgetown University. Formerly, he served as chairman and CEO of Theo. H. Davies & Co., the North American holding company for the Hong Kong–based multinational Jardine Matheson. He has been vice president for academic affairs at the University of Hawai'i and, before that, dean of its business school.

Educated at the College of William and Mary, Columbia University and the University of Pennsylvania, Heenan has served on the faculties of the Wharton School, the Columbia Business School, and the University of Hawai'i. His articles have appeared in such leading publications as the *Harvard Business Review*, the *Sloan Management Review*, the *Wall Street Journal*, the *New York Times*, and the *Christian Science Monitor*. He is author or coauthor of seven other books, including *Bright Triumphs From Dark Hours*, *Flight Capital* and *Double Lives*.

Heenan lives in Honolulu, Hawai'i. For contact information please visit www.LeavingOnTop.com.

To Sheila and the Heenan Clan

Contents

ACKNOWLEDGMENTS

MANY FRIENDS and colleagues contributed to this book. The earliest version of my manuscript was critiqued by Brett Uprichard, who brought a journalist's eye to the process. Warren Bennis, Dick Tomey, Marty Jaskot, and Jerry Porras provided both inspiration and important inputs. I also owe special thanks to Bill Hamilton, who edited three of my previous books. *Leaving on Top* benefited tremendously from his wisdom and rigor. Hats off, too, to Jim Bouton, Bill Snyder, Tom Leppert, Laurent Jacque, Bryce Arrowood, Tadanobu Kashiwa, Hiroshi Yasuda, Robert Witt, Dick Gushman, Zap Zlatoper, Clint Churchill, Marc, Eric, Nozomi, and Jennifer Heenan.

Many thanks to all those who allowed me to tell their stories. Others who assisted include Peter Boylan, John Agee, David Carey, Patricia DelGuidice, Ryan Klinkner, Nick Boyle, and Stephanie Chun.

At Nicholas Brealey Publishing, I had the pleasure of working with a talented team of wonderful professionals: Nick Brealey, Jennifer Delaney, and, earlier, Vanessa Descalzi. Renée Nicholls diligently copyedited the manuscript and saved me from many potential gaffes. Any remaining errors are entirely mine. Thanks, too, to Meryl Moss for marketing and publicity support.

Once again, Martha Miller's competence, diligence, and unfailing good cheer contributed greatly to the book's completion. She was assisted by Jenny Okano and Linda Perrin.

Finally, my wife, Nery, has been at my side throughout this project. As with my earlier books, she organized my interviews and read and commented on successive versions of the manuscript. To this loving and most constructive critic goes a very special *Mahalo*.

David Heenan
Honolulu
June 2012

FOREWORD

⟨⟩

T O LEAVE OR TO STAY? The answer—and the timing—will
vary for every individual. In my five decades of observing leaders in all walks of life, I've found that determining the right moment
to move on remains one of life's most gut-wrenching decisions.
Some people handle this basic human fear skillfully; others don't.

Oprah Winfrey got it right. She mastered the fine art of quitting at the top of her game. After 25 years of ruling daytime television, she gracefully exited *The Oprah Winfrey Show* last fall. "The
show has been my life," she said at the time. "And I love it enough
to know when it's time to say goodbye." Yet, within months, the
most powerful woman in the media took on the biggest risk in
her professional life—launching a new cable venture, OWN, the
Oprah Winfrey Network, for Discovery Communications.

Phasing out of one's comfort zone takes guts and self-
determination, strengths that Ms. Winfrey has exhibited countless times. All of us—at one time or another—have encountered
similar challenges. I used to think I wanted to be a university
president. And for seven long years, I did just that. The problem
was I wanted to *be* a university president, but I didn't want to *do*
a university president's job—a role often described as notoriously
hellish. A year before my seventh and final year, I had a moment
of truth. At four o'clock in the morning—weary of bone and tired
of soul—I found myself muttering, "Either I can't manage this
place, or it's unmanageable." Consequently, I shucked the brass

ring for opportunities that allowed me to achieve my brightest triumphs: to write, teach, and lecture on a wide variety of topics.

Ernest Hemingway once remarked that retirement was the ugliest word in the English language. Peering back through the shining ether of time, I've also become totally opposed to the idea of sitting in a rocking chair. Now, at age 87, I'm working just as hard as I ever have in my life, with more focus and passion around what I believe to be my mission. That's not to say that folks should stay in their jobs forever. Quite the contrary. I think a person should move on every five to seven years. Such movement forces one to keep learning—to get involved in new projects, new ideas, and challenging assignments.

In this well-timed book, David Heenan explores the art of the sweetly timed exit. A well-respected corporate executive, business-school dean, and former Marine, he has encountered his own share of successful sayonaras. It is this authenticity that allows him to lay out a comprehensive road map—a set of directions any of us can follow to confront one of life's most daunting challenges: the graceful exit.

Read this insightful book and you'll discover some simple truths about how and when to move on—as well as when to stay put. In light of the prediction that most people in the contemporary workforce will have eight or nine jobs by their forties, we can expect that moving on will become part of everyday life. Part meditation, part how-to manual, *Leaving on Top* illustrates through the prism of 20 diverse and interesting personalities that bidding adieu is not the end of the world. According to Heenan, it can serve as an important speed bump on the road to success. This is one of the rare books on this delicate—and often only whispered about—topic. It takes a David Heenan to write about this with such a graceful touch.

Warren Bennis
Santa Monica, California
June 2012

"I prefer to leave standing up,
like a well-mannered guest at a party."

—*Leontyne Price*

CHAPTER 1

TIME'S UP

"When the horse dies, dismount."

—ENGLISH PROVERB

People from the Southern parts of the United States talk about having to make "hurtin'" decisions: choices that tear at the soul. None is more painful than deciding when to leave on top—when to leave a beloved calling, whether it's business, entertaining, athletics, healing, or winning hearts and minds. The naked truth is that there comes a time when the door will slam on everyone. No one really wants to pack it in. And yet, everyone does.

"You've got to know when to hold 'em, know when to fold 'em, know when to walk away and know when to run," goes Kenny Rogers's timeworn song. *Leaving on Top* explores the psychological drama of quitting when you're ahead versus clinging to a role in which you are no longer effective and tarnishing a distinguished career. For the past several years, I have been scrutinizing dozens of traumatic, life-altering sayonaras—and how men and women of every stripe confront them. Some handle this basic human fear with dignity and candor; others don't. Through their gripping stories, you will better understand how to come to terms with one of life's most formidable challenges: *the graceful exit*.

In what Lance Armstrong called his "dream scenario," the embattled Texan would finish the 2010 Tour de France on the Champs-Élysées in Paris wearing the famous yellow jersey, or *maillot jaune*, thereby reinvigorating his bully pulpit to promote the worldwide fight against cancer. That dream gained credence the year before when the seven-time Tour winner re-emerged from a three-and-a-half-year retirement to capture an astonishing third-place finish in cycling's ultimate contest. However, at 38, he knew that his comeback was a gamble. Up to that point, the oldest rider to win the three-week, 2,000-plus-mile suffer-a-thon was Firmin Lambót, who had won it nearly a century ago in 1922 at the age of 36. Anything less than victory, teammates warned, could tarnish Armstrong's legacy.

Yet the aging icon portrayed his return to biking's most popular race as more than preserving the Lance brand or mollifying the ego of an aging athlete who missed the spotlight. After all, many other champions—Michael Jordan, George Foreman, Dara Torres, and Martina Navratilova—had come back successfully from retirement. Steadfastly denying taking performance enhancers and breaking his sport's rules, Armstrong was betting that his competitive fire and athletic experience could fend off the attack of younger legs. But it was not to be.

On a sweltering July day, Armstrong's dream was dashed after he crashed three times on the race's first foray into the sun-baked French Alps. Bloodied and bandaged, he plummeted to 39th place overall.

"My Tour is finished," the controversial superstar and cancer survivor lamented. "I've had lots of years where it's been very different, so I'm not going to complain." Armstrong's disastrous day in the mountains marked the end of an era: his days of the grueling two-wheeled challenge were over.

For centuries, youth and creativity have been inextricably linked. Youth brings vigor and vision. "The time of enterprise and hope," Samuel Johnson called it. That piercing truth is reinforced in today's culture, which facetiously calls the last trimester of life the "golden years." Sooner or later, all of us must face—like the oven bird of Robert Frost's poem—the problem of "what to make of a diminished thing." We all have a shelf life where we begin to lose our spark—and we wonder how to exit with grace.

Reflecting on the winter of his own distinguished career, John Updike noted that the "memories, impressions and emotions from your first twenty years on earth are most writers' main material; little that comes afterward is quite so rich. By the age of forty, you have probably mined the purest veins of this precious lode; after that, creativity is a matter of sifting the leavings."

Many great writers, musicians, physicists, mathematicians, and inventors tend to start strong and peak early. Certainly, wünderkinds often flame out prematurely in Updike's publishing world, where youth is almost always served. J. D. Salinger wrote *The Catcher in the Rye* when he was 32, and then went into seclusion. Harper Lee, at 34, stopped publishing after her Pulitzer Prize–winning masterpiece, *To Kill a Mockingbird*, one of the most beloved books in all of America's literary canon. Leo Tolstoy, too, wrote no big novels after *Anna Karenina* (completed 33 years before his death). In each instance, their creative stuff had been snuffed.

Yet, examples abound of other writers who were late to the spotlight, finding fame in their senior years. The novelist Thomas Hardy became a full-time poet in his late 50s and wrote what many feel is his greatest poem at the age of 61. Alex Haley's Pulitzer Prize–winning *Roots* was published when he was 55, and he had retired from the U.S. Coast Guard. After 30 years of teaching high school English, Frank McCourt was shocked to learn that, at 66, he had written a bestseller, *Angela's Ashes*, about his early childhood in poverty-stricken Ireland. It took even more decades before 96-year-old Harry Bernstein achieved literary success with a memoir, *The Invisible Wall*, profiling his own miserable childhood in an English mill town.

Creative output, therefore, does not crest and ebb at any predetermined time, and a decline in productivity is far from inevitable. Besides writers, many other individuals have fired their creative spark in their advanced years. Grandma [Anna Mary] Moses first picked up a paintbrush at 76 and was still painting when she was 100. Martha Graham was a working choreographer well into her 90s. Frank Lloyd Wright completed the Guggenheim Museum in New York at 91. Perennially cool jazz legend Dave Brubeck, now in his 90s, still plays before full houses. As actress Bette Davis famously put it, "Old age ain't for sissies!"

Furthermore, a growing body of research suggests that the fall of the creative curve can be postponed. Studies of brain plasticity—the lifelong ability of our gray matter to adapt to changing demands—are proving that our creative horizons need not narrow with age. "We never lose our potential to learn new things as we grow older," says Gay Hanna, head of the National Center for Creative Aging. "In fact, we can master new skills and be creative all our lives." What's more, the brains of people in their 50s and 60s apparently work better in many ways than those of younger adults. The brain actually feeds on novelty, and studies show that cognitive ills can be delayed—even prevented—by taking on new mental challenges, such as learning a new language, reading a difficult book, or tackling a new pursuit.

Painters, writers, composers, and sculptors—the gamut of creative types—work until they die. They often find life's best rewards late in the game. Works created by Paul Cezanne in his 60s, for example, command fifteen times the price of paintings he did as a young man. Even the award-winning Updike, who died in 2009 at 76, conceded that "an aging writer has the not insignificant satisfaction of a shelf of books behind him, . . . and the pleasure of bookmaking remains creation's giddy bliss." Still, the stereotype of aging and diminished productivity persists.

Confronting the final act to a productive career is also compounded by a culture in which one's profession is a real-life passport to identity, to selfhood, to self-esteem. "You are what you do," says management guru Warren Bennis. "If one leaves, one is nowhere, like a character in a Beckett play, without role, without the props of office, without ambience or setting." For many leaders their whole persona is wrapped up in their job. Their partners, staff, and others are their community. As a result, many equate saying goodbye with euthanasia and castration—and hang on too long. But how long is too long? "When you no longer have some snap in your garters," geriatric U.S. Sen. Russell B. Long once quipped.

On his 90th birthday, Justice Oliver Wendell Holmes gave a radio address in which he quoted a line of ancient Latin poetry: "Death plucks my ear and says, 'Live—I am coming.'" In grappling with their mortality, some would-be Methuselahs refuse to grow old without a fight—seeking out age-defying aids, from hair plugs and Harleys to Botox and little blue pills.

Others demonstrate that growing old and maintaining competence aren't mutually exclusive. Crusty codgers like Warren Buffett, Clint Eastwood, Betty White, and Sandra Day O'Connor are able to resist the gravitational pull of time, maintaining their enthusiasm and sharpness. They seem to get better with age and stay as professionally and socially engaged as possible. They refuse to ride into the sunset—and why should they? But they are true outliers.

For most of us, time does not move with merciful slowness. "No matter how you sugarcoat it," Bennis adds, "aging forces us to confront the essential tragedy of our species." While medical technology and genetic enhancements are moving individuals to a longer life (longevity has doubled since the mid-19th century), it's hard to reverse the clock. Like it or not, the 70s represents the end, not the beginning. Average life expectancy remains 78. It's rising, but not as fast, perhaps, as our expectations.

As we shall see, balancing the push and pull between timetables and dreams is an inexact science. It can be a mistake to call it quits too early, and it can be easy—as well as self-defeating—to stay too long. The trick to the graceful exit, says columnist and septuagenarian Ellen Goodman, who retired after 46 years of deadlines about social change, "begins with the vision to recognize when a job, a life stage, a relationship is over—and to let it go. . . . It involves a sense of the future, a belief that every exit line is an entry, that we are moving on rather than moving out."

"Don't retire, retread!" advises Robert Otterbourg, author of *Retire & Thrive*. He tells folks to shun the forbidding signposts: should have, would have, and could have. Moving on, as Goodman suggests, is not life's final chapter, but simply the end of one phase of adulthood and the beginning of another.

It's certainly too soon to order a coffin for Ed Koch, the former congressman and mayor of New York. Since leaving Gracie Mansion in 1989, the peripatetic octogenarian has had several lives: lawyer, talk-show host, columnist, movie reviewer, university lecturer, author (*I'm Not Done Yet!*) and TV judge on *The People's Court*. "It suits an old workaholic like me just fine," Koch writes of his many roles. Polymaths like the no-nonsense Koch forge new highways of their own choosing. His "last hurrah" is his current crusade to reform New York state government, a task many have tried—and failed—to accomplish.

"God writes straight with crooked lines" goes a Portuguese proverb, meaning the oddest happenings often make sense only in the long run. Leaders contemplating leaving on top recognize that the topology of life is ever changing. For them, the whole-life experience is an exploration, a journey of self-discovery. They would agree with the novelist, poet, and composer Paul Bowles, who said, "The point of life is to have fun, if there is any point at all. Enjoyment is what life should provide."

The central decision to bid *adios* to a certain position, therefore, should always begin with this question: *Will I enjoy more—and contribute more—today and tomorrow than yesterday?* If not, the timing is right to enter the next stage of life.

Career transitions are never easy. After being stripped of his cycling titles for doping and banned from competition, Lance Armstrong, at 40, faces the prospect of a tarnished legacy. Drug cheat or persecuted hero? Although his time is up as a professional athlete, his primary focus remains his high-profile attack on cancer, as attested by more than 70 million Livestrong wristbands. He has become an established celebrity outside sports. "Here's a guy who hangs out with Matthew McConaughey, Bono and Ben Stiller," said Neal Rogers, managing editor of *VeloNews* magazine. "A lot of people don't equate Lance Armstrong with athleticism anymore."

Nonetheless, jettisoning a longstanding career and heading into uncharted waters takes tremendous drive and confidence. Graceful exiters are highly motivated. Their spunk and spirit of self-renewal pays off. People who are able to reinvent themselves "have a way of reducing stress and of assuming that they're not so bound up in the power games of life that they're highly vulnerable to disappointments and setbacks," says Abraham Zaleznik, distinguished psychoanalyst and professor emeritus at Harvard Business School. "They have something more going for them."

These intrepid adventurers want to stretch their limits. Rather than being shackled to the past, they are on a never-ending search for higher mountains to climb and a bigger canvas to impact people. J. B. Fuqua, founder and former chairman of the multibillion-dollar Fuqua Industries, long advised business bigwigs to explore second careers to escape creeping corporate boredom. Having served four terms in the Georgia Legislature, the self-made entrepreneur combined business with philanthropy, becoming one of Duke University's biggest benefactors. "Becoming a CEO is not the end of the learning curve," he told his corporate colleagues. "It's more like a new beginning."

Fuqua brought a panoply of assets, including self-awareness and independence, that served both him and his multiple roles well. That kind of self-possession and personal equilibrium guarantees happiness, regardless of the métier an individual may once have pursued.

Similarly, Winston Churchill, arguably the greatest figure of the last century, long advocated the merits of exploring virgin territory. "The creation of new forms of interest are a policy of first importance to a public man," he wrote. A Nobel Prize–winning author, a mesmerizing orator, and an accomplished artist, Churchill was the quintessential Renaissance man. He made it his life's mission to reinvent himself. Beyond balancing the affairs of state, "the Last Lion," as William Manchester called him, insisted that personal experimentation was the true test of happiness.

Of course, the nature of work also influences when to call it a day. "The more spiritual the work," suggests author and talk-show host Michael Medved, "the better the chance for rewards that last a lifetime. The more physical the focus, on the other hand, the quicker the decline from youthful peaks."

For an athlete, time is rarely an asset. Boxers Rocky Marciano and Oscar De La Hoya, golfers Annika Sörenstam and Lorena Ochoa, and Hall of Fame gridders Jim Brown and Barry Sanders sidestepped the press of time—and left at the top of their game. Conversely, Muhammad Ali, Willie Mays, Joe Namath, and, more recently, Brett Favre ran out of gas and clung stubbornly to their fading careers. Many sports heroes accustomed to rigorous competition and fixated on adulation have a devilish time stepping out of the limelight once the cheering stops. "Nothing touches the thrill of the crowd roaring for you just after winning a boxing match," explains former heavyweight champion George Foreman. "Not even a billion-dollar paycheck."

Performers, as much as athletes, are slaves to the flesh—and the crowd. British conductor Sir Colin Davis and actor/director Sir John Gielgud, both octogenarians, continue to take their achievements to unprecedented heights and manage to perform on an astonishingly high note. Others, like Elvis Presley, Frank Sinatra, Bob Dylan, Rudolf Nureyev, and Arturo Toscanini, represent the all-too-familiar syndrome of those who hang on too long, leaving their fans with lackluster memories.

For many, letting go of a successful career means change, and such transitions are never easy. "Often they're frightening and painful," says Martin Groder, a Chapel Hill, North Carolina, psychiatrist and business consultant. "But on the other side of the struggle is a sense of rebirth and renewal." Therefore, those nearing the final role should start anew while they're still hale enough to face new challenges.

Far too many people, though, seek solace in the familiar. Rather than explore new directions, they cling to the safe, risk-free environments that can become self-constructed prisons. Eventually, these people lose their capacity for self-renewal, costing them soul and substance. Postponing the inevitable, they bury themselves deeper and deeper in their work, depriving themselves of emotionally rewarding experiences. Individuals so ensnared soon discover that the workplace, while a good servant, can become a bad master.

"Man cannot discover new oceans unless he has courage to lose sight of the shore," wrote André Gide. Graceful exiters are undaunted risk-takers. For years, Sony Corporation chairman and chief executive officer Norio Ohga had a rich life outside the company as a jet pilot, a calligrapher, an operatic tenor, and an orchestra conductor. Instead of haunting Sony's offices in Tokyo, he chose to fly around the world pursuing his musical interests. Not your average salaryman, this managerial maestro tapped his baton in leading symphonies on almost every continent and later chaired the Tokyo Philharmonic. When he left the top slot at Sony, Ohga simply rekindled his musical passions—and never looked back.

Similarly, astronaut Sally Ride jettisoned a promising career at NASA to explore new frontiers. After two trips in space and several fast-track management stints, the thirty-six-year old space pioneer left the space agency on top—assuming a series of opportunities: professor, physicist, author, and entrepreneur. "I have a tendency to be fascinated and totally involved in something for five or six years, and then look around for other new, interesting initiatives to dive into," she told me. Her last plunge: Sally Ride Science, a venture that provides training and career opportunities for young women interested in science, technology, engineering, and math.

In every instance, these enterprising personalities wanted to eliminate the nagging feeling that their lives could be more fulfilling. After 18 years as a practicing attorney, Ron Bass turned to screenwriting, penning the Oscar-winning *Rain Man* and films such as *Amelia*, *The Joy Luck Club*, and *Memories of a Geisha*. "I was a good lawyer, a negotiator. It was interesting and challenging," the Harvard Law School grad said. "But for me, the pinnacle was something allowing me to make the business of living—the business of what I do all day—exploring the meaning of life."

Of course, not everyone can be a modern-day da Vinci. What is a graceful exit for some can be a bumpy road for others. "Don't give up your day job," warned the late Steve Allen, reflecting on his own paradoxical career. The actor, TV show host, jazz pianist, composer of more than 6,000 songs, and writer of 48 books—as well as countless short stories, poems, and films—understood the downside of experimentation. "We ought not to make a firm commitment to a new field," he said, "unless we have an actual aptitude for it." Not everyone has the natural ability, independent of drive and intelligence, to forge a fresh identity. And pipe dreams can lead to disappointment.

More and more professionals, though, are coming to view a career as but one among many experiences. Wise leaders today define success not in terms of vocation, but in terms of happiness and personal fulfillment. To accept any other definition is to lose the control we have over our destiny. These bravehearts want to branch out after years of single-mindedness, shedding their primary careers to feed their souls. Getting their second wind, they want to experience the liberating effects of changing skins and shaping their own renaissance.

Yet leaving the C-suite is often especially troublesome. Few business moguls are in a hurry to consider succession. Many exhaust their welcome, hanging on well past their expiration dates. They dread the future, sensing that steady doses of golf or bridge in retirement aren't going to match the satisfaction of command. Shakespeare explained their reasoning simply: "How sweet it is to wear the crown."

But the emperor's crown today isn't nearly as comfortable as it used to be. We are witnessing a populist backlash against number ones. The wear and tear of the treadmill economy has made public lynchings commonplace, as top guns rise and fall with each business cycle. In 2012, CEO tenure continues to plummet. Almost one in seven of the world's largest companies will show their chief executives the door. As corporate chieftains have lost the aura of infallibility, it's become almost impossible for them to dig in their heels and enjoy significant longevity. "Many don't last as long as a refrigerated fruitcake," writes *USA Today*'s Del Jones.

Frozen in fear, imperious leaders try to postpone the inevitable. With feet of clay, they cling to their jobs well past the point of diminishing returns, refusing to give up the reins. Recall Occidental Petroleum's Armand Hammer, Peter Grace of W. R. Grace, Leona Helmsley (the "Queen of Mean"), and the legions of decrepit Japanese bosses. Long-term CEOs, often intoxicated by power and position, forget that, in the Greek myth, Narcissus wastes away—unable to avert his gaze from the pond reflecting his beautiful, but doomed, features. These antique autocrats remained embalmed in their jobs—not only tarnishing their legacies but also depriving their organizations of vital new blood.

Others, however, challenge the increasingly outdated notion that great enterprises are the lengthened shadow of a Great Man or Woman. Take Microsoft's Bill Gates. Although rock-star famous, Gates understood that much of the software giant's unprecedented success was due to a cadre of highly talented professionals working together to get important things done. A decade ago, he had no problem turning the reins over to his first-rate deputy Steve Ballmer. As Microsoft's president and top tactician, Ballmer was responsible for everything from getting the first Windows operating system shipped to keeping the company supplied with top-notch personnel. "Microsoft could lose Bill Gates," said former staffer Adrian King, "but it could not survive without Steve's sheer will to succeed. That's what makes the company unique."

In the 21st century, Microsoft and other vanguard organizations are in the business of ideas. A superb mentor, Gates knew full well that if he were to exit gracefully, Microsoft would need a deep cache of gifted coleaders like Ballmer. In many respects, one of Gates's greatest legacies may be the way he so carefully selected, then nurtured, the company's future leadership.

In the course of studying similar transitions, I was constantly reminded that there are many ways to say goodbye. Leaders—unlike solids, fluids, and gases—are anything but uniform and predictable. Because every exit strategy is situational, I chose to examine a wide range of extraordinary individuals in a cross-section of disciplines. Some mastered the art of moving on; others didn't. From these diverse portrayals, you'll discover the roadmaps for negotiating this difficult terrain. I'll explore each of these guides for leaving on top in the next ten chapters and amplify them in Chapter 12.

These inspiring and dramatic stories are for leaders in all walks of life—people who want to be prepared for the uncertain, but potentially invigorating, next stage of their lives. As you will see from the pages that follow, our characters and their callings are as different as chalk and cheese. We'll look at political patriarchs, men and women who seem to have great reluctance hanging up their spurs. From the late U.S. Sen. Strom Thurmond and Sen. Robert Byrd to the current "Two Dans"—Inouye and Akaka—from my home state of Hawaii, we'll see why the Halls of Congress often appears to be a surrogate nursing home, where seniority can become counterproductive. Appointed public officials, too, can wear out their welcome. J. Edgar Hoover, Adm. Hyman Rickover, and Gen. Douglas MacArthur typify civil servants who found it painful to hand over the joystick.

Less perilous day jobs involve "individual contributors"—professionals, for the most part, doctors, lawyers, professors, and others whose skills often grow with age. Among those we'll dissect is Dr. Michael DeBakey, once described as the nation's greatest surgeon, who lived to 99 rebuilding human hearts. Creative types, too, tend to enjoy prolonged fertility. Although, as noted earlier, some writers, artists, and entertainers fizzle out in early or mid-career, many have found that even a battered heart can still beat strongly. We'll compare those who escaped with dignity (Johnny Carson, for example) with others who overstayed their welcome (Carson's sidekick, Ed McMahon).

But first, we'll consider how those running some of the biggest companies left on top. From Howard Schultz and Anne Mulcahy to Richard Kelley and John Calley, there are many examples of

CEOs who knew their exit lines—retiring on their own terms and reinventing themselves with renewed vigor. Conversely, we'll look at several sad souls who refused to relinquish command and became figures of ridicule, even contempt.

Folks toiling in big-time sports—athletes, coaches, even broadcasters—have their own set of issues fading into the sunset. We'll look at a wide range of superstars who plied their talents at the highest level—Olympians Eric Heiden and Dara Torres, boxers George Foreman and Mike Tyson, high-profile coaches John Gagliardi and Joe Gibbs, and announcers Vin Scully and Bob Uecker.

In the course of my research, I found that, however they differ, most people usually take one of four distinct paths to this delicate endgame.

- **Timeless Wonders** treat moving on as synonymous with an early death. With their skills very much intact, white-haired sages like Henry Kissinger, Brent Scowcroft, Paul Volcker, and Lee Kuan Yew have much to offer—continuing to dispense wisdom well into their 80s and 90s. These über-oldsters feel absolutely no need to call it quits.

  "I know if I rest," says Singapore parliamentarian Yew, "I'll slide downhill fast. Those who believe I'll go into a permanent retirement should have their heads examined." Putting out to pasture also is not in the cards for 82-year-old Warren Buffett. "I love running Berkshire Hathaway," he says. "And if enjoying life promotes longevity, then Methuselah's record is in jeopardy." Despite battling prostate cancer, the Sage of Omaha recently identified his potential (but unnamed) successor, while reaffirming that he has no plans to step down.
- **Aging Despots** also want to stay in the game. But unlike timeless wonders, they are clearly past their prime. Reluctant to leave the spotlight and turn the reins over to the

younger generation, these geriatric Goliaths don't—or won't—go easily. Though they should be wise enough to know better, many feel they are owed immortality. On the global stage, Stalin and Sukarno, Mao and Marcos, are just a few examples. More recently, there are former strongmen Egypt's Hosni Mubarak, Tunisia's Zine El Abidine Ben Ali, and Libya's Muammar al-Gaddafi. These narcissistic dinosaurs don't go gently. No graceful exits for them. As the famous philosopher Charlie Chan explained, "He who rides on tiger cannot dismount."

- **Comeback Kids** represent people who departed, but later seek a return engagement. In some instances, they represent founders who want to restore their enterprises to their former glory. Encore executives include Apple's Steve Jobs, Starbucks's Schultz, and financier Charles Schwab. In other cases, hyperkinetic comebackers "unretire" for another rush of adrenaline. Football coaches Bill Snyder, Bobby Ross, Joe Gibbs, and Dick Vermeil boomeranged back for a late-career rally. Still others resurface for economic reasons. Witness the platoon of over-the-hill boxers—Joe Louis, Sugar Ray Robinson, Mike Tyson, and Evander Holyfield—who blew multimillion-dollar fortunes and returned to the ring in search of another payday.

- **Graceful Exiters** leave on top. They quit when they're ahead, moving on to something as opposed to moving away from something. Like our earlier examples—Norio Ohga, Sally Ride, and Ron Bass—these eclectic types believe that lifestyles can—and should—be elastic. Leaving the confines of an original career, they are on an emotional jailbreak to explore a broader sweep of interests.

"Life, as I see it, is not a location but a journey," Henry Ford once observed. "Everything is in flux and is meant to be. We may live at the same number on a street, but it's never the same person who lives there." Typically, a change of address involves immersing oneself in a totally new pursuit. Former Dallas Cowboy quarterback Roger Staubach, for instance, parlayed his stardom on the football field into a highly successful real estate career. His Staubach Company grew to a national powerhouse before he sold it to behemoth Jones Lang LaSalle in 2008 for $613 million.

Similarly, with 85 tournament victories worldwide and a place in the L.P.G.A. and World Golf Halls of Fame, Annika Sörenstam earned a restful retirement when she left competitive golf. But today, she is involved in more ventures than ever, with a golf academy, a charitable foundation, a clothing line, a wine label, a fragrance, and an international golf course design business.

People like Staubach and Sörenstam understand, in the most visceral way, the value of a personal makeover. They are the graceful exiters.

Nowadays, the longevity revolution brought about by modern science offers everyone an opportunity to chart new horizons. As life expectancy increases, so does career expectancy. Consequently, it's time to retire conventional definitions of "retirement." "Retire," in fact, stems from a French word with the bleak meaning of "withdrawing" or going into "isolation." To most people, the term conjures the frightening image of an early demise.

"Retirement is the enemy of longevity," claims 89-year-old David Murdock, the energetic owner of Dole Food Co. and Castle & Cooke. "It just isn't in my vocabulary. I think the excitement of life is creativity—creating things and making things happen."

Welcome, then, to the era of "un-retirement." Whether by choice or necessity, no one touts sitting in a rocking chair anymore—the hammock and the shuffleboard are passé. Adventurous leaders are not the retiring kind. They aren't ready to clock out.

Rather than vegetate, they view bidding farewell not as the end of the line, but as a path of continuity.

"The delight of opening a new pursuit imparts the novelty of youth even to old age," wrote British Prime Minister Benjamin Disraeli. Properly orchestrated, the ability to molt, to slide effortlessly from one life to another and leave on top, can provide exciting new opportunities along with a renewed sense of identity, structure, and community. The chapters that follow offer a framework for thinking about the next season of life—in clear, unemotional terms.

Leaving on top, Anne Mulcahy handed over the reins at Xerox to talented successor Ursula Burns.

Hollywood King Kong John Calley took periodic breaks from the movie business to recharge his batteries.

CHAPTER 2

LETTING GO

"Beauty lies at the top of the mountain."

—Mao Tse-tung

"ALL MEN ARE LIABLE TO ERROR," philosopher John Locke once wrote. "And most are, in many points, by passion or interest, under temptation to it." It is shocking how often those in power in organizational life are tempted to err by not leaving the stage or by failing to nurture superstar replacements.

Of course, egos drive people in every occupation. Power-hungry CEOs resist any diminution of command and find the prospect of stepping down downright depressing. These imperious personalities cling to their titles, determined to drive away any adjunct who begins to look too strong. Take, for instance, Sandy Weill, who brilliantly transformed a small Baltimore-based commercial lender into the behemoth Citigroup. His success unraveled with the firing of his loyal lieutenant, Jamie Dimon, the one-time darling of Wall Street and chairman and CEO of JPMorgan Chase.

In retrospect, Weill got high on celebrity in a culture where the urge to be the star often leads to the decline of institutions of all types. "Celebrity is a mask that eats into the face," warned John Updike. Pretentious bigwigs who behave like sultans, refuse to exit gracefully, and drive away potential replacements inflict irreparable damage on their organizations. No one was more articulate on this subject than Peter Drucker.

"CEOs are just hired hands," he reminded us. "They are servants of the organization. It's their duty to subordinate their likes, wishes, preferences to the welfare of the institution." Drucker's enlightened view of leadership reflects the current backlash against the once-popular image of the CEO as an indispensable titan surrounded by a pack of pygmies.

Despite the shift away from the Great Man theory of leadership, some high-powered executives still believe they will live forever. As they age, remaining in the game is Job One: it's their identity, and they refuse to leave on top.

Failing to see themselves with clear eyes, some CEOs look for evidence that confirms their urge to hold on, says Richard Staelin, a professor at Duke University's Fuqua School of Business, who studies "confirmation bias." Among the telltale signs that it's time to leave: poor financial results, slumping stock prices, health issues, family concerns, and the like.

With the global economy in the tank, the days of long-tenured chiefs are becoming increasingly rare. Once a sinecure, the C-suite has become a revolving door, as boards and shareholders become ever more demanding of CEOs. Witness the recent departures at Barclays, Yahoo, British Petroleum, UBS, Avon, and Best Buy. Nowadays, heading an important organization is like being one of the kings in ancient Crete who had extraordinary power and access to every perk and pleasure—but only for a time. After his year of absolute power, the king was put to death.

For contemporary CEOs, the pay and the perks are unbeatable while they are in office, but they can't count on being in office for long. According to consulting firm Booz & Co., as the tenure of the average chief executive becomes shorter and shorter (6.6 years in 2010 versus 8.1 a decade ago), the need for timely exits and succession planning becomes even more crucial.

"The trend is clear," writes *Fortune* satirist Stanley Bing. "It's now virtually impossible for a demented, high-profile narcissist to hold the position of CEO." His choice? "One who is willing to be trustworthy, loyal, helpful, friendly, courteous, kind, obedient, cheerful, thrifty, brave, clean, and reverent to his craven board, and then, when it's over, take his $100 million package and fade away in polite silence."

Anne Mulcahy, sans the exit package, would make Bing happy. She achieved what many corporate leaders find impossible: leaving on top and at the time of their choosing. Mulcahy spent her career transforming lethargic, scandal-riddled Xerox into a profitable, highly respected digital powerhouse. But in 2009, after 33 years at the Stamford, Connecticut, company, she stepped down as CEO and seamlessly handed over the reins to her deputy, Ursula Burns, and left the board a year later.

Growing up in East Rockaway, New York, Mulcahy never dreamed of a desk in the corner office. Her father was an English professor turned editor; her mother, a stay-at-home parent who handled the family finances. As the only daughter among five children, Mulcahy never backed off confronting her siblings. "She wouldn't let us exclude her from anything, even shooting basketball hoops," recalls her oldest brother, Thomas Dolan, later president of Xerox's global solutions group. "Dinnertime in our house was a time for debating ideas, and Anne was as outspoken as the rest of us."

"My upbringing was my greatest advantage," Mulcahy told *The New York Times*. "I was comfortable around men, and I learned to love contention." That said, she enrolled in the all-women Marymount College in Tarrytown, New York. After her junior year, she managed a 15-month stint with government-run Vista, working with preschoolers, prisoners, and juvenile delinquents in impoverished parts of rural Kentucky. She then returned to Marymount, graduating in 1974 with a degree in English and journalism.

Her venture in the world of work brought her to Boston, where she applied for a sales position at Xerox. A few years later, she met and later married Joe Mulcahy, a regional sales manager for Xerox in New York. He retired from the company in 1987.

During the early '90s, Mulcahy served in a variety of sales, marketing, and human resource positions. In 1997, she was promoted to chief staff officer, responsible for coordinating a large swath of Xerox functions. The next year, she became corporate senior vice president. Prior to that, she oversaw customer operations for Latin America, Europe, Africa, and Asia.

"Every time I was tempted to leave, they'd find something interesting," Mulcahy says. One of the highest-ranking women at Xerox, she became president of the company's $6 billion general markets group in 1999. A year later, she was elevated to president and chief operating officer of the entire enterprise.

"Anne is the best line operator we have," Xerox chairman and CEO Paul Allaire said at the time. The troubled document-processor needed plenty of operating help. The company was in terrible shape, losing hundreds of millions of dollars, with its stock approaching single digits. Hewlett-Packard, Canon, and Ricoh were nibbling away at its markets. An earlier attempt to overhaul Xerox's once-powerful sales organization had flamed out, and the Securities and Exchange Commission (SEC) was fighting the company over its questionable accounting practices.

Mulcahy threw herself into the fray, hitting the office as early as 6 A.M., rarely out before 7 P.M., often working through the weekend. In short order, she won plaudits for reinvigorating the sales force, pruning business losers, bringing new products to market, and slashing costs.

In 2001, Xerox's board chose the 47-year-old veteran to lead the company. Six months later, it added the chairwoman's title. Mulcahy candidly admitted she had never planned or expected to be the top gun, let alone one who was asked to reverse the company's fortunes.

Unlike Athena emerging from the head of Zeus, Mulcahy didn't arrive fully formed. "It was like being drafted into a war," she said. "I certainly hadn't been groomed to become a CEO. I didn't have a very sophisticated financial background, and I took the position feeling equal parts of excitement and dread." Nor did her promotion ease the market's unease about the company. Its stock plummeted 15 percent on the day of her appointment.

When Mulcahy took office, Xerox was teetering on bankruptcy. It had piled up almost $19 billion in debt and only $100 million in cash. Moody's rated its bonds as junk. Customers remained unhappy, employees were demoralized, and the economy had started to sputter. On top of that, the SEC continued to press ahead with its protracted probe of accounting improprieties.

But the new boss proved relentless in pursuing a fix. Recognizing her lack of financial expertise, she enlisted the treasurer's office to tutor her on the finer points of finance. Although many outsiders advised her to declare bankruptcy and cut research and development, the tough, independent thinker refused to do so. Instead, she quickly addressed the firm's liquidity issues, raising $2.5 billion in cash. Through a "back to basics" approach and a renewed focus on operating efficiency, she cut capital expenditures, attacked Xerox's bloated infrastructure, and trimmed its total debt. Just eight months into her tenure as chief executive, she settled the company's lengthy SEC investigation, agreeing to pay a $10 million fine.

To gain support for her no-nonsense recovery plan, Mulcahy personally met with the top 100 executives. "I spent the first 90 days on planes, traveling to various offices and listening to anyone who had a perspective on what was wrong with the company," she recalls. In return for their full and frank criticism, Mulcahy demanded a 100 percent commitment to her bold turnaround. "I gave people a choice to make," she said. "Either roll up your sleeves and go to work—or leave Xerox." Only two of the top 100 bailed.

Progress was almost immediate. Despite the continued economic slump, Mulcahy led the company to a profitable year in 2002, its first since 1999. While the improvement failed to buoy its stock, Wall Street pundits were optimistic about the firm's future. "I give Xerox the best chance of all of my fallen angels for turning itself around," said Carol Levenson, a director of the corporate bond-research firm Gimme Credit, at the time.

The upshot was that Xerox, though still weak, was off the critical list. "We've got a lot more to do," Mulcahy said. "But finally, we're not in crisis."

The tenacious leader pressed on, inspired, she contends, by reading her favorite book, Caroline Alexander's *The Endurance*, which chronicles how, against all odds, adventurer Ernest Shackleton rescued his men in an Antarctic ice storm in 1916. She remained determined to create an organization that would march into the 21st century, happy with what it could offer customers and employees. Continuing to make sharp staff and business cutbacks, she sold off part ownership of Fuji Xerox, restructured Xerox PARC, its Palo Alto research center, and farmed out much of its manufacturing to Flextronics International, a Singapore-based outsourcer. Along the way, she began shifting the iconic document company away from copying and printing to becoming the leader in managing digital content.

"Don't defend yourself against the inevitable," she says. Rally the troops and customers to a new vision that will result in reinvention. To that, she also warns about the dangers of isolation, the undoing of many CEOs. "It is imperative that leaders surround themselves with at least a few good critics," she says. "People around you want to please. If you're not careful, you can begin to delude yourself and lose touch."

Keeping close to her customers and employees, Mulcahy soon won converts. By 2006, Xerox was earning annual profits of more than $1 billion, prompting *Money* magazine to term it "the great turnaround story of the post-crash era."

Although the company was firmly stabilized, Mulcahy recognized the fine line between gratification and doubt. "I'm more motivated by fear of failure than a desire to succeed," she told Stanford Business School students. "My experience at Xerox has taught me that crisis is a powerful motivator. It intensifies your focus, your competitiveness, your relentless desire to attain best-in-class status. I want to do everything I can to make sure that we don't lose that now that we're back on track."

Mulcahy remained focused. Under her tenure, in four years Xerox's debt levels fell from 10 times its equity just before she took the reins to less than two times, while red ink continued to turn black. Magazine profiles lauded her as a model CEO, commending her for Xerox's painful turnaround. *Chief Executive* selected her CEO of the year in 2008.

After 33 years at Xerox—eight in command—Mulcahy stepped down from the top post in 2008 and left the board the following year. "To retire at the age of 57 is a gift," she told *Bloomberg Businessweek*. "[But] to stay around until I was 65 would be a disservice to Xerox, a disservice to my successor."

Her handpicked replacement, company president Ursula Burns, had been the heir apparent for some time. "For the better part of the past decade, she has been at my side helping to turn Xerox around and, more importantly, transform Xerox for a new era," Mulcahy told company shareholders. In facilitating the change of command, the departing chief made her successor's success her own. This was the first time a female chief executive had replaced another female CEO at a *Fortune* 500 company. What's more, Burns, at 50, was the first African-American woman to run a large business. (At the time, Xerox reported revenues of $17.6 billion.)

Today, many organizations continue to pooh-pooh succession planning. In 2011, only 35 percent of 1,318 executives surveyed by Korn/Ferry International said their companies had such a plan. Yet a seamless change of command is the hallmark of every great enterprise. Elevating a company insider like Burns—recently ranked the eighth most powerful woman in business by *Fortune*— can pay handsome dividends. "It's an admission to bankruptcy to have to go outside to recruit top management," said management guru Drucker. In addition, recent research by Spencer Stuart, Booz & Company, and others indicates that internal candidates outperform—and outlast—outsiders.

While making her farewell as chief executive look effortless and drama-free, Mulcahy found that leaving on top carried its own challenges. "I loved every minute of being CEO," she said. "The biggest surprise is how hard it is to give it up. I almost understand why so many successions go badly. It's really, really hard to give up power. You get up with a bounce in your step every day because you know you can make a difference."

With no hobbies, this self-proclaimed "one-trick pony" worried that her life had been totally "invested in the job." "It's bittersweet," she said of her departure, "but I feel really fortunate."

Careers are a pyramid, not a ladder. With an enviable track record and a broad base of experience, Mulcahy had built a strong foundation from which to forge a new life. As a seasoned board member—from Target and Citigroup to The Washington Post Company and Johnson & Johnson—this remarkably adaptive leader brings unique skills to any organization. In 2010, she was mentioned as a possible replacement for Larry Summers as head of the National Economic Council—a rumor Mulcahy quickly dismissed. More recently, as further testament to her exceptional ability, *Fortune* placed her on its first-ever Executive Dream Team, a lineup of global superstars from the corporate world. Today, Anne chairs non-profit Save the Children.

∽

F. Scott Fitzgerald's famous observation that there are no second acts in American lives carried no water for John Calley. The veteran movie executive and producer, whose wildly eclectic and successful career spanned 50 years, led three major studios and championed films, including *A Clockwork Orange*, *The Remains of the Day*, *Spider-Man*, and *The Da Vinci Code*. But after 11 years in Hollywood, the cerebral executive did something that powerful people often talk about but almost never do: He gracefully exited the silver screen.

For a dozen years, the retired movie mogul lived as a virtual hermit in his 35-room mansion on Fishers Island, in Long Island Sound. He spent his summers sailing to various places around the world, sometimes living on his boat for six months at a time. For the most part, he shunned the entertainment industry, rarely watching television or movies. But in 1993, bored with his reclusive lifestyle, Calley, at 66, was lured back to Hollywood to engineer an incredible second and third run at troubled United Artists and Sony Pictures.

Calley's peripatetic path began on July 8, 1930, in rough-and-tumble Jersey City, New Jersey. An only son, he was raised by his working-class mother, who divorced her car-salesman husband just six months after the boy was born. Raised during the Depression, the young Calley was called on at an early age to help support the struggling family. In the late 1940s, he attended Columbia University before briefly serving in the Army.

At age 21, he entered the entertainment industry at rock bottom—as a mail boy in NBC's New York headquarters. Soon he was bumped up to a clerical job, where he introduced a cost-saving idea that eliminated several hundred thousand dollars a year. From that point on, Calley was like a match to dry wood. Over the next several years, he was given a series of increasingly responsible jobs and eventually became director of nighttime programming. At 27, he moved to California-based Henry Jaffe Enterprises, where he oversaw developing and producing musical entertainment for films. Then it was back to New York for a stint in advertising. The allure of Hollywood, however, proved too strong, and Calley returned to Los Angeles to give producing a try at Filmways, known mostly for its TV comedies like *The Beverly Hillbillies*.

By the mid-1960s, Calley emerged as a boy genius, producing important Filmways hits such as *Ice Station Zebra*, *The Americanization of Emily*, *The Cincinnati Kid*, and his last project there, the zany wartime classic *Catch–22*, directed by Mike Nichols. His ascendency coincided with a seismic shift in Hollywood's balance of power, as more and more clout was given to the new generation of young filmmakers.

"Kids were kings," Calley said in a 1999 interview with *The Los Angeles Times*. "We were all young. It was our time, and it was very exciting."

In 1968, he began a long and fruitful run heading production at Warner Bros. There, he helped create 120 movies, including *A Star is Born*, *The Exorcist*, *Deliverance*, *Blazing Saddles*, *All the President's Men*, and *A Clockwork Orange*. The polar opposite of the stereotypical image of the monstrous Hollywood mogul, Calley's notable lack of pretension and low-key manner separated him from the pack. He eschewed fancy offices, Gulfstream jets, and $3,000 suits, while his calm, artistic approach endeared him to agents, filmmakers, directors, and screenwriters. Under Calley, Warner Bros. became the studio of choice for luminaries as different as Stanley Kubrick, Clint Eastwood, and Sydney Pollack, who for years were among his closest confidants.

"As a studio head, he was unfailingly supportive and didn't try to do the filmmaker's job," says director Nichols. "When he believed in someone, he trusted and supported him—and when, very rarely, he had a suggestion, it was usually a lifesaver. In fact, that's what he was: a lifesaver."

As Warner's topper, his cool quotient also enabled him to soothe some of Hollywood's most prickly personalities. Among them: Steve McQueen ("a nightmare") and Orson Welles ("an enormous pain in the ass"). In the final analysis, Calley's grace, wit, and sensitivity won them over and added to his growing reputation.

Then, in 1980, having just signed a lucrative seven-year contract with Warner Bros., Calley made a graceful exit. "What drives a CEO is what I call a 'golden spur,'" explains New York–based leadership consultant John Wareham. "He gets to be CEO to prove something to the world. But when he reaches that stage, it's usually a good time to leave."

Citing his record of accomplishment plus an unhappy marriage, burnout, and boredom, Calley, then 50, left on top—selling his house, his furniture, and his dog to his lawyer. He spent much of the following decade decamped in his giant home on Fishers Island, the billionaires' haven on Long Island Sound. He avidly traded in commodities and foreign currencies and traveled to Europe on his sailboat, out of touch with the film world. He eventually settled in Washington, Connecticut, as a gentleman farmer.

"When I left Warners, what I wanted to do was create a vacuum and see what, if anything, would fill it," he said in a 1994 interview with *The New Yorker*. "It didn't scare me, but I found myself withdrawing more and more from life as we know it. I began to think that it would be interesting to go back and see what effect, if any, an activist approach to life would have on me."

During his hiatus from Hollywood, he maintained contact with his longtime colleagues. Concerned about "becoming a vegetable," Calley produced a movie from time and time with Nichols, including the critically acclaimed *Postcards from the Edge* and *The Remains of the Day*. The latter was nominated for eight Academy Awards.

Retirement wasn't the Promised Land. In 1993, at the urging of talent agent Michael Ovitz, the restless Calley resurfaced as president and chief operating officer of moribund United Artists (UA). "I like the idea of chaos," he said at the time. "I was also attracted by the fact that the company was to be sold in a few years."

With a tiny staff and a cost-conscious eye, Calley began to resurrect the ailing studio so its parent company, MGM, could flog it—"putting rouge on the corpse," he said. In no time, he brought UA back from oblivion, first by reinventing the James Bond franchise with the blockbuster *GoldenEye*, then backing *The Birdcage*, which his old pal Nichols directed, and low-budget *Leaving Las Vegas*, which won an Oscar for Nicholas Cage.

"He turned UA around on a pittance. 'Unheard of!'" Nichols told *Newsweek*. "And he enjoyed it." Calley gave MGM/UA enough cachet to attract a surprising $1.3 buyout from Kirk Kerkorian in 1996. Calley, in turn, walked away with big bucks.

Given his textbook turnaround at United Artists, no less than six major studios came after Hollywood's Mr. Fixit. In October 1996, the 66-year-old producer seemed determined to show his vitality and became the new leading man at Sony Pictures. When he reported to work, he told the Japanese owners something they'd never heard an American studio boss say: "I don't want to redecorate the office." After a string of money-losing flops, the company was hemorrhaging badly. Costs had skyrocketed as a result of lavish office renovations, expensive parties, and overly generous production deals. One former executive used the corporate jet to send flowers to his girlfriend. As a result, Sony was forced to take an embarrassing $2.7 billion write-off in 1994.

The new honcho saw his immediate task as controlling costs. "It's about only making films that you are intensely supportive of," he said, which meant not overpaying for scripts or stars. "There's a finite pool of talent," Calley explained. "There have never been more than 15 to 20 really good movies made in any given year. Everything else that works is a fluke."

Applying his sharp pencil and artistic eye, Calley quickly began cranking out a string of popular hits. Just six months after he took over as president, Sony's two studios, Columbia Pictures and Tri-Star Pictures, brought in a combined $447 million at the box office—a record pace for the film industry. The success of movies like *Jerry Maguire* and *Anaconda* helped the company snare 20.7 percent of the market.

"It's my life again," said the supercharged Calley of his strong debut at Sony. His proven formula of filmmaking fueled his success. Rather than producing safe commercial fare, he continued to make risky, gut-level bets on innovative directors and writers, and then gently and quietly steered them. "Working with him is like rolling in feathers," one screenwriter said.

At Sony, he delivered a string of important films. With colleague Amy Pascal, he launched the first *Spider-Man* blockbuster, which became a lucrative franchise. Upped to chairman and CEO, he then produced *As Good as It Gets*, *Men in Black*, *Air Force One*, and many others. Under his leadership, Sony's home entertainment and international television business also soared along with its domestic TV group, with hit shows like *Wheel of Fortune*, *Jeopardy!*, and *Mad About You*.

"It's been a terrific experience," Calley said of his role in leading Sony's bounce back. His skills clearly hadn't atrophied. But in 2003, after seven years at the helm, the 73-year-old dropped out once again, having watched Sony move from among the smallest major studios to the box-office leader. "I've been lucky over my career to be able to transition back and forth between my two great passions—managing studios and producing movies," he said at the time. "It feels like the right time to close that chapter and begin a new one."

Calley returned to independent producing. With Nichols, he made *Closer*, which brought Oscar nominations to its stars, Natalie Portman and Clive Owen. He then produced *The Da Vinci Code*, which drew more that $758 million at the global box office, and its sequel, *Angels & Demons*. He also churned out the popular TV miniseries *The Company*, based on the book by Robert Littell.

In his final years, he battled cancer. "I visited him in the hospital, but nothing had changed," said Sony chairman Sir Howard Stringer. "He never felt sorry for himself. He had a parade of medical problems, but he soldiered on."

Startlingly honest and, in super-agent Michael Ovitz's words, "frighteningly egoless," the three-act legend was feted in 2009 by the Academy of Motion Picture Arts and Sciences, which gave him filmdom's highest honor, the Irving G. Thalberg Memorial Award. The Academy recognized "his intellectual rigor, sophisticated artistic sensibilities and calm, understated manner," calling the longtime studio head "one of the most trusted and admired figures in Hollywood."

Unable to attend in person because of his illness, Calley appeared on video. On September 13, 2011, the studio lion died at 81 in his Los Angeles home after his long illness. Tributes poured in from, among them, film veterans Clint Eastwood, Candice Bergen, and Buck Henry, who noted that "the problem with making a comedy with John is that he was usually funnier than the actors." Added Stringer, "John Calley will be remembered in the history of Hollywood as an extraordinary studio chief, who ran three studios with a maximum of taste and a minimum of tyranny."

The businessman with the soul of an artist was one of a kind. Few people get the chance to lead one studio in a lifetime. From

boy genius to Hollywood King Kong, Calley led three studios—
and left a lasting mark on each one.

Now in his second stint as CEO, Howard Schultz wins plaudits for returning Starbucks to its former glory.

Dr. Richard Kelley

Dr. Richard Kelley left a successful medical practice to supercharge his family's growing hotel empire.

CHAPTER 3

FOUNDING FATHERS

"Company founders look upon retirement as
something between euthanasia and castration."

—LEON A. DANCO, FOUNDER,
THE CENTER FOR FAMILY BUSINESS

"THE GRAVEYARDS ARE FULL of indispensable men,"
Charles de Gaulle reportedly once said. Steve Jobs was the
exception. The mercurial genius, who died last October at the
age of 56, said in his youth that he wanted to "put a ding in the
universe." He did just that, presenting the world with a wave of
well-designed products it didn't know it wanted and couldn't live
without. With his death, it's hard to imagine a world without the
indispensable Jobs.

Battling pancreatic cancer, the Apple chairman and co-
founder stepped down as chief executive two months before his
passing, handing the reins to longtime deputy Tim Cook. Yet
the world continues to watch and see how well Apple sustains its
incredible success without the vision and guidance of its inventive
leader. Few mortals can match the astonishing career of Steve Jobs,
a genius who will be remembered with Edison and Einstein. Yet

lesser founding fathers, blinded by hubris, consider themselves equally indispensable and often have great difficulty hanging up their spurs. As Fidel Castro, who ruled Cuba for 47 uninterrupted years, once explained, "Revolutionaries never retire." In the business world, octogenarians Sumner Redstone, the chairman of Viacom and CBS; Rupert Murdoch, News Corp's top dog; Castle & Cooke CEO David Murdock; and Mesa Power founder T. Boone Pickens show no interest in taking the gold watch and collecting their pension. Bailing out goes against the grain.

Company founders, after all, fought hard to build their businesses and, understandably, are reluctant to hand over their "baby." "As an entrepreneur, your company is your child," says Jarkko Veijalainen, one of the founders of Finland's 3 Step IT Group, a multimillion-dollar recycler of office equipment. "It takes great mental effort to loosen the apron strings." Just like parenting, knowing when to give the next generation its due is one of the most daunting challenges for corporate creators.

Howard Schultz continues to deal with that challenge. Forty years ago, the zealous entrepreneur nurtured a few small Seattle coffee shops from infancy to a global brand. Under his leadership, Starbucks experienced more than 13 years of breakneck growth. Along the way, the company was cited as a great place to work, of ethically sourcing and roasting the highest-quality coffee beans, and of crafting beverages for millions of global customers who frequented its cozy stores for refreshment and a sense of community.

In 2000, Schultz stepped down as the chief executive, happy to turn one of the world's most recognizable brands over to a handpicked successor. Several years later, Starbucks saw its headlong growth go into reverse, as the company suffered from a rough economy and its own strategic missteps. In 2008, the founding father unexpectedly returned to the chief executive role—promising to take the business back to its roots and make Starbucks beloved again.

Howard Schultz's autobiographies, *Pour Your Heart Into It* (1997) and *Onward* (2011), painstakingly expound his illustrious career. Born in 1953 and raised in a subsidized Brooklyn, New York, housing project, the youngster grew up in a poor, impoverished family. "We were pretty much destitute," Schultz recalls. "I always felt like I was living on the other side of the tracks."

A football scholarship to Northern Michigan University was his ticket out of poverty. After graduating in 1975, he got a sales job at Xerox and then went to work for Hammarplast, a Swedish manufacturer of drip coffee-makers. Noticing that a small Seattle company, Starbucks Coffee, Tea and Spices, was ordering unusually large quantities of its equipment, he decided to pay it a visit.

Schultz immediately was impressed by the aroma of freshly ground beans that permeated Starbucks's original store, in Seattle's historic Pike's Place Market. But what really caused him to fall in love with the business was the care the quirky owners put in choosing and roasting coffee beans, as well as their dedication to coffee connoisseurship.

"I walked away saying, 'God, what a great company, what a great city, I'd love to be part of that,'" says Schultz. It took a year to convince Starbucks's owners to hire him, at 29, as director of marketing in 1982. A year into the job, he had another epiphany. On a business trip to Milan, he discovered "the romance of the Italian coffee bar," which not only served excellent espresso but also, as a meeting place, was part of the country's societal glue.

Upon returning to Seattle, he tried to convince the owners to develop a retail chain that sold beverages in addition to just selling whole-bean and ground coffee. Although a pilot store went well, Starbucks's bosses balked at a national roll-out, saying they didn't want to enter the restaurant business.

Frustrated, Schultz quit in 1986 and started his own coffee bar, called Il Giornale, after Milan's daily newspaper. A year later, he returned to Starbucks and bought the company for $3.8 million.

He then merged its six stores with his three Il Giornales, keeping the Starbucks name. By the end of the year, the 34-year-old entrepreneur had 11 stores, 100 employees, and a dream to create a national brand.

"I wanted to elevate the quality of coffee in America," he wrote in *Onward*. "Yet I also believed that Starbucks would thrive not just because of our coffee, but also because of our guiding principles. I was determined to create a different kind of company— one that would be committed to shareholder value and making a profit, yet [act] through a lens of social consciousness."

Under Schultz's aegis, Starbucks quickly spread the gospel of high-quality, customized coffee drinks to urban areas around the country. His new wave of coffee houses conveyed a friendly, relaxed atmosphere that many customers, particularly young professionals, found welcoming, even virtuous. By the early 1990s, Starbucks was soaring as one of America's fastest-growing companies—grinding "coffee into gold," gushed *Fortune* magazine, and rewarding stockholders with astonishing profits.

Beyond creating a gathering place that served a great cup of coffee, Schultz pursued his dream of "building a company with soul." He knew that baristas were critical to the business, so he treated them well, offering unprecedented stock options and health insurance, even to part-timers who worked 20 hours a week or more. These moves boosted loyalty and led to extremely low turnover.

Schultz claimed that the model for his fast-growing chain with a bohemian ambience was McDonald's, but with a few key differences. He shunned franchising, the lifeblood of the ubiquitous burger-maker, and stuck primarily to company-owned stores. He also refused to advertise nationally, preferring instead to rely on word-of-mouth kudos from loyal customers. Finally, Starbucks clung to a fairly upscale clientele, with a host of premium products.

Few could quibble with the results. The corporate Empire of the Bean performed brilliantly. By 2000, Starbucks had 2,100 stores in 13 countries, with revenues approaching $2 billion. Since 1992, the year of its initial public offering, the company had grown at a compound annual rate of 49 percent, unprecedented in retailing. Confident of the firm's future and feeling "a bit bored [and] ready to take on new challenges," Schultz, at 46, stepped aside as CEO in 2000, kicking himself upstairs, while retaining a role as nonexecutive chairman and chief global strategist. His successor: president and chief operating officer Orin Smith, a 10-year Starbucks veteran.

During Smith's first five years at the helm, Schultz had every reason to feel satisfied with the new regime. By 2005, Starbucks's stock was trading close to historic highs of about $30 a share. Its sales had risen by more than $1 billion over the preceding year, as it opened stores in its home market twice as fast as it had in previous years. Its long-term target of owning 15,000 units in the United States, as well as at least 15,000 internationally, seemed reasonable. Apparently, nothing could stall Schultz's baby.

As the years progressed, however, forces of change began to appear on the horizon—subtle, but visible nonetheless—indicating that the invincible Cult of Schultz was heading into choppy waters. By 2006, overall store traffic was down, and cost-conscious customers weren't spending as much for pricey espressos, lattes, and cappuccinos. Growing competition from other specialty coffee shops—Peet's, Coffee & Tea, Caribou Coffee, among them, as well as the Big-Boy fast-food chains, such as McDonald's and Dunkin' Donuts—was inflicting pain. But the bigger culprits were internal: The company had grown too fast, opening cookie-cutter stores and failing to adequately train new employees, build a strong management team, and keep operating costs down. Once-loyal customers voiced their dissatisfaction over long wait-times and an erosion of the concept's original charm and intimacy.

Starbucks was clearly losing its luster. By late 2006, its stock began a seemingly relentless descent, losing more than half its value in 15 months. The following year, "comps," or same-store sales—the industry's most important metric, which gauges how fast sales are growing at stores open at least a year—fell by double digits. Along the way, hubris set in, says Rohit Depshande, a professor of marketing at Harvard Business School. Starbucks was "so focused on growth by opening new stores that it lost touch with its core customers," he claimed. *The Wall Street Journal* agreed, chiming in with its front-page story: "At Starbucks, Too Many, Too Quick?"

"We got swept up," Schultz told *Business Week*. "We stopped asking: 'How can we do better?' We had a sense of entitlement." Then came the recession, as people tried to stem their spending. It compounded the coffee-maker's struggles and exposed the company's overreach to the world.

Although still occupying his modest office in Starbucks's headquarters on an industrial lot south of Seattle, Schultz, as non-executive chair, often felt "like an outsider looking in." But as the company's fall from grace became increasingly clear, Starbucks's biggest shareholder began to re-engage in the business. After months of counseling senior executives and outside experts, he began to map his return as the company's CEO. One of his most trusted advisers was Michael Dell, another founding father who had recently returned to run Dell, Inc. "Michael had a unique perspective and insight about what I could expect," Schultz says of his longtime friend.

During a series of three-hour bike rides on Hawaii's Big Island, Dell suggested that the returning executive initiate a "transformation agenda": a bold series of action-oriented initiatives that could trigger a meaningful turnaround. Over the next few weeks, Schultz fashioned such a plan—one designed to fix troubled stores, rekindle an emotional attachment with customers, and address longer-term issues like overhauling the C-suite and revamping the supply chain.

On a Sunday evening in early 2008, he summoned the company's senior executives to his home to unveil his strategy and secure their commitment. "Are you in, or are you out?" he asked. Eight of his top 10 people eventually chose to depart.

On March 19, 2008, 6,000 Starbucks shareholders gathered at McCaw Hall in Seattle and greeted Schultz's return from his eight-year hiatus with vigorous applause. "I humbly recognize and share both your concern and your disappointment in how the company has performed and how this has affected your investment in Starbucks," he told them. "And I promise you that this will not stand."

True to his word, Starbucks's encore executive immediately started to get things back on track. He halted the marathon of new store openings, shuttered more than 800 stores in the U.S., laid off more than 4,000 employees, and slashed $581 million in costs. A month after his return, he closed every Starbucks in the nation to retrain baristas on the art of pouring the perfect shot. To freshen up its product, servers were ordered to dump brewed coffee after 30 minutes. New, expensive machines were bought to make better coffee and restore a sense of theater to the coffee-making experience.

In addition, the chain began offering discounts, conducting more market research, hitting the social media, and—in a dramatic break with the past—advertising the quality and freshness of its line. Stung by various reports that rated its snobbish, heavily roasted coffee behind competitors, including McDonald's, Starbucks created a new signature blend, Pike Place Roast. In another switch, the company also freshened up its units, with local woods, furniture, and art, to rekindle the feel of a neighborhood store. It also began upgrading its supply of specialty beans, as the independents were doing, and phased out "non-core products," such as hot sandwiches, CDs, books, and DVDs.

Despite the sagging economy, Starbucks's motivator-in-chief showed his willingness to exhort the troops and re-energize the business. Against the advice of many, he sent 10,000 store managers to New Orleans for an expensive ($30 million), three-day leadership conference in October 2008. Besides galvanizing company leaders to his new vision, he encouraged his staff to perform community service to a city still recovering from Hurricane Katrina. Employees, Schultz included, volunteered 50,000 hours and invested more than $1 million in local projects, including fixing up houses and cleaning streets in the Ninth Ward.

"If we hadn't had New Orleans, we wouldn't have turned things around," Schultz recalls. The experience was "the crucible . . . one of the smartest things we did to reinstall the values of the company."

In another risky bet, Starbucks began developing an instant coffee, which many observers considered the kiss of death. But Schultz had his eye on instant's delicious $20 billion market. In 2009, the company launched its new product, Via, which soon proved to be a big hit.

These steps, as dramatic as they were, were only part of a complete personal and corporate makeover. Shultz conceded that he could no longer run Starbucks through the Cult of Howard. For years, even when he wasn't actively running the company, he still seemed omnipotent. For his transformation to be a success, the founding father knew he needed to share power with a new breed of supercharged, independent thinkers. Although he would continue as Starbucks's guiding light, he began relying more and more on a cadre of carefully selected, high-performers from inside and outside the industry.

Schultz had gotten religion. He began to embrace big-company ideas like focus groups, which he used to reject. Delegating and accepting the input of others became commonplace. "What leadership means is the courage it takes to talk about things that, in the past, perhaps we wouldn't have, because I'm not right all the time," he told *The New York Times*.

The litany of changes, however, was not a panacea. As Schultz had accurately predicted, "No silver bullet will transform Starbucks overnight." Despite his triumphant return, same-store sales continued to slump, and the company's share price kept falling. But the re-energized chief stayed the course. By mid-2009, the chain began trending back into positive "comp" territory. In fiscal 2010, its operating margin of 13.3 percent was the highest in company history. In addition, it reported revenues of a record $10.7 billion and operating income of $1.4 billion, enabling the beverage giant to offer its first-ever dividend to shareholders.

In the course of two years—despite painful internal troubles and a worsening economy—Starbucks had returned to sustainably profitable growth. The 17,000-unit coffee-maker's performance was "nothing short of remarkable," wrote Deutsche Bank's Marc Greenberg, "and quite honestly the most significant business turnaround we have witnessed."

"We have won in many ways," Schultz triumphantly told 1,100 employees at the company headquarters in January 2011. "But I also feel it's important to remind us all of how fleeting success and winning can be."

In 2012, Starbucks entered middle age with a keen desire to improve the way its customers and its stockholders respond to the brand. Under Schultz's aggressive leadership, the coffee-maker is not standing still. Having once lost its mojo, Starbucks is continuing to reinvent itself. Besides making a frontal assault on the high-growth economies of China and India, the company has introduced a bold move to attract the hang-out-in-the-evening crowd with renovated stores serving wine and beer, as well as a limited menu of tasty morsels. In addition, Starbucks is developing a wide variety of goods that will be introduced in its retail shops then rolled out to the grocery trade, opened a chain of juice bars, and purchased a small baking chain.

Besides leading Starbucks's makeover, Schultz, at 58, has been on a mission to boost job creation and fight political dysfunction in Washington, D.C. The Seattle billionaire, No. 854 on *Forbes*'s world's wealthiest list, recently pledged $100,000 of profits from the Starbucks stores in low-income areas to add jobs in these communities. His national goal: 3,500 new hires this year. In addition, his "Create Jobs for USA" takes the program one step further, providing microlending to small businesses in underserved markets through Community Development Financial Institutions, or CDFIs. The Starbucks Foundation jumpstarted the effort with an initial $5 million donation. Perhaps even bolder, Schultz has been urging his fellow bosses to stop donating money to politicians until Washington starts sorting out its economic problems. To date, a reported 150 CEOs have taken his no-giving pledge.

Schultz worries that, having made a fortune after being born poor in Brooklyn, he could soon become "a poster child for an American dream that no longer exists . . . [and] that little bit of insecurity makes me motivated." But don't expect the public-spirited leader to take his eyes off his baby. He will not be exiting Starbucks in the near term.

"I'm here to see this [transformation] through," the founding father promises. "I'm not leaving soon." But there's a bigger motivation to all this than just making money. "It's the respect," he explains. "The legacy."

❧

Sigmund Freud is said to have fainted only twice in his life—both times when he perceived a threat to his legacy. Rupert Murdoch take heed. As the Murdoch episode attests, retaining a family legacy can be the source of bad blood and clashing visions of succession. With nine out of 10 businesses in the United States family-owned (including some *Fortune* 500 companies), avoiding jagged leadership transitions is of paramount concern.

Few families have passed the baton more effectively than the Kelley clan. These hoteliers extraordinaire have been the driving force in the behemoth Outrigger Enterprises since opening their first property in Hawaii in 1947. Patriarch Roy C. Kelley democratized tourism in the Islands, figuring out ways to offer rooms affordably to the masses. Since then, family members have run the tightly controlled hotel chain that now operates a portfolio of 45 properties in Hawaii, Australia, Guam, Fiji, Indonesia, Thailand, Vietnam, and China.

The first voyagers arrived on Hawaii's shores around A.D. 400, after sailing for months in huge canoes propelled by sails made of *hala*, or pandanus plants. Migrating from the Marquesas and Tahiti far to the south, these early migrants became the people known as Hawaiians. In 1929, an equally enterprising explorer, Roy Kelley, arrived in the Islands with his wife of four months, Estelle. It was Black Friday, September 12, the day the stock market crashed.

Kelley was born in Redlands, California, in 1905 and raised in a threadbare family environment. Working his way through the University of Southern California, he earned a degree in architecture and graduated at the top of his class. Unable to find work in Los Angeles, he and his wife sailed to Honolulu on the *City of Los Angeles* with $108 in their pockets. The young couple quickly settled in to a $45-a-month cottage in then sleepy Waikiki. For the next several years, Roy worked for a local architectural firm, designing a number of landmark buildings in Honolulu. In the early '30s, he dabbled on the side in real estate, developing several small apartment buildings. By 1938, he had gone off on his own, primarily designing upscale residences.

After World War II, the young architect shifted from building houses and apartments to hotels. In 1947, he built the 37-room

Islander Hotel in Waikiki. It was the first new hotel on the strip in 20 years and, with room rates at $7.50 a night, the first to focus on middle-income family travelers. Next came the Edgewater, Waikiki's first hotel with an automatic elevator and—wonder of wonders—a swimming pool. On its heels: the 10-story Reef Hotel, Waikiki's first high-rise, and, across the street, the 18-story Reef Towers.

With the advent of jet travel in 1959, the small chain grew dramatically. Kelley, a true entrepreneur with a gambler's instincts, made perhaps his biggest coup in 1963, when he coyly maneuvered the negotiation of a long-term lease on prime, beachfront property between the Moana and Royal Hawaiian hotels. The owner, Queen Emma Estate, had been in extensive discussions with Sheraton Hotels for a long-term lease. When those talks broke down momentarily over lease rents, Kelley jumped in to steal the show—and Outrigger Hotels Hawaii was born.

For the next 30 years, Kelley never stopped buying land and building on it. He combined his ability as an architect and supervisor to design and build hotels at half the cost of the competition, providing inexpensive accommodations for the flood of guests arriving on new jumbo jet planes. Revered by budget-conscious tourists, while reviled by others for creating his cheek-by-jowl hotel empire in Waikiki, the feisty founder remained unapologetic about his vision to make Hawaii travel increasingly accessible to visitors from around the world.

"The Kelleys created affordable properties that were open to everybody," says Frank Haas, a local tourism expert and University of Hawaii dean. "They did it by linking with airlines and tour companies, plus offering a basic hotel without room service, restaurants, or even bell service in some places. That's what put Hawaii on the map."

Hands-on in every respect, Kelley and his indefatigable wife ran a mom-and-pop operation, with Estelle performing or supervising many tasks. Kelley, for his part, worked long hours—doing menial jobs and manual labor. His idea of a corporate office was sitting behind the front desk of his hotels, overseeing operations and stepping into everything from greeting guests to humping luggage.

"He always focused on customers first," says David Carey, president and CEO of Outrigger Enterprises. And he always expected the same level of *hookipa*, or hospitality, from his staff. His children—Richard, Jean, and Kathleen—also pitched in at the hotels, and seven-day work weeks were practically a family tradition.

As the chain grew and redefined Hawaii as an attractive, affordable tourist destination, Outrigger Hotels remained very much the tightly held domain of Roy and Estelle Kelley. Gradually, they eased away from day-to-day control and, in the late 1980s, passed the baton to their son Richard, known as "Doc" Kelley.

"Doc's" move into Outrigger's C-suite took a path less traveled. Born on Dec. 28, 1933, in Honolulu, he grew up in a small wood-frame house in the bowels of Waikiki. As a youngster, while attending prestigious Punahou School (which boasts President Barack Obama, Steve Case, and Michelle Wie among its alumni), he toiled in the family business. No silver spoon here, he grew up in the culture of customer service and operational discipline, doing everything from clerking at the front desk to folding linen.

"It wasn't whether I was going into the family business; it was at what age," he told me. "But there was never any pressure to make a career out of the hotel business."

In a circuitous route to the industry, Richard went on to study medicine at Stanford and, in 1960, earned an M.D. from Harvard. That led to internships in Boston and San Francisco before returning home in 1962 to complete his residency at Honolulu's Queen's Medical Center. There, he served as a pathologist and lab director, while also teaching at the University of Hawaii Medical School. In his precious free time, he maintained close contact with the family business—visiting new sites, attending important business and industry meetings, and the like. If that weren't enough, he took evening courses in finance, real estate, and business law—subjects not offered in med school.

During the early 1970s, feeling a bit bored with medicine, Kelley hung up his stethoscope and joined the Outrigger group. His father retained the chairmanship, with the son assuming the presidency and chief executive roles. Later, in 1986, the retired physician became board chairman.

"Looking back on it now," says Richard, "what's extraordinary was the smoothness of the transition. My father was a very strong authority—accustomed to being the sole leader, dictatorial, unopposed. But he knew things had to change, and the succession is a great tribute to him."

In many respects, Kelley believes the fact that both he and his father had carved their own separate careers outside the hotel industry made the handover work. As a former architect, "my dad respected me for earning—as he did—my own identity as a physician. He accepted me as an equal. We had a common ground—and amazingly never got in each other's way."

Reaffirming the company's dedication to service, the outspoken and feisty ex-doc led the company's expansion in Waikiki and beyond. Besides acquiring additional properties on Oahu, Outrigger spread to the Neighbor Islands, initially the Big Island and, later, Kauai. Diversifying further, the group entered the condominium resort sector in 1990. In the process, Kelley professionalized the business, introducing computers, formal training, and human-resource management.

Three years later, Dr. Kelley gracefully exited his day-to-day responsibilities and moved the chairmanship to Denver, along with Outrigger's reservations center. As nonexecutive chair, he spent about a third of his time in Hawaii, a third in Denver, and another third on the road. "I'm free to do a lot of things I haven't had time to do before," Kelley said at the time, "like calling on major clients and actively participating in hotel- and travel-industry organizations."

His handpicked successor was son-in-law David Carey, who had joined the company as executive vice president and general counsel in 1986 and had become president two years later. In short order, the Stanford grad, with joint J.D./MBA degrees, was fully indoctrinated in the Kelley tradition: Run a tight ship and give frugal visitors a memorable experience.

Under Carey's leadership and Kelley's watchful eye, Outrigger grew internationally, upgraded its image, and diversified its product offerings. Renamed Outrigger Hotels & Resorts to reflect its changing face, Carey opened the company's first hotel outside the United States in 1990 on tiny Majuro Atoll in the Marshall Islands. That, in turn, led to a number of new resorts across the Pacific. The same year, Outrigger spun off 15 of its moderately priced Waikiki hotels into a new *Ohana*, or family, brand to differentiate them from the chain's increasingly upscale portfolio.

In the new millennium, Carey continued to champion the company's diversification, with an important strategic alliance with Fairfield Resorts, the world's largest time-share provider. To add management depth, he convinced another doctor, Chuck Kelley, grandson of the founders, to jettison medicine and join the family business in 2002. Chuck's initial duties focused on promoting Outrigger hotels to major medical groups; later, he assumed responsibility for investor services.

Despite its multiple initiatives, Outrigger has never lost sight of its home market of Hawaii. In 2005, the company began a massive $535 million upgrade of Waikiki. Its Beach Walk development transformed an old, worn-down 7.9-acre parcel into a sparkling new showplace, combining shops, restaurants, and entertainment venues.

Although exponential growth often triggers the demise of family-owned businesses, Outrigger proved the exception. Fending off unpredictable outside shocks—9/11, recessions, credit squeezes, even natural disasters—the group adapted to the changing landscape, as Hawaii's visitor count exploded from 22,000 when the Kelleys arrived to 7 million–plus today. "Outrigger stayed focused on reality," says local economist Paul Brewbaker, "while others lived in a mythical version of reality."

CEO Carey agrees. "We moved with the market. We're a vastly different business today," he says. "We're in Hawaii. We're international. We run upscale hotels. We run condominiums. We really don't run very many budget hotels anymore."

Doc Kelley, in large part, has kept the clan in sync with Outrigger Enterprises' transformation. It was the good doctor who established the family advisory board, on which any family member (and their spouses) "in good standing" can learn about corporate strategy and then offer ideas and feedback on the firm's direction and vision. And like his father before him, Kelley continues to instruct future generations on the inner workings of the hotels.

"My father knew that if you pay attention to people, that motivates them to do the very best," says Dr. Chuck Kelley, who succeeded his dad as nonexecutive chairman in 2011. "He clearly recognized the enormous impact that Outrigger has on its employees, the family and the community at large."

Tick. Tick. Tick. That was the clock running. A decade ago, Richard Kelley was diagnosed with Parkinson's disease, which affects more than a million Americans. Faced with his own mortality, he now enjoys an active but more limited role as chairman emeritus.

"I'll never let the disease get me down," the 77-year-old doctor-turned-hotelier told me. "I've been very, very lucky and have benefited greatly from magnetic therapy treatments. In the meantime, I'm focusing on issues of responsibility, integrity, honesty and dedication. I try to pass those values on to our family and employees."

"We cannot change the cards we are dealt, just how we play the hand," wrote former Carnegie-Mellon professor Randy Pausch, in his best-selling book, *The Last Lecture*. Roy Kelley, who died in 1997, and Estelle, who died a year later—both at age 91—would be proud of how well their offspring have played their cards. With a minimum of bickering and a maximum of pride, subsequent generations have left on top—transforming the Outrigger brand into an 11,000-room, trans-Pacific empire and enhancing the family legacy.

At age 85, John Gagliardi, the oldest active coach in U.S. sports, shows no signs of slowing down.

Hall of Fame coach Joe Gibbs twice traded in professional football for another highly competitive team sport: auto racing.

CHAPTER 4

STILL IN THE GAME

"I'd give a year off my life to win."

—HALL OF FAME FOOTBALL COACH GEORGE ALLEN

H E HAS MORE WRINKLES than most college football coaches, is a little more hunched over, walks with a shuffle, and, like many octogenarians, he's a little hard of hearing. Yet, at age 85, John Gagliardi, the oldest active coach in U.S. sports, shows no signs of slowing down—that is, when he isn't making the occasional trip to the bathroom during a game. In a notoriously pressure-packed profession, coaching legends rise and fall with each new cycle. Few exit on their own terms. If and when he decides to go, Gagliardi will be the exception.

As the 2012 season approached, the bespectacled senior entered his 64th overall season with 484 wins, the most ever among college or professional football coaches. In a testament to the virtues of immobility, Gagliardi has spent almost his entire adult life at Saint John's University, a picturesque Benedictine Catholic men's college with 1,900 students, 70 miles northwest of Minneapolis. Over the years, he has compiled a gaudy .779

winning percentage (484-133-11), which put him ahead of former coaches Bobby Bowden, Bear Bryant, and Pop Warner.

Using unconventional coaching methods and without the aid of scholarships, Gagliardi has won two NCAA Division III national championships and two NAIA titles and, in 2006, became the first active coach inducted into the College Football Hall of Fame. The Division III Player of the Year Award also carries his name. His last losing season was in 1967.

In a profession filled with nakedly ambitious coaches and silver-tongued mercenaries who leap from one lily pad to another, Gagliardi seems an aberration. Shunning plenty of opportunities to move to a high-profile program and a potentially stratospheric salary, he has remained fiercely loyal to Saint John's. As a result, he is revered as something akin to a saint in Collegeville, Minnesota, the leafy hamlet that houses the small, proud, academically rigorous institution.

Gagliardi's deeply planted roots in Division III football have allowed him to fly under the radar of big-time sports and sidestep the stresses and strains that often accompany them. At slower-paced Saint John's, he has avoided recruiting wars, barracuda boosters, reality-deprived expectations, call-in-shows, and acrimonious websites. Perhaps more important, his lower-division lifestyle has permitted him to mold his own program, unencumbered by meddling administrators and the relentless pressure to win.

But Gagliardi is celebrated as much for his contrarian coaching methods as for his remarkable longevity. Right from the start, he went against the book so often that it's easy to overlook his incredible success. During his unrivaled tenure, he has operated far outside his sport's mainstream, with a winning formula predicated on a staggering list of 108 *No's*. Among them:

- *No* tackling in practice.
- *No* practicing in full pads. A practice jersey and sweat pants will do.

- *No* practicing outdoors if it's too hot, too cold, too wet, or if there are too many bugs. (You've got to experience Minnesota's lake country to appreciate this.)
- *No* mandatory weightlifting, running, or wind sprints.
- *No* cuts. Up to 180 players will make the roster, and they all dress for home games.
- *No* whistles or yelling at practice.
- *No* playbooks. His quarterbacks call most of the plays.
- *No* conventional calisthenics before games.

While fearing a coach is commonplace in the testosterone-infused world of male sports, Gagliardi also insists that no one call him "Coach." Even 17-year-old freshmen refer to him as "John."

"We don't have a mission statement or a big philosophy. We just do it," says the smiling sage, who has forgotten more about the game than many of his overpaid peers will ever know.

Pigskin's ancient standard-bearer has been plying the same unorthodox principles since arriving in Collegeville in 1953. Far from the preening crowd, he has made his mark without bravado or bullying. Insisting that his old-school values haven't gone out of style, he refuses to take a knee. When asked about a graceful exit, Gagliardi—or Gags, as he is known—pauses and says with his trademark smile, "I don't think about retirement. After losses, though, I have thought about suicide." Then he laughs, the way he often does whenever he hears suggestions that there is an age at which coaches should call it quits.

Like Betty White and Jimmy Dean, who are profiled in a later chapter, the coaching Methuselah acquired his maverick mind-set in the Great Depression. He grew up the fifth of nine children to Italian immigrant parents. His father, Ventura, settled in southern Colorado, initially as a coal miner and then a blacksmith. Finally, he ran an auto body shop. Auto repairing was what Gags thought would be his life's work. "It was a pretty good living," he recalls. "My brother, brother-in-law, and uncle worked there and had a pretty good life."

But things changed in 1943, when his football coach at Colorado's Trinidad Catholic High School was sent off to World War II. At 16, the high school senior convinced the principal to let the boys coach themselves. The principal agreed, naming Gagliardi player-coach. The youngster quickly eliminated many of his favorite dislikes: warm-ups, extensive calisthenics, and wind sprints. He also allowed players to drink water during practice. "Frankly, I didn't know what I was doing," he admits. "I was just trying to do something that I thought was right." His experiments paid off: Gags led the team to its first-ever league championship.

He stayed on to coach another year and to pick up another league championship. Then, it was off to attend Colorado College, where the clever wünderkind found time to direct St. Mary's High in Colorado Springs to two more league championships.

After graduating in 1949, Gagliardi, at 22, became the head coach and athletic director at Carroll College in Helena, Montana. The school had not had much success, and there were serious moves afoot to drop football. But four years later, Gags had led the Fighting Saints to three conference titles. If that wasn't enough, he also headed the baseball and basketball teams and won conference championships in those sports as well. "It was evident," one sportswriter predicted, "that the bigger schools would soon be after him."

Leave it to the Benedictine monks at Saint John's to come calling. In 1953, now all of 27 years old, Gagliardi trekked to rural Minnesota for the grand salary of $4,400. "I hated to leave Carroll because I really enjoyed it," he said. "But I figured, well, it's a great adventure. Bigger school, bigger opportunities."

However, some warned the young coach that the Johnnies were a lost cause—a professional black hole. In truth, the program had been mired in mediocrity. The previous head coach, Johnny "Blood" McNally, an ex–Green Bay Packer and a charter member of the Professional Football Hall of Fame, was put off by the Benedictines and the school's lack of scholarships. He told Gagliardi,

"These are a bunch of tight, German monks. They want to win, but they won't give you a nickel. I don't know if anyone can win here."

So Gags entered fully aware of the risks. But he had, after all, experienced transformations firsthand. After settling into spartan quarters in St. Mary's Hall, the new coach changed the air in Collegeville. He immediately whipped up the team's energy level. His attitude rubbed off on his players. In short order, he had them believing there were no limits to what they could do. "Ordinary people doing ordinary things extraordinarily well" became his mantra.

After Gags deployed his evolving list of infamous *No's*, his team quickly bought into his player-friendly system. In his first season, he won six of his seven conference games and the conference co-championship—its first in 15 years. During those early years, he also coached track and hockey. Even though he had never played hockey, his team's record over five seasons is still the best winning percentage of any hockey coach in the school's history.

But it was in Clemens Stadium, surrounded by pine trees and nestled in a natural bowl, that Gagliardi made his greatest splash. After 1953, it became clear that he was no one-season flash. For the next 58 years, the best little coach in America continued to eschew many of football's most sadistic traditions at the expense of his opponents. Combining deep squads that mixed hellacious defense with a high-octane offense and unselfish team play, Saint John's gridders became a small-college powerhouse. In 1962, Gags had his first undefeated team, followed by two more undefeated teams that won national titles in '63 and '65. A couple more undefeated championship squads came in 1976 and 2003. Then, on November 8, 2003, 13,000 loyal fans crammed into the tiny stadium to witness history in the making. That chilly day, in 18-degree weather, Gagliardi surpassed Grambling head coach Eddie Robinson on the all-time win list with his 409th victory.

For Gagliardi, execution, not physicality, is the key to success on the gridiron. "Football is a game of mistakes," he explains. "And somehow you've got to eliminate them." If you stand behind him in practice, you can see his consistent demand for perfection. With studied calm, he moves about, watching from different angles, talking to players. A stickler for details, he insists on meticulously timed repetitions and drills. Distractions are not tolerated. By game time, his teams are prepared for whatever's thrown at them.

What's more, Gags draws on a mismatch of overlooked, small-town players to accomplish his magic. No blue chippers here. Saint John's rosters typically are stocked with undersized overachievers—the anonymous castoffs of bigger Division I and II programs. From these cracked bricks, he builds teams that—clawing and scratching—produce handsome results and bring fans to their feet.

"We found some real gems in the boonies," says Gagliardi. He likes to ask heartland recruits if they have the nerve to ask out the best-looking girl in school. Invariably, he says, the ones who say "yes" reflect the confidence he seeks.

Although the Johnnies may not be as gifted as high-profile schools, they almost always make fewer mistakes—fewer turnovers, penalties, and misalignments. Consequently, Gagliardi has shown that a small-town program can make a big-time impact with modest talent.

As with any bright triumph, there was also an important message. During his extended tenure at Saint John's, the philosopher-coach has always insisted that the winning is not the final reward. It's the game of life that counts. "We want you to be a better person today than yesterday," he tells every student-athlete. "And be better tomorrow than yesterday—be a topflight person at all times."

In an era of glib coaches who often infest collegiate sports, Gagliardi's unvarnished sincerity is perhaps his most endearing quality. He may not have coached at the highest level of college football, but his ability to lead is unmatched.

"John is what the coaching profession is all about," Joe Paterno told *The New York Times*. "He's loyal to his institution. He's loyal to his players. He's had tremendous influence on not only the people who have played for him, but the people who have played against him. He's been a wonderful example."

Victorious coaches like Gagliardi are presumed to live on a career ladder, climbing as they toil, always seeking a better job until they reach the top rung of success. As Gags built respect and a winning record at Saint John's, opportunities came his way to coach at bigger, marquee programs. In the 1950s, West Point made some advances. Before Notre Dame hired Ara Parseghian in 1964, Fighting Irish alumni approached Gagliardi about the job. He had chances to coach in the National Football League. Miami Dolphins owner Joe Robbie wanted him to lead his team, and Bud Grant of the Minnesota Vikings also wooed him. But he said no.

The closest Gagliardi came to leaving was in the early 1980s, when he was offered the coaching job at the University of San Diego. But after a campus visit, he turned down more money and sunny weather to remain in frosty Minnesota.

Saint John's had become home. There were, Gags reckoned, no greener pastures. He and his wife, Peggy, had four grown children, who lived close by. His son, Jim, was—and continues to be—his offensive coordinator, and the majority of assistant coaches once played for him. As the victories kept piling up, Gagliardi had become a local institution, the glue that held the town together.

In an era of galloping egos, especially in coaching, this quiet, unassuming man put quality of life above conventional notions of success. He weighed ambition against the status quo and found ambition wanting—as wise people usually do. He had a good life, a happy family, a wonderful working environment, and the respect of his community. In effect, he downshifted before the concept became popular. He bent his goals around his life, not the reverse. He defined success on his own terms.

Interestingly, Gagliardi isn't the only Saint John's coach to enjoy an extended run in Collegeville. Basketball coach Jim Smith ended his 48th season in 2011. This year, Jerry Haugen enters his 35th year as a baseball coach. Cross country/track and field coach

Tim Miles has been on the job 33 years, while soccer coach Pat Haws recently retired as soccer coach after 32 seasons. Of the university's 13 coaches, 10 have the longest tenure in their sport in the school's Minnesota Intercollegiate Athletic Conference.

Saint John's University *is* Collegeville, a quaint burg once described as "Lake Wobegon with a monastery." There are no first-class amenities, no glitzy restaurants, nightlife—or buzz. The tiny, top-notch liberal arts school is tucked off I-94 in the Minnesota hinterlands. Dominating the woodsy, 2,400-acre campus, considered to be one of the nation's most attractive, is Abbey Church with its arching bell tower.

Chartered in 1857 by Benedictines, the university for years was known as "the Priest Factory" for churning out men of the cloth. Though the number of monks has dwindled over time, the remaining 150 or so continue to yield a powerful influence. Benedictine fathers and brothers living the order's tradition of *Ora et Labora*—prayer and work—serve as the primary faculty and administrators. A monk lives on every floor of every dormitory as an adviser, on call 24/7. "I think that resonates with men like John Gagliardi," says Father Timothy Backous, the school's former athletic director.

Saint John's graduates also have had an important and far-reaching impact. A roll call of distinguished alumni includes former U.S. senator and presidential candidate Eugene McCarthy, actor Jack Webb, movie director Stephen Sommers, Grammy-winning folk singer John McCutcheon, and John Agee, president of Carlson Holdings.

Today, more than one-third of the student body participate in intercollegiate athletics—90 percent, when club sports and intramurals are included. As impressive, 80 percent of Saint John's students graduate in six years (well above the average for peer institutions), and 98 percent of the student body receive some form of financial aid to help cover the $50,000-plus annual tab for room, board, and tuition. (As mentioned, the school does not award athletic scholarships, which Gagliardi refers to as "athletic welfare.")

What's more, Gags has rarely had a player not graduate, most of them in just four years. Nor does he lose players to ineligibility. "We get good kids," he told me. "We want guys who don't need rules." No babysitting or bed checks here. Nor are there academic scandals, recruiting violations, or under-the-table payments. It is understandable, therefore, that Gagliardi and many of his fellow coaches remain content to spend their days in this comfortable Midwestern community known for its small-town hospitality.

Yet football's pooh-bahs have a hard time understanding how any coach in his 80s can maintain his enthusiasm and sharpness. But if you think that Gagliardi is getting too old for all of this, think again. Not only do his competitive juices still rage, he's on a mission to prove that, like wine, coaches can improve with age.

Still, the ageless wonder knows that he can't coach forever. So when might we see a graceful exit? For now, there's no *arrivederci* in sight. The Hall of Fame coach says he'll continue doing what he's doing as long as he's healthy and productive. He figures he's got another decade or two.

In the meantime, Gagliardi isn't worried about dying on the job. "The monks have given me a lifetime contract," he quips, pausing for a senior moment. "But if we start losing games, they can give me the last sacraments—and declare me dead."

∽

Sometimes we are lucky enough to know that our lives have changed: to discard the old, embrace the new, and bask in the rewards. But few successful leaders, particularly in their fifth and sixth decade, are able to comfortably refashion themselves. Joe Gibbs is an outlier, constantly searching for, in his words, "an examined life."

In the 1980s and early '90s, as head coach of the Washington Redskins, he led the team to four NFL championships and three

Super Bowl titles. In 1992, he exited professional football, taking his talents to another highly competitive team sport: auto racing. In short order, his Joe Gibbs Racing team became one of the most successful in NASCAR, with three major championships. Then, after an 11-year hiatus from the gridiron, Gibbs came back to lead the Redskins. That encore met with mixed success, causing the Hall of Fame coach, once again, to trade in the smells of the locker room for those of burned rubber.

Joe Jackson Gibbs was born on November 25, 1940, in Mocksville, North Carolina, near Asheville. Raised in a God-fearing family by strict, but caring, parents, he spent most of his life outdoors and developed a love of sports. "What I lacked in natural ability, I made up for in competitiveness," he says. "I've never lost that."

As a youngster, Gibbs moved with his family to southern California, where he starred as a high school quarterback. From there, it was on to junior college and, later, San Diego State University, where he played for offensive-minded Don Coryell. Following graduation in 1964, he joined Coryell's staff as offensive line coach. That led to three two-year stints as an assistant at Florida State, Southern California, and Arkansas. It was during this crusade that Gibbs became a born-again Christian.

In 1973, Coryell tapped his former protégé to join his staff at the St. Louis Cardinals in the National Football League. After five years there, he served as offensive coordinator for the Tampa Bay Buccaneers under legendary coach John McKay. In 1979, he rejoined Coryell, this time with the San Diego Chargers.

As the Chargers' offensive coordinator, Gibbs spearheaded their explosive passing attack, labeled "Air Coryell." For two years, the team smashed multiple offensive records, averaging more than 400 yards per game. In 1980, Washington Redskins owner Jack Kent Cooke offered Gibbs the head coaching job, including a three-year contract, starting at $100,000 a season.

Although Gibbs had no head coaching experience, Cooke was impressed with his high-powered offense at San Diego and his innovative reputation within the NFL. In addition, he was attracted to his enthusiasm, outgoing personality, and commitment to work notoriously long hours. The owner also was determined to hire someone who could develop the young players who dominated the Redskins' roster.

As the 17th head coach in team history, the 41-year-old Gibbs would soon realize that pro football coaches are de facto CEOs of multimillion-dollar operations, with dozens of employees and more than 60 highly diverse players. Perhaps no one individual has more responsibility in American team sports than an NFL coach. He must "supply players with tactics and purpose," writes Nicholas Dawidoff of *The New York Times*. "Because 50 percent of all NFL games are decided by eight points or fewer, the man with the brilliant plan is king—the face of the organization." But above all, he must win: there is no cushion for short-term failure.

Inheriting a club that compiled a 6-10 record the previous season, its worst in 17 years, the rookie head coach quickly encountered the harsh realities of being top gun. His first season began inauspiciously when the team lost its first five games, and Gibbs actually feared for his safety. "The press was calling for my head," he recalls. "The fans wondered where this no-name had come from and whether he could succeed at all." Redskins' owner Cooke, however, gave his new coach a public vote of confidence (which is the usual protocol before a firing). That message seemed to steel the team. Gibbs then installed an innovative one-back offense and a position called H-back, and the Skins rallied to finish the season with an 8-8 record.

In year two, the bookish-looking coach won the hearts of Redskins fans, winning the team's first Super Bowl. His surprising success continued in 1983 with another trip to the Super Bowl, only to be upset by the Los Angeles Raiders. Nine winning seasons followed, with two more Super Bowls in 1987 and 1991.

"Great coaches," Pro Hall of Fame coach Bill Walsh observed, "demonstrate personal drive, expertise and knowledge. In return, great players will sacrifice for a hands-on-coach, because they identify with him as an integral part of the team."

Gibbs, if anything, was Mr. Hands-On. In the NFL, there is no such thing as diminishing returns to the endless work. Laboring ridiculous hours, Gibbs did his best scheming at night (often until 3 A.M.), slept on his office cot, and left nothing unscripted. "By the end of each week, we'd have a game plan developed down to the exact plays and formations for every situation. *Nothing was left to chance*," he wrote in his bestseller, *Game Plan for Life.*

With his victory parade, the *Washington Post* called Gibbs "the most popular man" in the nation's capital. But victory doesn't mean wisdom. Outside the Beltway, the meticulous mentor stumbled, often falling into the money trap. "I started hungering to set myself up financially," he says. "I wanted to be comfortable, even rich. Problem was, I knew nothing about the financial world."

In a world where nobody wins forever, Gibbs knew that the grinding, year-round scrutiny of coaching often leads to an ungraceful exit—and financial insecurity. To hedge the downside, he embarked on a string of ill-fated business ventures: oil and gas investments, racquetball clubs, nursing homes. "We lost a lot of money," he says, "I was looking in the wrong places for my financial security and relying on my less-than-perfect instincts to discern a good deal."

Barely escaping bankruptcy, the humbled coach shelved future get-rich-quick schemes—drawing strength from his religion. Henceforth, he vowed to focus on football, with the "understanding that God is the ultimate owner of everything."

In addition to financial missteps, the relentless workaholic began to experience health problems. Toward the end of the 1991–92 season, he started getting tremors, which the Mayo Clinic diagnosed as prediabetic symptoms. Stress, he was warned, could lead—and eventually did—to full-blown diabetes and more serious complications.

The day a leader forgets his core values, he'll disappear like dew on a sunny morning. Seeking to avoid burnout, Gibbs promised his wife, Pat, that he wouldn't fall prey to the rigors of the job. He also wanted to reconnect with his two sons, J.D. and Coy. From that time on, he says, he "began to strive for a better balance between my work and my family."

"We must be willing to get rid of the life we planned to have the life that is waiting for us," wrote scholar Joseph Campbell. Looking for greater work-life balance, Gibbs began plotting a graceful exit from coaching a year before his final season with the Redskins. He wasn't looking forward to endless rounds of golf or sipping pina coladas, though. His career, after all, had been defined by the pressure of team competition.

Calling the family together, Gibbs's sons professed an interest in auto racing, which also appealed to their dad, a former hot-rodder. "J.D. suggested we put together a NASCAR race team," Gibbs recalls. Mrs. Gibbs approved the new avocation, but only on assurance that none of the family would participate in the terror-filled driving.

In 1992, Joe Gibbs Racing entered U.S. motor sports at the highest level. "We had no idea what we were doing," Gibbs says. "We had nothing. No cars, no drivers, no money, just an idea." The would-be race-track baron soon discovered that NASCAR racing is extremely expensive. After several stops and starts, he was able to convince Norm Miller, owner of Interstate Batteries, to sponsor his fledgling venture.

With Gibbs continuing to coach the Redskins, veteran Dale Jarrett was designated lead driver on the 16-man team. That first year, Gibbs Racing entered NASCAR's first and most prestigious event, the Daytona 500—a spectacle on a par with football's Super Bowl. For most of the race, Jarrett led the pack over the 2.5-mile super speedway. However, roaring around the track at almost 200 m.p.h., he piled up, escaping injury but unable to finish the race. "In the blink of an eye, our hopes were smashed," Gibbs says. Winless that year, he wondered if there was a second act in motor sports.

Meanwhile, back in Washington, Gibbs was attempting to defend the Redskin's Super Bowl crown from the previous year. But it was not to be. The team finished out of the money, with a disappointing 9-7 record. Along the way, coaching lost its luster. Weary of the long hours and eager to return to the family's racing business, Gibbs retired in early 1993, surprising many in the Redskins' organization and around the league. Nonetheless, he had left a formidable legacy.

Gibbs was one of the winningest coaches in NFL history. During his first 12-year stint, his record was 124-60, with a post-season mark of 16-5. His combined winning percentage of .683 ranked behind only Vince Lombardi and John Madden at the time. Gibbs was also the only NFL coach to win three Super Bowls with three different quarterbacks—Joe Theismann, Doug Williams, and Mark Rypien. In 1996, he was enshrined in the Pro Football Hall of Fame.

Leaving D.C., Gibbs made tracks for Huntersville, North Carolina, where his NASCAR organization was based. After the rough ride in its inaugural year, Gibbs Racing came back with a vengeance. With Jarrett again behind the wheel at Daytona's marquee track, the Gibbs clan witnessed intense, last-lap dramatics. With three laps to go, Jarrett pulled into the lead and roared across the finish to take the checkered flag. It was an emotional moment in the winners' circle, with the family, sponsors, and race team crying and hugging.

In the years that followed, Gibbs watched the organization grow and prosper, notching two more NASCAR championships. The coach-turned-owner was enjoying his new life and professed no desire to return to the gridiron.

Throughout his retirement, though, he managed to stay in touch with pro football. For a few years, he did color commentary of televised NFL games for NBC Sports. Every winter he was asked by team owners to coach again, but he kept breaking their hearts. The Carolina Panthers nearly lured him out of retirement in 1995, offering to move his entire racing team to the team's Charlotte home.

Even though he had left football, the game never left him. In 1999, he joined a group that attempted to buy the Redskins but failed. Three years later, Gibbs and a small group of investors purchased a 5 percent interest in the Atlanta Falcons from owner Arthur Blank for $27 million. The following year, Blank interviewed him for the Falcons' vacant coaching position.

Almost simultaneously, Washington Redskins coach Steve Spurrier abruptly resigned, creating another opportunity for Gibbs. He quickly passed on the Falcons job, explaining to Mr. Blank that his loyalty still rested with the Skins. On Dec. 31, 2003, Washington owner Daniel Snyder flew his private plane to North Carolina and, in a stunning move, lured the former coach out of retirement.

"The desire to coach has always been with me, after being away from the game for 11 years," Gibbs said at the time. "The Redskins are very dear to me and my family. We're very excited about this opportunity to return to where we have so many friends and loyalties."

No doubt, Snyder's lucrative offer carried some weight. Gibbs's five-year contract, worth $28.5 million, made him the NFL's highest-paid coach. He also received the title of president. But the returning coach was not stirred solely by dollar signs. The challenge of rescuing a sinking ship—a team that foundered after his retirement, reaching the playoffs only once—carried great appeal.

Despite his heroic stature in the nation's capital, some doubted whether Gibbs could recapture his past triumphs. History, after all, was littered with examples of leaders who tarnished their strong reputations with unimpressive second acts. Recall Napoleon's failed comeback at Waterloo. Encore executives can easily be bogged down by a legacy of previous strategies, when the organization needs a new strategy—a true break from the past.

"More often than not, the experience, skills and temperament that yield triumph in Act One turn out to be unequal to

Act Two's difficulties," says leadership expert David A. Nadler. "In fact, the approaches that worked so brilliantly in Act One may be the very opposite of what is needed to bring Act Two to a happy resolution."

Although the father figure was back, Gibbs realized the game had changed during his extended absence from coaching. "There had been major shifts in both offensive and defensive styles and game plans; even differences in how we went about getting players, with free agency and a shorter draft," he concedes. "But what hadn't changed was human nature. [Players] were still driven by the same things: money, fear, greed, self-interest and praise."

Leaving his racing team in the hands of his eldest son, J.D., Gibbs began to unravel the mess in D.C. He quickly assembled one of the largest and most experienced coaching staffs in the NFL. His turnaround then depended on getting the right players, followed by the right strategy—and then executing.

Hoping to revive the old magic, he sensed the need for a new game plan. The difficulty was implementing one. Blending a mish-mash of unproven rookies with pampered veterans, Gibbs experienced what was, up to that point, the worst season of his career, with a 6-10 record. The turnaround came the next year, when the Skins went 10-6 and earned a trip to the playoffs. Disappointment returned, however, in 2006, when the team faltered to 5-11.

Heading into December, the Skins had just five games to go in the 2007 season when Gibbs was awakened with the shocking news that 24-year-old Sean Taylor, the team's All Pro safety, had been murdered in his home. The coach and team were deeply shaken. "How do you stay prepared and keep an emotionally rocked team together?" Gibbs wondered.

In what has been described as the Hall of Famer's finest month of coaching, Gibbs somehow managed to rally his troops and conclude the season with four straight victories and a 9-7 regular season mark. But the job's stresses and strains, plus the extended absence from his family, made the 67-year-old mentor again reevaluate his priorities. He also worried about the health of his three-year-old grandson, Taylor, who was battling leukemia.

On January 8, 2008, standing in an auditorium at Redskins Park before a gleaming row of Super Bowl trophies, the iconic coach announced his retirement, citing family issues. "I felt like they really needed me," he said in an emotional farewell. "Although I hate to leave something unfinished."

Unlike Gibbs, many leaders suffer from a misplaced sense of duty to stick it out and complete the mission. "I've hardly ever come across an occasion in which people thought the CEO had chosen to leave prematurely," Nadler says. "The consensus is usually that the CEO had stayed around too long."

The man who helped create the modern NFL agreed to serve as an advisor to Redskins owner Snyder. But he refused to keep an office at Redskins Park, saying he didn't want to loom over his successor. Mastering the art of the graceful exit, Gibbs returned to North Carolina to reconnect with his family and his racing team. Despite his departure, a recent *Washington Post* poll of D.C. sports fans cited the ex-coach as "the greatest sports figure" in the city's history.

Today, NASCAR rivals the NFL in popularity. What was once a mom-and-pop pastime has been transformed into a commercial behemoth, fueled by a rapid, television-inspired rise. Few organizations have profited more from the sport's resurgence than Joe Gibbs Racing, which has grown to 440 employees. Last year, the enterprise was valued by *Forbes* at $155 million, No. 3 in the industry.

"Happiness is not having what you want, but wanting what you have," Rabbi Hyman Schachtel once said. Whether on the gridiron or the racing track, Joe Gibbs always remained true to his core values. "God is first," he says. "Family and loved ones are second—my occupation is third."

Heavyweight champion George Foreman found happiness outside the ring as an entrepreneur and marketing genius.

Troubled ex-fighter Mike Tyson tries to remake his life in the unlikely sport of pigeon racing.

CHAPTER 5

FIGHTING BACK

"I love boxers because they face fear—and they face it alone."

—BROADCASTER NICK CHARLES

"FIRST SECURE AN INDEPENDENT income, then practice virtue," goes an old Greek proverb. Boxers, historically, are notorious for plying their trade too long—seeing their incomes evaporate and dreams of virtue disappear. Joe Louis, "The Brown Bomber," was the standard bearer of fighters who racked in millions, overstayed their welcome, and ended up broke. In this life-or-death sport, rare is the boxer who walks away on top, championship belt in hand, finances intact.

George Foreman is the exception: a prizefighter who knew what it was like to get knocked down—in the ring and in life—and how to exit gracefully. When his salad days were over as heavyweight king, Big George rebounded handsomely, sidestepping an earlier flirtation with bankruptcy. Reinventing himself as an entrepreneur and marketing genius, he proceeded to find much greater wealth (an estimated $250 million) and happiness than he had experienced during his boxing career.

Mike Tyson took a much different course. The once-gifted man-child and former heavyweight champ found it hard to leave the ring, squandering an unimaginable $400 million. Gorging himself on all manners of vice, the self-proclaimed Baddest Man on the Planet descended into the world of nonstop clubbing, drinking, and cocaine—culminating in a lengthy police record and jail time. Since hanging up his gloves, the newly clean, sober vegan is now fighting a different fight, attempting a makeover in the unlikely sport of pigeon racing.

In many ways, both men had much in common. They both experienced troubled, impoverished childhoods, with raucous, dysfunctional families. In their early teens, as brooding hooligans, both champions-to-be were in and out of trouble with the law. Thanks to aging mentors, boxing was their salvation. Devastating opponents with brutal, staccato punches short on artistry but long on force, Foreman and Tyson achieved mainstream fame—working their way up a list of formidable foes. But, after winning the heavyweight crown, one of the greatest trophies in sports, they each experienced a dizzying sequence of ups and downs: multiple marriages and divorces, numerous offspring, embarrassing losses, title defeats, and financial mismanagement. While professional pugilism had brought them fame and fortune, it had not prepared them for a graceful exit and a meaningful life outside the ring.

Foreman, for his part, evolved successfully from street fighter to boxing champion to celebrity pitchman. Born to J.D. and Nancy Foreman on January 10, 1949, in Marshall, Texas, the fifth of seven children, he grew up on the mean streets of Houston's Fifth Ward. "The Bloody Fifth," he calls it, "where every weekend someone got shot, knifed or killed." The dirt-poor youngster would blow up a brown paper sack to make it look full when he had no lunch to take to school. "We couldn't afford a TV or a separate bed for me," he remembers. "Having a bedside lamp seemed like the height of luxury."

A junior high dropout, Foreman took his frustrations out as a mugger and street brawler and had constant run-ins with the law. Luckily, he was rescued by President Lyndon Johnson's Job Corps program aimed at troubled inner-city youths. At 17, he traveled to California to meet Job Corps counselor Charles "Doc" Broadus, who taught him how to box. Under his careful training, Foreman rapidly crafted an impressive amateur record. In less than three years, he captured a gold medal at the 1968 Olympics in Mexico City. In celebrating his victory, Foreman danced around the ring waving an American flag. "I wanted everyone in the world to know I was American, and was proud of the opportunity that I was given." An unforgettable image.

The following year, the 20-year-old bruiser made his pro debut under the guidance of veteran trainer Dick Sadler. Regrettably, he copied sparring partner Sonny Liston's intimidating, bad-boy image, which did nothing to ingratiate him with either the press or the public. Using a piercing stare, the 6-foot-4-inch brawler, at 250 pounds, growled to his opponents, "I'm going to kill you." Undefeated, and with an impressive knockout record, the surly, hard-edged heavyweight went on to beat the bejesus out of heavily favored Joe Frazier in two brutal rounds to capture the title in boxing's premier division in 1973.

Big George then defended his title successfully twice during his initial reign as champion. By 1974, his record was 40-0, with 37 knockouts. But by this time, free-spending and carousing had seduced the former street thug. "It embarrasses me to think of all those years I was buying silk suits and alligator shoes," he recalls. "Numerous cars I just parked, and let the dust build up." Despite advice to remain faithful to one woman, the insecure infidel later admitted that he "just didn't grasp it at the time. You get five girls just because so-and-so had them. It wasn't desire or physical urgency. It was ignorance." Consequently, he would pile up a string of five marriages and 10 children.

With 24 straight knockout victories under his belt, Foreman traveled to Zaire in 1974 to defend his crown against the mythic Muhammad Ali in what was to become known as the "Rumble in the Jungle." As if in some morality play, the '70s villain got his comeuppance, and most of the world rejoiced when Ali flattened him in eight rounds. It was Foreman's first defeat and only knockout loss of his career.

"From being feared to being pitied was a long fall," he says. "And with disappointment comes evil." The loss so depressed him that he went into a tailspin. "Life was complete emptiness and darkness. I was on my own, helpless—just dead."

After taking the year off, Foreman returned to the ring in 1976, winning a number of fights, including a rematch over the formidable Frazier. For his next bout, he took on a lesser fighter named Jimmy Young before a raucous crowd in Puerto Rico on Saint Patrick's Day, 1977. In a shocking upset, Young decked and defeated the former champion.

After the fight, Foreman had an epiphany, claiming to have seen God in his dressing room. Shortly thereafter, he retired, becoming a minister and "fighter for God." Following this spiritual transformation, the born-again slugger preached for a decade in Houston, devoting himself to his family and parishioners. In 1984, he founded a youth center that bears his name, a place for Texas street-smart youngsters who need direction to stay on track.

Though mindful of the money problems of boxing legends like Joe Louis, Foreman made a series of economic blunders: "Oil wells, gas wells, banks—flop flop, flop!" After squandering $5 million, he barely avoided bankruptcy. "I lost all my money, and when you lose your money, you think you're done," he recalls. "I was only fractions, fractions away from being homeless."

Entangled in financial woes, the former knockout king desperately needed funds to support his family and youth center. After a 10-year layoff (in which he had ballooned to 315 pounds),

Foreman astonished the boxing world by announcing a comeback at age 38. He said his return to the ring was intended not only to restore his depleted finances but also to prove that nobody was too old for a second chance. Although most pundits contended that his "unretirement" was a mistake, Foreman soon proved that he could still dispose of his adversaries. Eventually slimming down to 245 pounds and improving his stamina, he racked up 18 consecutive knockout victories.

Along the way, Big George discovered a hidden talent for salesmanship. In the early 1990s, he began to sell everything from grills to mufflers on television. He also landed a lucrative, high-profile announcing gig with HBO Sports that would last a dozen years. In addition, he remade his public persona from the formerly aloof, ominous Foreman to a bald, loveable, gentle George.

"I knew I needed to rebuild my tough-guy image," he wrote in his autobiography, *Knockout Entrepreneur*. "I wanted to show the new George—a George Foreman who smiled, who loved, and who still competed hard, but a George Foreman whom no one would ever again have to fear."

His desire to reclaim the heavyweight mantle initially was stalled by Evander Holyfield in 1991. But a few years later, Foreman again startled the world by knocking out undefeated 26-year-old heavyweight champion Michael Moorer in the 10th round with a ferocious right to the jaw. In an instant, he had regained the title he had lost to Muhammad Ali two decades earlier. At 45, Foreman became the oldest heavyweight champion in history, as well as the fighter with the most time between one world title and the next. He would hail his victory as one "for all my buddies in the nursing home and all the guys in jail."

With renewed vigor, the kinder, gentler bruiser successfully defended his title, "never throwing a punch in anger or attempting to injure anyone," he said. "Sometimes I got booed during my comeback because I wouldn't destroy my opponents as I'd done in my earlier years."

In the final showcase of his fistic talents, Big George took on 25-year-old Shannon Briggs in Atlantic City, New Jersey, in 1997. After 12 rounds, in which he consistently rocked the challenger with awesome power punches, almost everyone at ringside saw Foreman as the clear winner. However, Briggs was awarded the fight in a highly controversial decision.

"Of course, I was discouraged and disappointed to hear the referee's voice reverberating throughout the arena," he recalls. "For a few minutes, I had my own personal pity party. I wanted to dive under the canvas and escape the millions of eyes watching me. But that boxing match was history."

At 48, Foreman again announced his retirement. But unlike most punch-drunk pugilists, he had an exit strategy. "A good fighter knows when to throw in the towel," he says. "I immediately looked to the future. When one dream dies or comes to an end, you can't wallow in despair. Dream a new dream, and then work hard to see it come to pass."

Although he would receive several overtures to return to the ring, including, at 55, an offer to fight ex-champ Larry Holmes, Foreman—with considerable urging from his wife Joan—remained true to his word. Having earlier laid the groundwork for a graceful exit from the fight game, he resumed his career as businessman, minister, and family patriarch. Drafting off his mainstream fame, the self-described "grillionnaire" saw the now infamous George Foreman Lean Mean Fat-Reducing Grilling Machine become the largest-selling household appliance in history. In 1999, he sold his interest to the manufacturer for $137.5 million in cash and stock (after he had already pocketed more than $60 million as its ardent pitchman). At the time, it was the biggest deal for any athlete.

Thanks to his likeable public personality, the retired boxer also made millions touring on the lecture circuit and endorsing a wide range of household names: Nike, McDonald's, Doritos, KFC,

Oscar Mayer, Motel 6, and Meineke Car Care, among them. In addition, he launched his own line of environmentally safe cleaning products, an exclusive line of personal care products, a health shake, a prescription shoe for diabetics, a restaurant franchise, 13 books—and the list continues to grow.

Croesus-rich, Foreman today owns a fleet of 60 high-end cars, a fancy watch collection, two homes and a ranch in Texas, and another home on the Caribbean island of St. Lucia. Nevertheless, he says he doesn't know—and doesn't want to know—his net worth. His earlier brush with bankruptcy remains deeply etched in his psyche. "I'll never feel secure again," he reminds himself every day. "I've got to earn, earn, earn!"

"Try not to become a success," Albert Einstein once said. "Try to become a man of value." Graceful exiters like Foreman find activities that they love and do well. They find people and causes they believe in and serve with all their hearts. They give their energy to projects that improve people's lives, not diminish them. They find ways to savor all of life, not just the rewards of work. Simply put, they define success on their own terms.

Despite his recent wealth, Foreman defines success primarily in noneconomic terms. "Don't let making money be your only motivation," he warns. "Do something you can be passionate about beyond the mere accumulation of money. Success is helping people believe that they can do something great. But don't wallow in your present success. Get on to the next thing!"

Besides managing his various business interests, Foreman tends to his ministry and charitable work, including his "Knock-Out Pediatric Cancer" initiative. With a household of 10 offspring, including five sons named George, it came as no surprise when cable network TV Land signed the ex-champ to star in its 2006 reality show *Family Foreman*. The retired boxer was tabbed as "someone who reinvented the second half of his life," TV Land president Larry W. Jones said. "There are so many ways to describe

George Foreman—but viewers have never seen how he juggles all of these demands while being a loving father." The show ran for two years.

"Boxing is an unnatural act," F. X. Toole once wrote. "Everything in it is backwards to life." Retired warhorse Foreman is the exception. Never one to look backwards, he has been propelled forward beyond the boundaries of boxing by his popularity and sense of self. At age 63, one of the world's most beloved athletes and personalities remains on a constant quest to reinvent himself. "Keep answering the bell," he tells his audiences today. "The key to success in boxing—and life—is to keep getting back up. Always dare to do something different. A never-give-up attitude will bring you victory."

"The people who go to fights don't just go to see some guy win," W. C. Heinz wrote in 1951, "they go to see some guy get licked, too." Ironically, prizefighters are often remembered more for losing a great fight than winning a bad one. Clearly, Mike Tyson's legacy—and, to a great extent, his downfall—was shaped on February 11, 1990, in Tokyo, when a quintessential underdog, James "Buster" Douglas, knocked out the then-undefeated and seemingly invincible heavyweight champion in the 10th round. The most spectacular upset in boxing history would change his life forever, demonstrating once again how fickle fame can be.

Tyson's rise to prominence didn't come easily. As a youngster, he grew up in the rough-and-tumble Bedford Stuyvesant and Brownsville sections of Brooklyn. His father abandoned the family when Mike was two, leaving his alcoholic mother prey to multiple boyfriends who beat her up regularly. As a picked-on, fat, bespectacled kid with a high-pitched voice and lisp, Tyson quickly learned to defend himself against older and bigger boys.

By his early teens, he had been in numerous scrapes with the law and arrested 38 times. At 13, he was sent to a juvenile lockup in upstate New York. There, he was introduced to boxing and, in time, to the stern, paranoid-driven trainer-manager Constantine "Cus" D'Amato. "Cus was my father, my backbone," Tyson recalls. "He did everything for my best interests. If it weren't for him, I would've been a bum."

Disciplinarian D'Amato forgave the youngster's troubled path, inviting him into his 14-room Victorian mansion on 15 acres in the Catskills, and eventually assuming the role of legal guardian. This quirky boxing version of Father Flanagan was assisted by co-trainer Kevin Rooney, another D'Amato protégé, and managers Bill Clayton and Jim Jacobs. Together, as Team Tyson, they developed a master strategy that would take their star pupil to the top of the heavyweight division and, initially at least, make him wealthy beyond his wildest dreams.

With a frenetic training and fighting schedule, Tyson began to develop his signature boxing style. Combining stunning speed with superior athleticism, he emerged as not only a one-punch knockout artist, but a marvelous defensive fighter. The promising pugilist worked out furiously in D'Amato's Spartan gym above the Catskill Police Station and became a deeply devoted student of the sport, watching endless hours of films of the game's greatest fighters. "Tyson learned from the best," reported Joe Layden of *The New York Times*, "and his ascent to their ranks seemed an absolute certainty."

Tyson made his professional debut in 1985 at age 18 in Albany, New York, dispatching in 107 seconds a chunky fighter named Hector Mercedes. "I knew he had potential," Rooney said at the time. "I just didn't know how good he'd be." Later that year, after Tyson had run his record to 11-0, mentor D'Amato died of complications from pneumonia. It was a knockout blow to the young boxer—the genesis, many speculate, of the many troubles that lay ahead.

Under Rooney's tutelage, Tyson slowly moved away from low-wattage opponents to borderline contenders, flattening them with a combination of outstanding hand speed and lethal punching power. Because of his strength and skill, he intimidated many fighters, with his contests often likened to public executions: "violent, primal, cathartic."

On November 22, 1986, "Iron Mike" received his first title shot in the sport's glamour division against Trevor Berbick in Las Vegas. Using a fury of vicious uppercuts and body shots, Tyson knocked out Berbick in the second round, becoming, at 20, the youngest man to win the heavyweight crown. His one-sided victory caused one ringside reporter to describe him as "a heavyweight champion fit to stand alongside Dempsey, Tunney, Louis, Marciano and Ali."

Expectations for the new champ ran high. His managers quickly launched an ambitious campaign to take on all worthy challengers. In short order, the full-of-fury Brooklyn kid defeated the likes of James "Bonecrusher" Smith, Tony Tucker, Tyrell Biggs, and former heavyweight king Larry Holmes.

With each victory came the glare of an increasingly bright, pop-culture spotlight. In 1987, Nintendo released the video game *Mike Tyson's Punch-Out!!* Casinos and networks—notably Home Box Office and pay-per-view outlets—vigorously bid for the right to feature a Tyson contest. On June 27, 1988, the former street brawler found his scowling, sweat-soaked puss on the cover of *Time* magazine.

Team Tyson immediately negotiated a bout that, at the time, was the richest fight in history. The so-called "Battle for the Ages" matched Tyson's aggressive infighting with Michael Spinks's skillful counterpunching and fast footwork. The much-anticipated match took place in Atlantic City on June 27, 1988. However, in just 91 seconds, Tyson KO'd the former heavyweight champion, who promptly took his $13 million purse and never fought again.

Tyson, for his efforts, pocketed $20 million in a fight that many consider to be the pinnacle of his boxing career.

But during his ascension as a modern-day "Raging Bull," demons began to surface. "I have this thing inside me that wants to eat and conquer," he said. "I just want to conquer people and their souls." This mantle of invincibility would reveal a poisonous, self-destructive personality.

Following a glory period in the late '80s, Tyson's overpowering ring style was matched by his equally reckless personal life. After D'Amato's death, he lost his confidante and co-manager Jacobs, and then he fired longtime trainer and taskmaster Rooney. In their stead, the mercurial fighter took on a cast of second-rate managers and, worse, handed his burgeoning financial empire over to flamboyant ex-con Don King. (A decade later, Tyson sued King for $100 million and was awarded $14 million.)

In 1989, the boxer's first marriage to TV actress Robin Givens disintegrated after only a year. A soap-opera hell, the tumultuous tabloid-sensation union had Givens describing Tyson on national television as "manic depressive" and their life as "torture, pure hell, worse than anything I could possibly imagine." Later, she accused him of domestic violence—a claim Tyson denied.

With his marriage scuttled and Team Tyson dissolved, the trajectory of his life continued to spiral downward. A notorious womanizer, Tyson began to exchange his Spartan gym for the high life, carousing with strippers, getting drunk and high. Lacking direction and with his training habits in disarray, the most feared boxer at the time ventured to Tokyo in 1990 to take on the quintessential underdog, Buster Douglas. *Sports Illustrated* quipped that Tyson, a 42-1 favorite, would go through the challenger "faster than a plate of tuna in a sushi bar."

Douglas, however, wasn't having any of this. In this David-and-Goliath replay, David would take the full measure of Goliath. Energized by the loss of his mother just 23 days before the bout, the emotionally charged Douglas knocked out the undefeated titleholder in a monumental upset.

Just as George Foreman's second rise to the top of the heavyweight ranks was occurring, Tyson's boxing career was declining. The Douglas loss had taken the heart out of him. "He's a tragic figure of what I call the sky above and the mud below," said boxing pundit Larry Merchant after the fight. "Tyson had the talent and ambition to escape his background, and to reach very high, but he couldn't deal with it. He fell to the earth."

Following his defeat by Douglas, Tyson's noxious habits began to reappear. In 1992, he was convicted of raping 18-year-old beauty queen Desiree Washington and served three years in the Indiana Youth Center. After he was paroled, he had a series of victories over a tasty menu of "tomato cans," in boxing lingo: easily defeated, unworthy opponents. But with more lucrative pay-per-view bouts on the horizon, Tyson decided to take on the dangerous ex–heavyweight champion Evander Holyfield twice, losing both times—the latter under a disqualification for biting his foe's ear.

After his shocking defeats, Iron Mike was required to undergo a psychiatric evaluation, where doctors concluded that he was chronically depressed and unable to deal with the burdens of celebrity. Yet, despite his emotional problems, Tyson remained a money-making machine. By this time, he had acquired mansions (including one with 38 bathrooms), Bengal tigers, expensive jewelry, and dozens of exotic automobiles. The entertainment industry fueled his wayward lifestyle.

"His pay-per-view events were some of the biggest in history," according to Matthew Blank, the chief executive of Showtime, which produced several Tyson fights. "His ups and downs were extreme, but Mike brought a huge amount of drama both in and out of the ring."

Promoters rekindled the drama when Tyson confronted heavyweight king Lennox Lewis in Memphis in 2002. In the pre-fight hoopla, he had audaciously warned Lewis, "I want to eat your heart and eat your children." But on a toasty June night, an enraged Lewis dominated the much-anticipated fight, knocking out the challenger with a right hook in the eighth round. At the time, the contest was the highest-grossing event in pay-per-view history, generating $107 million.

In his final stab at another possible title match, the befuddled boxer took on journeyman Kevin McBride in Washington, D.C., on June 11, 2005. Mustering his typical prefight bravado, Tyson warned his opponent, "I'll gut you like a fish." However, the contest was a complete mismatch. In the sixth round, Tyson crumbled both physically and emotionally—refusing to fight. Saying that he no longer had "fighting guts or heart," the ex-champion quit the ring. "My career's been over since 1990," he said, alluding to his loss to Buster Douglas. "I want to move on with my life."

Nevertheless, there were huge bills to pay. Worth hundreds of millions at his peak, Tyson was reduced to bankruptcy in 2003—owing creditors $27 million. He had maintained a monthly budget of about $400,000 before the filing. "I've got nowhere to live," he lamented. "My whole life has been a waste."

To pay off his mounting debts, the unmajestic former heavyweight king tried to leverage the Tyson brand, descending, as one pundit noted, "into the lower circle of entertainment hell." In 2006, just 15 months after his loss to McBride, he launched a barnstorming series of exhibition fights. Although his physical condition was "terrible" and he "truly hated fighting," he conceded that the money "would be useful" and might even alleviate his chronic depression.

Little more than a circus sideshow, Tyson's "World Tour" quickly sputtered out. His post-boxing career descended into further darkness, as he was the victim of his chronically toxic tendencies. He gorged himself on all manner of vices: sex, booze, drugs. He was, he admits, "addicted to everything." During decades of excess, Tyson managed to marry three times and sire eight children by several different women. As Wife No. 3 and current business partner Kiki, 35, puts it, "He's slept with every kind of woman you can think of."

In the latest chapter of a life run amok, the stocky slugger sought solace in the desert, moving to Henderson, Nevada, less than half an hour from the Las Vegas Strip. No sooner had the former boxer settled into his $3 million abode (once owned by ex–NBA player Jalen Rose) than he got the call that Exodus, his four-year-old daughter (from an earlier relationship), had stopped breathing. She was strangled when her neck was caught in a cord from a treadmill. Tyson immediately caught a plane to see her at St. Luke's Medical Center in Arizona. By the time he got there, Exodus was dead.

The tragedy seemed to transform Tyson. When he returned home to Henderson, he took a pledge: no more destructive, dysfunctional behavior. With the help of Kiki, whom he married in June 2009, Tyson began to channel his energies into leading an ordinary, even humdrum, lifestyle. Taking refuge in convention, he insists he is thankful to have been given a second chance at life. Drug-free, sober, and vegan, the 46-year-old boxing veteran is a chiseled 235 pounds, having shed 130 pounds in the last few years.

Tyson's finances remain in tatters, though. "I'm totally broke," he says. Debt-ridden, he owes millions in back taxes and is adhering to a strict payment plan. Struggling to make ends meet, the ex-warrior works the promotional circuit: a soul-baring one-man show in Las Vegas and on Broadway, personal appearances across the U.S., and meet-and-greet dinner tours in Europe.

Recognizing—as George Foreman had—the potential of reality television, Tyson recently began starring in the six-part *Animal Planet* series called *Taking on Tyson*. The show examines his lifelong love of pigeons and follows him in the practice of pigeon racing ("the sport of princes in Europe," he says). The owner of

3,000 birds, Tyson "has always kept pigeons and knows everything about them. The first thing I ever loved in my life was a pigeon. It's a constant with my sanity in a weird way."

If "boxing has become America's tragic theater," as Joyce Carol Oates once wrote, Mike Tyson could be cast as the leading man. Yet, a full 25 years removed from his professional debut, the once invincible figure who soared to uncommon heights says that he now feels "awesome"—and that's a little scary. The gentle giant with the famously tattooed face claims to have found an inner calm, which, he admits, is odd for an athlete notorious for his multiple addictions and brushes with the law. "But if I'm not disciplined," he says, "I won't survive."

In his present quest for self-renewal, Tyson likes to cite the last line of his favorite poem, "Don't Quit":

> *Stick to the fight when you're hardest hit.*
> *It's when things seem worst that you must not quit."*

Cynics contend that Tyson's rehabilitation and departure from boxing are hardly sure things. He still carries daunting psychological baggage from his once-scandalous life. He remains bitter and, at times, introspective about the opportunities he has squandered. "I should have made better decisions," the remorseful ex-champion says today. "I've embarrassed 500 years of my family. But you can't dwell on the past. I want to count for something. I want to do nice things so my kids can respect me."

Father Time keeps coming, but will the new Mike Tyson punch back? It remains to be seen whether he will learn—as we all have—that the road to respect has many on-ramps and off-ramps. Stay tuned!

Speed skater Eric Heiden traded in the glare of Olympic fame for a successful career in sports medicine.

Timeless wonder Dara Torres, 45, refused to hang up her Speedos.

CHAPTER 6

AFTER THE GOLD

"I was very satisfied with my Olympic career.
I left no stone unturned and never looked back."

—NINE-TIME GOLD MEDAL WINNER MARK SPITZ

SAYING GOODBYE IS NEVER EASY. It's an admission to the world and yourself that you may not be the same person you used to be. Nobody wants to think that their talent, energy, or desirability has diminished. But it's particularly hard for world-class athletes, whose skills seem to deteriorate much more quickly. That's why so many of them—engulfed by the scary prospects of an ordinary life—refuse to leave on top.

"Athletes compete, then retire and go on to a real life," says former tennis great Chris Evert. If only that that were so. "I have virtually never met an athlete who willingly walked away from sports," argues agent Leigh Steinberg. Who can forget, for instance, the embarrassing melodrama of NFL legend Brett Favre? His greatness unquestioned, the 41-year-old grandfather tarnished the legacy of a thrill-filled 20-year career with his protracted, on-again, off-again, exit from professional football. Favre and many other sports heroes remind us that letting go is a basic human fear. Perhaps for no one is it more torturous than an Olympic athlete.

For most Olympians, the Games represent far more than just patriotism. They serve as the crucible for plying one's talent and toughness against the best in the world. As the perfect-10 gymnast Nadia Comaneci, winner of five gold medals, once put it, "I didn't just want to compete to make history, I wanted to compete to be the best."

Yet many Olympians—used to rigorous competition—have struggled with "civilian life" after stepping down from the podium. Oksana Baiul, winner of gold in figure skating in 1994, battled alcohol before getting back on her feet. Eventually she launched a clothing line and skated professionally. U.S. cross-country skier Bill Koch also went on to join the rag trade. But when asked if there was ever anything as rewarding as Olympic competition, he offered a resounding, "No!"

Fan support also can be intoxicating. Many Olympians are shattered when the cheering stops and while bidding adieu. The finality can be devastating. In one of the most complete surveys of the so-called "golden hangover," researcher Steven Ungerleider interviewed 57 U.S. Olympians in 12 sports, from ice skating to swimming. He found that 40 percent of the group admitted having serious problems after exiting the Games. "Many reported that this was the only life they knew and it was inconceivable to do anything else," Ungerleider wrote.

Eric Heiden, one of the greatest Olympic athletes in history, is the exception. At the 1980 Winter Olympic Games, he won all five individual gold medals in speedskating—the equivalent of a sprint, a marathon, and everything in between. In the process, he set five Olympic records and one world record, and he defeated every one of the 144 athletes competing in the five events. Yet, at age 21, the world's greatest speed skater retired.

What was he thinking? his fans wondered. Why would this national icon—still in his prime—walk away from Olympic fame and the adoration of millions of his countrymen?

Fortunately, Heiden was singularly positioned to make a graceful exit. Ever since he was a boy, the unassuming doctor's son from the Midwest had a vision of doing something for others: a wish, though not fully articulated at the time, to heal others, rather than speed by them.

Born on June 14, 1958, in Madison, Wisconsin, Eric Arthur Heiden grew up in a sports-conscious family. "Some families play music, some dance; we did sports—*playing* sports, not observing," he recalls. At age two, Eric started skating; at eight, he joined the Madison Speed Skating Club. Six years later, he began dreaming about the Olympics. His coach, former gold medalist Dianne Holum, put him through a rigorous five-hours-a-day training regiment so he could catch up with his European counterparts. When there was no ice, he practiced in his basement on a six-foot-wide plastic sheet, where, in his stocking feet, he would simulate skating in place. In between, he punished himself—running hills, lifting weights, and cycling.

At 17, Heiden began his Olympic speedskating career in Innsbruck, Austria, where he finished seventh in the 1,500 meters and nineteenth in the 5,000 meters. The next three years, he became unstoppable, capturing the world championships from 1977 to 1979, the first American to do so. His tenacity and superior stamina made him the undisputed king of a sport that epitomized power, pain, and poise.

Consequently, Heiden came into the 1980 Lake Placid Olympics as the overwhelming favorite. On February 15, he entered his first and most vulnerable event: the 500 meters. Battling 1976 Olympic gold medalist and world record holder Yevgeny Kulikov, Heiden turned on the heat in the last 100 meters, setting a new Olympic record and beating the Soviet skater by 0.34 seconds.

The next day, the Wisconsin native racked up another gold, besting Norwegian world record holder Kay Arne Stenshjemmet in the 5,000 meters. On February 19, he won the 1,000 meters, his favorite distance, by 1.5 seconds. Two days later, he trumped Stenshjemmet again in the 1,500 meters for his fourth gold medal.

Heiden almost missed out on his final gold. The night before his last event, he watched the U.S. men's hockey team's "Miracle on Ice" upset of the Soviet Union. The next morning, after sleeping through his wake-up call, he was finally roused by worried friends who got him to the rink just in time.

The muscular skater didn't disappoint. On a bitter cold, snowy day, he calmly and methodically smashed the world record by 6.2 seconds, winning in 14:28:13. "That's the last world record I had ever expected to beat," he says.

In just nine days, Heiden accomplished what no other athlete at the time had done, earning five gold medals in a single Winter Olympics. Generally, at the elite level, skaters hone their skills for either the short or long races. Nobody before or since has won all five events. Heiden was able to combine powerhouse starts, long-distance endurance, effortless style, speed on the turns, and coolness under pressure—the result of his extraordinary ability to concentrate, endure pain, and train hard. On every front, he had honed his skills to the quality that da Vinci called the ultimate sophistication.

In becoming an Olympic icon, Heiden took home more gold from those Games than Finland, Norway, the Netherlands, Switzerland, West Germany, Italy, Hungary, Japan, Bulgaria, Czechoslovakia, and France combined. His sister, Beth, won a bronze medal as well, giving the Heiden clan exactly half of the speedskating medals awarded at Lake Placid. Three years later, Eric was inducted into the Olympic Hall of Fame.

"The first man ever to turn ice into gold," Dave Kindred of the *Washington Post* called him. Heiden, though, refused to cash in. Unlike earlier U.S. Olympic stars Mark Spitz and Bruce Jenner, the modest Midwesterner generally shunned lucrative endorsements, which he felt brought unwanted pressure and demands. To this day, he remains proud that he was fueled by the sheer enjoyment of the sport, not the often corrosive effects of sponsorship dollars.

Admitting that he was "pretty fatigued" after the Games and sensing he had "peaked at the right time," Heiden bid adieu to a sport that required intense dedication and maturity. What's more, he never felt comfortable with celebrity and the madness surrounding his newly acquired fame. Nor did he want anyone putting him on a pedestal.

"I didn't get into skating to be famous," the Wisconsin native says. "It's not a sport you want to get famous in. If I wanted to be famous, I would have stuck to hockey." As for gold medals, his rather cavalier answer: "What can you do with them? They just sit there. When I get old, maybe I could sell them if I needed the money."

Some misinterpreted his remarks, but this reluctant hero simply longed for anonymity. "I really liked it best when I was a nobody," he has explained. There's something to be said for a gifted athlete not intoxicated by fame, a public figure who shuns the limelight.

Although the low-key Olympian wanted a clean break when he hung up his skates, he refused to vegetate. The self-professed overachiever kept adding to his résumé.

Like many speed skaters, Heiden had trained as a cyclist to stay in shape. With his history-making feat at Lake Placid behind him, he began a second career racing bicycles. One of the first successful crossover athletes, Heiden thrived on cycling competition and quickly rose to the top. He narrowly missed a spot in the

1980 Moscow Summer Olympics, which were later canceled by
President Jimmy Carter.

In 1985, the transformed skater won the U.S. professional
cycling championship and took part in the grueling Giro d'Italia.
A year later, he competed on Team 7-Eleven in the Tour de
France. Just five days from the finish, he survived a frightening
crash on the descent, which left him with a concussion. (Thirteen
years later, he was inducted into the U.S. Bicycling Hall of Fame.)

During his spare time, Heiden played professional hockey in
a Scandinavian league. Yet, for all his athletic prowess, he believes
that it was his mental toughness that separated him from the
field. "There are a lot of times you want to give up," he says. "But
when you think about all the people who supported you, the time
and effort you put in, you can't give up. You talk your way out of
quitting."

That same mental toughness prepared him to change skins
once again. So, what next? Some former Olympians make a living
off their former glory, giving motivational speeches and making
corporate appearances. Others cling to sports, often coaching,
unable to let go—postponing life decisions that their contempo-
raries made years before. Not Heiden. While cycling, he began
to pursue his lifetime dream of healing others. By 1991, he had
earned his medical degree from Stanford University and launched
his third career as an orthopedic surgeon, following in the foot-
steps of his father, a longtime practitioner in Madison.

In 1996, Dr. Heiden completed his residency at the University
of California Davis, developing a much-admired sports medicine
program. This led to a stint as team physician for the NBA's Sacramento Kings and the Sacramento Monarchs of the WNBA, as
well as the U.S. Speedskating and USA Cycling teams.

In 2006, Heiden and his wife, Karen, also an orthopedic
surgeon, moved to Utah with their two children, Zoe, 10, and
Connor, 8. The couple built a thriving sports medicine practice at

the Orthopedic Specialty Hospital, located in both Murray and Park City. Heiden and a colleague, Dr. Massimo Testa, shared their medical secrets in a recent bestseller, *Faster, Better, Stronger*.

Despite his many athletic accomplishments, the former Man of Gold says his strongest identity and pride come from his post-athletic career, where he is able to help others attain their dreams and goals. "It's pretty rewarding," says the 54-year-old surgeon. Yet, when reminded of his racing victories, he admits, "Winning five gold medals, that's pretty impressive. I still wonder sometimes how I did it."

Just how much those medals mean to him became evident at the 2002 Winter Games in Salt Lake City. Heiden declined to participate in the opening ceremony, believing he embodied the Olympic ideal and should have been selected to light the Olympic flame. The celebrated 1980 hockey team was chosen instead. Heiden now admits he "was probably too stubborn" in refusing to appear. However, that hasn't diminished his love of sports, which, he believes, if carefully managed, can lead to success on a much broader canvas.

"Many of the skills I learned in medicine came through sports," the Renaissance athlete explains. "You can use those same skills in other pursuits. Perseverance, overcoming obstacles and staying focused can produce success anywhere."

Eric Heiden epitomizes the Greek ideal that sports should be a preparation for life in general. After stepping off the medal stand, he transferred his tough-as-nails mind-set to triumphs in medicine and beyond. Leaving on top, the reluctant hero left his fans cheering—and discovered a meaningful life after sports.

༄

No weepy retirements, no ugly endings for Dara Torres. America's fastest female swimmer, with three world records and 12 Olympic medals (four of them gold), had set her sights on the 2012 London

Olympics. Over the years, she had retired and unretired time and again, yet her competitive spirit remained undiminished. She continued to summon the focus and motivation to train at the highest level. The Wonder Woman of swimming would be 45 when the London Games began.

If Torres made the U.S. team, she would have become the oldest Olympic swimmer. She first became the oldest Olympic female swimmer in the 2008 Games, when she took three silver medals and, at 41, came within a blink of winning the 50-meter freestyle gold. None of this has come without pain, though. In the last two years, she has had surgeries on both shoulders, a thumb and left knee reconstruction (in which her kneecap was recentered and cartilage restored via transplant). Undeterred, the legendary gold medalist had "every intention" of representing the Red, White, and Blue in London.

Dedicated or delusional? Courageous or crazy? Most Olympic swimmers have long since retired by the time they turn 30, let alone their mid-40s. Yet Torres, known for being both ultracompetitive and compulsive, had no plans to get out of the pool. She readily brushed off critics, who for years thought she was swimming against the tide, preferring, instead, to inspire everyone to stay fit, age gracefully, and pursue their dreams.

As we have seen, leaving on top—for most athletes and nonathletes—is an uneasy, often unwanted change. Nor was the hyperfocused Torres immune to trying to stretch her remarkable career. Her hunger to lock horns athletically was as acute in 2012 as it was in 1982 when, at age 14, she set her first world record. She refused to retire, and with her aquatic talent and age-enhanced moxie, why should she?

In her book, aptly titled *Age Is Just a Number*, Torres reveals how the dream of Olympic gold first came to her—how she battled bulimia, demanding coaches, testy teammates, two divorces, the loss of her beloved father, and her first, hard-won pregnancy. With humor and candor, she speaks frankly about being an older athlete in a younger athlete's game. For instance, she recounts walking into a warm and stuffy ready room in Beijing before the 50 freestyle final and eyeing competitors less than half her age.

"Anybody else hot? Or is it just me?" she asked the girls. "I feel like I'm in menopause." A few minutes later, Torres went out to trump all but one of them. "People talk about my age, my age, my age, but it worked to my advantage," Torres said after the race. "This was the most important thing in their life, but I'd been there so many times before, my age was a total advantage mentally."

The first American swimmer to have competed in five Olympic Games said she enjoyed competing more than ever. Despite a schedule packed with speaking engagements, sponsor commitments, and time with her six-year-old daughter, Tessa, she seemed to get better with age. U.S. National Team coach Mark Schubert told her, "There's no reason to retire when you're improving so much."

As taut and toned as much younger swimmers, the age-defying fitness freak would not go away without a fight. Obsessive-compulsive? Absolutely. But the hourglass of her career wasn't losing sand fast. Unlike many aging athletes, Torres had been given the rarest of gifts: the ability to perform at the top of her game when she could most appreciate it.

To grasp what has driven this exceptional athlete, it helps to understand her journey to swimming prominence, a story that is both primal and mythic. Born in glitzy Beverly Hills, the fifth of six children and the older of two girls, she was heavily influenced by her parents, Marylu Kauder, a former model, and Edward Torres, a successful real-estate developer. Living in the lap of luxury—the family mansion had 10 bathrooms—Torres shunned the fancy West LA lifestyle for active sports.

At age seven, tomboy Dara started following her brothers to swim at the Beverly Hills Y and later joined the Culver City Swim Club, under coach Terry Palma. She began swimming six days a week, and Palma's guidance quickly paid off. In 1980, Torres set a national age-group record for 11- to 12-year-old girls. She still has the gold-crusted blue ribbon framed on her office wall in Parkland, Florida.

The next year, Palma took her to her first National Team event at Harvard University. The up-and-coming 13-year-old tied for sixth and began "to realize I had the ability to be not just a good swimmer, but an exceptional swimmer if I applied myself." In 1982, she broke the world record in the 50-meter freestyle and earned a place on her first U.S. National Team.

Back home, at the tony Westlake School for Girls (now Harvard-Westlake School), Torres smashed a host of California marks, setting records that remain to this day. To up the competition, the family made the difficult decision to leave prestigious Westlake for laid-back Mission Viejo, California, where the talented high school junior could better prepare for the 1984 Olympics under Mark Schubert, coach of the Mission Viejo Nadadores and current head coach of the U.S. National Team.

Under Schubert's tightly structured approach, Torres began to appreciate the work ethic demanded of elite athletes. That first year at Mission Viejo, at 16, she recorded personal bests in both the 50- and 100-meter freestyle. The following year, she secured a spot on the U.S. 4x100-meter freestyle relay team and won a gold at the Los Angeles Olympics. Her leg in 55.92 seconds represented another personal best.

After the Games, Torres enrolled at the University of Florida, where she garnered 28 NCAA all-American swimming records— the maximum number possible during a college career. But success came with a heavy price. Coach Randy Reese, a notorious taskmaster, wanted his ladies lean, with mandatory weigh-ins before each practice. Any added pounds meant "the breakfast club," shorthand for extra morning workouts. Acknowledging that she would do anything to avoid the club, Torres developed bulimia, which would haunt her for "five horrible, obsessive years."

Despite her eating disorder, Torres entered the 1988 Olympics in Seoul as the odds-on favorite in the 100-meter freestyle. Describing the Games as "excruciating" largely because she "couldn't figure out what or how to eat," she underperformed—placing a disappointing seventh in the 100-meters. Again, she picked up medals, but only in relays.

With the Olympics over and college behind her, Torres began her first retirement. In 1990, she moved to New York, working as a production assistant for NBC Sports. However, inspired by Olympic ice-skater Brian Boitano's comeback at age 27, she decided to train for the Games again. In 1991, the now bulimia-free swimmer set her sights on the 1992 Barcelona Olympics.

At 25, and already referred to by her teammates as "Grandma," Torres was elected team captain. Swimming once again in the 4x100 freestyle relay, she garnered another gold. "Mission accomplished," she said at the time. "Now I could put my Olympic ambitions behind me and move on with my life."

She moved back to New York with her husband, Jeff Gowen. In short order, Torres began to make a name for herself outside swimming as a TV commentator and print model. She also became the first athlete to appear in the *Sports Illustrated* swimsuit issue. To stay fit, she worked out at the Reebok gym, played hoops, and ran and cycled in Central Park. Along the way, though, her marriage crumbled.

In 1999, seven years into retirement, the 32-year-old divorcee plotted her second comeback. To pursue her dreams, she put her modeling and television career on hold and moved to California to train under highly respected Richard Quick. Her return triggered a wave of negative vibes from jealous teammates, particularly

Olympian Jenny Thompson. Nevertheless, under Quick's tutelage, Torres became bigger, stronger, faster. After only five months, she bested her 50-meter freestyle time by 0.3 seconds—faster than her existing world record set 15 years earlier.

At the 2000 Sydney Olympics, the Comeback Kid displayed her full potential, scoring five medals, including three bronzes for individual events. "At age 33, I'd accomplished more than I had at age 17, 21 or 25," she says. "But I was also exhausted" and came home "faced with emptiness" and—like many fellow Olympians—confused about "what to do with my life."

To complicate matters, Torres sensed that her success after a seven-year hiatus from elite swimming had put her under suspicion for doping. "Behind my back people were saying that I must be using something," she says. The Sydney star quickly became the face of innuendo, her achievements grist for the rumor mill. Though it was emotionally "very hurtful," Torres managed to put the drip-drip-drip of unfounded drug charges behind her as she plotted her third retirement.

Over the next five years, the now-beached Olympian was married and divorced again, this time from an Israeli surgeon, Itzhak Shasha, who had cared for her father during his final years. To stay in shape, the compulsive exerciser hit the gym again—big time. For her, training wasn't simply an escape, but a lifelong ritual. "Some people have religion," she explains. "I have the gym. I love the challenge, the structure, the sense of accomplishment as you set, work toward and attain your goals."

In 2005, after trying for years to have a baby, Torres bore a daughter, Tessa, with her partner. Years earlier, she had always promised that if she ever got pregnant, she would start swimming again. True to her word, four weeks after giving birth, she was back in the pool, swimming three or four times a week at the Florida-based Coral Springs Aquatic Complex, under the watchful eyes of Michael Lohberg, a six-time Olympic coach. During her training, the four-time Olympian managed to lose the 36 pounds she had gained during her pregnancy.

Two and a half months later, Torres broke a world age-group record at the Masters World Championships at Stanford. Her time was good enough to make the Olympic Finals qualifying mark and got her thinking about earning another gold.

Swimming at the Olympic level at her age, Torres understood, was "all about recovery" from training and competition. Consequently, she made the kind of adjustments older athletes must make, cutting her swimming workouts to five times a week, down from the 10 to 12 water workouts in her teens and 20s. "You may feel like you have to do what a 20-year-old does, but you just can't," she admitted. Also, she took two days a week completely off.

As important, Torres engaged a strength and conditioning coach to help her fight the typical decline in muscle mass that usually begins in the 30s. Her regiment included not simply weight machines, free weights, and standard floor exercises, but a combination of medicine balls, bands, and resistance cables. The goal of these four 90-minute sessions each week was to strengthen core muscles in the abdomen and back, which give a swimmer's arms and legs a better platform to work with.

Then there were two full-time personal stretchers or "mashers," a physical therapist, and a massage therapist. Before and after Dara's swims, they twisted and pulled her torso and limbs in a vigorous resistance sequence that has been described as "a cross between a yoga class, a massage, and a Cirque de Soleil performance." All this was designed to ease her body's recovery by flushing out toxins and lactic acids.

Added to Team Torres were swimming coach Lohberg and a sprint coach, Chris Jackson. Their more traditional duties were to analyze ways in which hundredths of seconds could be whittled away—improving everything from rapid-fire starts to more fluid flip turns.

Of course, this required big bucks. Her talented staff ran a combined tab of nearly $100,000 a year. Fortunately, Dara remained a well-paid motivational speaker outside the pool—receiving an average $25,000 a pop, according to her agent, Evan Morgenstein—with lucrative sponsorships from Speedo and Toyota.

Torres's regimented recovery schedule of proper nutrition, hydrating, stretching, and massage paid off at the Olympic Trials in 2007. Just hoping to qualify for a relay spot, the 41-year-old mother won the 100-meter freestyle. Two days later, she broke her own American record—for the ninth time—winning the 50-meter freestyle.

Everyone who marveled at Torres's supercharged motor wondered how the middle-age mom would do at the 2008 Beijing Olympics. From the moment she arrived in China, the sculpted swimmer stood in awe of the festival. "I loved Beijing," she said. "I loved the Olympic Village. I couldn't wait to get out and race. I felt that deep, appreciative, happy-to-be-there enthusiasm of a woman who was supposed to have hung up her Speedos many years before."

To preempt any speculation that she might be taking performance-enhancing drugs, Torres volunteered for an enhanced, state-of-the-art drug-testing program. "I am clean and wanted to be tested to show you can perform with hard work, dedication and good people," she said at the time.

Thanks to her rigorous training and talented retinue, the U.S. team co-captain won the 50-meter freestyle silver, missing out on what would have been her first individual Olympic gold (she had four from relays) by one-hundredth of a second. She declared afterward that she was done—that she was going to leave the lanes to the younger set.

Yet only weeks later, in another familiar change of heart, Torres returned to competition and set her sights on a strong finishing kick at the upcoming London Olympics. If she made the team, the 45-year-old would have become the oldest Olympic swimmer—the equivalent of climbing Mount Everest, one step at a time without oxygen. Torres can make the team "without question, because she knows how," predicted Jack Bauerle, the 2008 U.S. women's Olympic coach, before the team trials. "You're not going to find many people more driven."

But on July 2, Father Time caught up with Dara Torres. At the U.S. Olumpic trials in Omaha, she came up just short in her bid to make the team for a record six times. Torres finished fourth in the 50-meter freestyle, nine-hundredths of a second from second place and a trip to London. The timeless wonder's long career had finally ended.

"This is really over," Torres said. "That's it! I'm going to enjoy some time with my daughter, have a nice summer and cheer on the U.S. team."

Broadcasting icon Vin Scully prepares for his 64th season in Dodger Blue—with no plans of retirement.

Colorful ex-jock Bob Uecker parlayed a mediocre playing career into four decades of stardom as the Milwaukee Brewers announcer.

CHAPTER 7

BROADCAST NEWS

"Almost everything I know about spring is in baseball."

—THOMAS WOLFE

O N   A   S C O R C H I N G   S U M M E R day, an old man begins his arduous climb to the top of gracefully aging Dodger Stadium. Unlike almost everyone else, he is not wearing a badge, security identification, or media credential. When he reaches his perch, the legendary Vin Scully comes to life. Gazing out at the Los Angeles skyline, bounded by the San Gabriel Mountains, the dean of baseball broadcasters begins to share stories of America's national pastime. All in a day's work: it's a routine he has proudly performed for 63 years.

One of the most recognizable voices in announcing, Vincent Edward Scully is one of a subset of timeless wonders: baseball broadcasters whose endurance with one or more teams made them greater symbols of their franchises than most players. "You can replace a player, but that voice—you can't," retired Seattle superstar Ken Griffey Jr. said of sportscasters. Ernie Harwell, Mel Allen, Red Barber, Harry Kalas, Harry Caray, and Jack Buck were other longtime icons of the mic who seemed like extended members of the family. But Scully, at 84, remains the grandmaster—the longest serving broadcaster with any one team. He is revered by generations of fans, players, and peers, and his unique style and melodic approach to calling games have served as a model for legions of baseball announcers.

"He's the reason I decided to do what I do for a living," says veteran broadcaster Charley Steiner, now in his eighth year as Scully's partner in the Dodgers booth. "We had a small house in Long Island with a very large Zenith radio. I sat there kind of like the old RCA Victor dog and listened to his voice." Working with Scully, he adds, "is like playing pepper with Babe Ruth."

Today, football may garner the highest television ratings, but baseball remains the country's verbal pastime. "The game has a natural affinity to narrative," says Fordham University English professor and sports buff Leonard Cassuto. "Each contest unfolds like a measurable story, and the gaps in the action leave room for embroidery of all kinds."

For six decades, the venerable Scully has crafted memorable word pictures that allow audiences to visualize the action on the field. He has the astonishing ability to speak for hours at a time, seemingly without stopping to breathe; he can broadcast games, recounting pithy anecdotes, without so much as a pause. His picturesque prattle has turned millions of neophytes into serious aficionados of the game. Bridging the era between the Golden Age of radio and the modern era dominated by television and the Internet, Scully remains at the top of his game, the recipient of countless awards and accolades.

They say that if you watch baseball long enough, you'll see something you've never seen before. Maybe that's what has kept Vin Scully so young—the promise of what the next game might bring.

Scully became addicted to sports at an early age. Born in the Bronx on November 29, 1927, he has said that his lifelong love affair with the microphone goes back to his early years listening to football games on the radio. On Saturdays, he would "crawl under the radio" listening to the sirens of the day: Graham McNamee, Ted Husing, Harry Wismer, and Bill Stern. "I would listen, and the crowd noise would come down like water out of a showerhead," Scully told broadcast historian Curt Smith. "I hadn't seen a crowd, but I loved its roar—it gave me goose bumps."

Baseball won him over at the tender age of nine. "I was walking home from my grammar school in Washington Heights, and there was a Chinese laundry," he recalls. "The owner had posted the score on a piece of paper on the window. I don't know what number it was, but the Yankees beat the Giants—and they scored in double figures. I can still see it. I stopped and looked at the lopsided score and thought, 'Oh, those poor Giants.' From that moment on, I became a Giants fan."

When he wasn't shuttling off to see the Giants play at the Polo Grounds, 25 blocks from home, Scully attended Fordham Preparatory School in the Bronx. Named the "wittiest" and "most popular" senior, he played centerfield on the baseball team, while excelling in drama, debate, and elocution. In 1944, he entered Fordham University with the aid of a partial scholarship. There, he announced baseball games over the campus radio station and also got some experience in the field by playing for the Rams for two seasons.

With graduation soon approaching, Scully sent out résumés to roughly 125 radio stations along the Eastern seaboard. Only one, CBS affiliate WTOP Radio in Washington, D.C., responded. Living that summer in Georgetown, he opened the station at 5:30 A.M., closed it at 1:00 the next morning, and—in between— worked as a fill-in. But opportunity knocked.

Scully was introduced to CBS Radio's sports director and voice of the Brooklyn Dodgers, Red Barber, who took an interest in the 21-year-old greenhorn from Fordham. Barber tapped him to broadcast the Maryland–Boston University football game on November 12, 1949, at Fenway Park in Boston. Expecting an enclosed press box, Scully had left his coat, hat, and gloves in his hotel room. When he arrived at the stadium in raw, 40-degree weather, he discovered he would be broadcasting from the roof, exposed to the elements. Cable trailing behind him, he walked back and forth along the roof calling the action. Fighting frostbite and bone-chilling winds, Scully never mentioned his discomfort or his working conditions to his listeners. All in a day's work.

By the time Maryland had wrapped up a narrow victory, Scully dejectedly climbed down from the building. "I was sure I'd blown the greatest opportunity of my life." Two days later, though, a Fenway official apologized to Barber for the shoddy treatment accorded Scully. "That turned out to be a big break," the young New Yorker remembers. "In Red's mind, 'This kid never mentioned anything about the booth, the cold, nothing.' That really impressed him." A couple of days later Barber called Scully: "You'll have a booth this week: You're doing Harvard-Yale."

Vin Scully had left his mark. Two months later, Barber's broadcast partner in Brooklyn, Ernie Harwell, left to work for the New York Giants. Barber remembered the young redhead who hadn't made a fuss. In his autobiography, *Rhubarb in the Catbird Seat*, he wrote, "I always had the dream of taking an untutored kid who showed some promise and of putting him on the air for what he was, a neophyte learning the trade. Scully was the perfect choice. He was a green pea, but a very appealing green pea. It was obvious he had something on the ball; you didn't know precisely what it was, but he had it."

Dodgers owner Branch Rickey saw it too, telling Barber after meeting with Scully, "You have found the right man." And that was the start for the fledgling announcer.

In 1950, Scully, at 22, joined the Dodgers as its No. 3 announcer, sharing the booth with Barber and Connie Desmond. His salary: $5,000. At the time, gasoline cost 27 cents a gallon, a postage stamp was just three cents, and the minimum wage was a paltry 75 cents an hour.

Barber, the folksy yet flinty Southern gentleman, mentored Scully. He told him that if he wanted to be successful, he should never root for the home team, never listen to other announcers, shun players socially, and keep his opinions to himself. The athletes, Barber explained, provide the story. The sportscaster's job is to add information and identification, sometimes entertainment—in effect, to act as a sports enhancer. To this day, Scully calls Red Barber "the most influential person in my life."

When Barber got in a salary dispute with World Series sponsor Gillette in 1953, Scully took his spot for the Fall Classic. At age 25, he became the youngest person to ever broadcast a World Series game (a record that still stands). After 15 seasons, Barber left the Dodgers to work for the New York Yankees, and Scully eventually became the team's principal announcer.

At antiquated Ebbets Field (now the site of a housing development), the dapper Scully, clad in tie, jacket, starched shirt, creased trousers, and polished loafers, arrived four to five hours before a game for his crucial prep mode: stopping by the front office, field, clubhouse, then booth. Digesting a mound of baseball statistics, he threw himself into the details, contemplating how to transform them into poetry at game time. His most memorable moment behind the microphone was in 1955, when he said the words Brooklyn fans had never heard before, and would never hear again: "Ladies and gentlemen, the Brooklyn Dodgers are champions of the world."

The following season, at Yankee Stadium, Scully again found himself in the enviable position of calling what he would later say was the greatest individual performance he had seen: Don Larsen's perfect game against the Dodgers. Mel Allen called the first five innings, with Scully handling the last four. "I think we can both just go now," Vin said to Allen in their postgame wrap-up, admitting to "feeling wilted like a rose."

California, here we come. Although he had cut his teeth in the New York area, Scully decided to accompany the Dodgers when the team moved from Flatbush to Los Angeles in 1958. "It was an uneasy time, not knowing whether we'd be accepted. For a time, I had a suitcase in the closet. But California just took to us."

The transplanted Easterner quickly burst into prominence, demonstrating his regular-guy persona and unmatched credibility. He transitioned seamlessly from the frantic pace of Brooklyn to the easy air of laid-back L.A., where fans arrived famously late and left early in hope of beating the traffic. Because folks had difficulty following the action during the team's first four seasons in the cavernous Los Angeles Memorial Coliseum, it soon became customary for them to bring transistor radios to the games to hear Scully describe what was happening. One writer suggested that "the Portable Vinny" might have been the single largest influence on transistor radio sales in Los Angeles. In the traffic-bound metropolis, generations of listeners, held captive to their car radio, were soon won over to Dodger Blue.

"After a year in L.A.," Scully says, "I started to feel at home." Team attendance and fan interest soared. "The Dodgers made the greatest impact on Southern California's millions since the 1933 earthquake left them shimmying and shaking," wrote Pulitzer Prize winner Jim Murray of the *Los Angeles Times*. His golden voice had transformed the City of Angels into a true baseball city. "He was more than just their announcer when the Dodgers came West," Murray added. "He was the link to the great Dodger past, explaining the new family on the block."

Four years later, the Dodgers moved into its drop-dead gorgeous, 56,000-seat stadium in Chavez Ravine two miles from city center. In short order, they set a major-league attendance record:

2,755,184. That popularity, as well as Scully's well-chronicled contributions, brought the New York Yankees calling.

In 1964, the Yankees offered Scully the opportunity to succeed Mel Allen as their lead play-by-play announcer at a handsome salary and long-term contract. "I thought long and hard about it," he remembers. "But I had a young family and we had all just really adjusted here. In the end, I turned it down."

Although baseball broadcasters often live in a state of perpetual boyhood, Scully began to recognize the dangers of being pigeonholed. With Allen's unexplained dismissal and ungraceful exit from the Yankees, he became more introspective about his future. "I always thought of Mel as a good-natured man who was totally consumed by the business," Scully said. "I looked at him as a warning never to get caught up just being a baseball announcer."

Yet, Scully came to appreciate that broadcasting baseball— properly managed—could become a gateway to greater opportunity because the sport's unique rhythm and deliberate pace allowed announcers to explore its nuances and subtleties, requiring greater depth. Networks, with bigger paydays and national exposure, sought those skills and represented a logical next step. And the Voice of the Dodgers—with an established track record announcing World Series and All-Star Games—was a natural candidate.

In the 1970s, Scully began to hone his credentials in other sports, while his baseball career continued to blossom. From 1975 to 1982, he called National Football League games for CBS Sports television. One of his most famous calls came on January 10, 1982: Dwight Clark's touchdown catch in the NFL Championship game. The multitalented announcer also anchored network tennis and PGA golf in the '70s and '80s. In every instance, he demonstrated an unquenchable curiosity to learn everything about the events he covered. For example, to get up to speed on tennis, he read eight books by Billy Talbert and Tony Trabert, played

Santa Monica tennis pro Bob Harmon, and then aired the Jimmy Connors vs. Rod Laver Tennis Classic on CBS.

In 1983, Scully traded in CBS for NBC, hosting the *Saturday Baseball Game of the Week*. Teaming up with Joe Garagiola, he was on hand for several key moments in baseball history. One of his most memorable calls came in Game 1 of the 1988 World Series, when a hobbled Kirk Gibson's two-out, two-strike, two-run homer gave the Dodgers a victory over the highly favored Oakland A's.

"High fly ball into right field, she is gone," Scully said before remaining silent for more than a minute and allowing the crowd reaction to speak for the moment. The next words he uttered continue to be played almost nightly at Dodger Stadium: "In a year that has been so improbable, the impossible has happened."

Over the years, Scully took on more diverse assignments. He co-hosted the Tournament of Roses Parade in 1967, hosted *It Takes Two* in 1969–70, and, in 1973, *The Vin Scully Show*, an afternoon talk show. In 1977, he landed CBS's *Challenge of the Sexes*, covering a range of events: bowling, gymnastics, billiards, skydiving, and swimming. Scully portrayed himself in the 1999 film *For Love of the Game*, and his patois could be heard in a variety of films and TV shows. He also lent his voice to Sony PlayStation's MLB video game.

"Broadcasters are the greatest brand ambassadors you can have," says San Diego Padres president Tom Garfinkel. A series of Dodgers owners have appreciated Scully's vital contributions to the brand. To accommodate his various interests, the team modified his busy schedule. In recent years, he works a reduced load of 110 games a year. He calls all nine innings of every Dodgers television game at home and in Western division parks. His first three innings are simulcast on the radio.

Yet, after more than a half century behind the mic, his love of sports and his zest for broadcasting remain undiminished. "The nicest residual of this job if you've been at it a long time is to have someone say, 'When I hear your voice, I think of summer nights with mom and dad in the backyard.' Or, 'I think of fishing with my father.' That's a wonderful feeling to think you serve as a bridge to the past for so many people."

The Baseball and Broadcasters Hall of Famer doesn't know how much longer he'll work. He still considers sportscasting less a job than a labor of love. However, with each passing year, the labor becomes more burdensome. He also thinks a lot about his wife, Sandra, and the loneliness she must feel on game day.

"But the problem is that I love my job. It still gives me goose bumps," Scully admits. "Can I give it up? I don't know." Last season, after re-upping for a $3 million salary, he hinted he might retire after the 2013 campaign. But for the time being, any plans to exit gracefully are on hold, as his golden voice continues to boom away from the Vin Scully Press Box at Dodger Stadium. "God's been awfully good to me," he says, "allowing me to do the things I love to do."

Baseball could go on without Scully, but it would never be the same. With his departure, the Dodgers, now under new ownership, would lose a sizeable chunk of its identity. Someone eventually will succeed him, but no one will replace him. Till then, the magic of the baseball diamond keeps the veteran announcer forever young. "The roar of the crowd absolutely intoxicated me," he says. "And it still does."

❧

Bob Uecker feels more fortunate than most ex-jocks, because he has no feelings of frustration, of promise unfulfilled. He knows he got the most out of his talent—and it wasn't much. He played only six unremarkable years as a catcher in the major leagues but eventually found a way to parlay his blend of quick wit and homespun wisdom into stardom in the broadcast booth, on radio and television, and in the movies, as well as in beer commercials.

Unlike many fringe athletes, he knew when to exit gracefully and how to maximize leverage of the game he loved.

No one's more amazed than septuagenarian Uecker that he's been around baseball so long. "To last as long as I did with the skills I had was a triumph of the human spirit," he quips. It was in Milwaukee that this hometown boy began to achieve iconic status. As a youngster, he grew up watching the minor league Milwaukee Brewers. A hot-shot athlete, but an indifferent student, Uecker enlisted in the army in 1954 at age 19. His performance in various military leagues caught the attention of the Milwaukee organization that later signed him to a minor league contract for a $3,000 bonus.

For the next five years, he bounced around the Milwaukee farm system: from Boise to Wichita, from Eau Claire to India-napolis. "I was fortunate in the minors to have managers who encouraged me and moved me along to the next rung," he recalls. "They were always trying to convince someone in the front office that I could play, even if I wasn't always convinced myself." In 1961, he moved up to the Milwaukee Braves, which had relocated from Boston in 1953. That stay, however, was short-lived, one manager Chuck Dressen sent him back to the minors with the deathless words, "There is no room in baseball for a clown!" Little did Dressen know that Uecker's mastery of turning humor into hope and his mediocrity as a ballplayer ("I had slumps that lasted into the winter") would lead to a Hall of Fame career.

In 1962, Uecker returned to the majors, the first Milwaukee native to suit up for the Braves. For the next six seasons, he caught for four teams, including the 1964 World Champion St. Louis Cardinals. His hitting—never stellar, with a .200 lifetime batting average and 14 home runs—declined steadily over his career. He's still in the top 10 for most passed balls by a catcher in a season. But in his defense, he was catching pitcher Phil Niekro, whose specialty was the knuckleball, a very difficult ball to catch. "The best way to catch a knuckleball," Uecker would later jest, "is to wait until it stops rolling and then pick it up."

A major challenge for the marginal player is that it's hard to tell when you've begun to slip, he says. "But I knew when my career was over. When my baseball card came out, there was a blank space where the picture was supposed to be."

In 1967, the Atlanta Braves released the "good wit, no hit" catcher. "When the fringe athlete retires, no one feels cheated," Uecker wrote in his autobiography, *Catcher in the Wry*. "The adjustment to the Real World is more gentle when the time comes to take off the uniform. The fringe player doesn't miss the cheers, and his standard of living doesn't undergo a dramatic change. My highest salary in baseball was $23,000. In a few years, I would be earning more than that, from telling people what a failure I was."

The next few years, Uecker transitioned smoothly to his new life in Atlanta, working for the Braves speaker's bureau and doing color commentary on their telecasts. In addition, he sharpened his acerbic wit in a number of area comedy clubs. In 1970, Milwaukee Brewers owner Bud Selig hired him as a scout.

"Worst scout I ever had," said Selig, now the commissioner of Major League Baseball. His new hire was notorious for turning in reports that were unreadable and covered with food stains. "Yeah, I did scouting if you could call it that," Uecker admits. "For every guy, I wrote, 'Fringe major leaguer,' so in case he made it, nobody could say, 'How'd you miss that guy?' I could say I didn't."

The next year, Selig moved his underperforming scout into the broadcast booth, with Merle Harmon and Tom Collins. Initially, he had the common former player's role of color analyst: the wing man to play-by-play announcers, filling pauses with analysis, background, and the occasional exclamation. But by 1972, he had assumed play-by-play responsibilities, keeping fans informed of who did what and every other important detail. Uecker works with the diligence of a beat writer. He is regularly where the stories are—in the clubhouse, in the dugout, and around the batting cage before games. His preparation, complemented by a wink and a knowing smile, has made the ex-catcher a perennial fan favorite.

His exuberant voice with comic undertones gained national notoriety from his many Miller Lite beer ads; as the voice of *WrestleMania* for more than 20 years; as announcer Harry Doyle in all three *Major League* films; as Pittsburgh sportswriter George Owens for six seasons of the 1980s sitcom *Mr. Belvedere*; as the host of two syndicated TV shows, *Bob Uecker's Wacky World of Sports* and *Bob Uecker's War of the Stars*; and as a frequent guest—64 appearances—on *The Tonight Show*, where Johnny Carson dubbed him "Mr. Baseball."

It is in the Brew City, though, where Uecker has minted his greatest success. For more than 40 years, he has served as radio broadcaster for his hometown Brewers, forging an unbreakable bond with fans. Part comic, part encyclopedia, he can offer a dazzling array of esoteric statistics and colorful anecdotes of hundreds of players and teams. Most of his humor is self-deprecating, like his oft-repeated line that "I'd take my kids to the game, and they'd want to come home with a different player."

In recent years, however, a string of health issues has caused the colorful 76-year-old to sober up—at least a little. In 2010, he had three-quarters of his pancreas removed after benign tumors were found on it. "They put me on a little bit of insulin," he told *The New York Times*. "A lot of people want to shoot me. Now I shoot myself." A few months later, surgeons replaced his aortic valves and performed a coronary bypass. That was followed by another heart operation later in the year. With his ticker repaired, his return to the booth was widely hailed.

"You feel like a part of your family is back," said one longtime fan. "It's like your father had a heart attack and now he's back home." His former on-air partner and straight man, 33-year-old Cory Provus, agreed: "He's the best remedy for a bad day."

Clearly, the press box is Bob Uecker's pastime. This year, the Hall of Fame broadcaster plans to work every home game plus selected road trips. With no hint of retiring, Milwaukee's timeless wonder hopes to extend his career to his 80th birthday and beyond: Vin Scully territory.

"I'm a baseball guy and I'm going to do whatever I have to do to make myself happy," Uecker says. "Happiness is being with the team and being with our ownership. It's a great life."

Outspoken doctor–cum–legislator Sen. Tom Coburn rails against "careerism" in Washington.

Sen. Daniel K. Akaka

Octogenarian Daniel Akaka of Hawaii had a difficult time bidding Aloha to the U.S. Senate.

CHAPTER 8

SENIOR STATESMEN

"Politicians, old buildings and prostitutes
become respectable with age."

—MARK TWAIN

FOR THE SAKE OF THE COUNTRY, George Washington
knew his exit lines. Not only did our Founding Father do
much to define the American presidency, but he respected the
office and avoided anything that might tarnish it. Then, to top it
off, he left the job voluntarily. No law required him to step down,
and running against him would have been impossible. Retiring
after two terms, Washington enabled the transfer of power by
electoral process.

"That crowning achievement," writes historian William Hogeland, "set the standard, albeit less celebrated by history." Truth
be told, Washington never lusted for the presidency and hoped
to resign after his first year. Only his unique ability to moderate
the intense bickering between Thomas Jefferson and Alexander
Hamilton caused him to serve a second term.

Yet America's first president knew when enough was enough.
He fully understood Article I of the Constitution, which explicitly

asserts that "no title of nobility should be granted." Rather than attempt to forge a political dynasty, "Honest George" refused to overstay his welcome. He simply retired to his plantation at Mount Vernon and distilled whiskey.

While Washington exemplified the art of leaving on top, contemporary politicians often have great difficulty finding the right moment to hang up their boots. The problem stems, in part, from an eroding sense of self-awareness, forgetting the time-tested warning: "Remember, thou art mortal." Often isolated from their critics, who do pols turn to for advice? Overprotective staffers? Gushing constituents? Close family and friends? The more others validate their favorite lawmaker's value, the more special and therefore secure he or she feels.

Whether through poor counsel or personal insensitivity, politicians are often the last to find out when it is time to go. Many get caught up in the buzz; others think they are owed immortality. But every country goes through periodic purifications. Recall when Margaret Thatcher declared, from the doorstop of 10 Downing Street, the official residence of the British prime minister, "I fight on, I fight to win," only hours before finally losing the confidence of her cabinet—and giving up the fight altogether.

Great leaders like Baroness Thatcher rise and fall. Americans are fed up with the Mickey Mouse way in which our elected officials in Washington are displaying their dysfunctional approach to the debt and budget crises. Disenchanted with the political process, John and Jane Doe recently registered the highest level of congressional disapproval on record: 92 percent.

"The political status quo, whatever it did over the past 50 years, has arrived at a dead zone," claims *The Wall Street Journal*'s Daniel Henninger. Washington's traditional impulse to spend more of the public's money has shifted to one of penny-pinching and belt-tightening. In the new paradigm, officeholders face the unenviable choice of slashing spending or raising taxes to eliminate the country's persistent deficits. The premium today is on timely compromise and statesmanship rather than procrastination and political posturing.

Youth is almost always served, except in Washington. Although Americans tell pollsters they are fed up with Congress and crave fresh faces and new ideas, the nation continues to rely on long-serving, multiple-term politicos. According to the Congressional Research Service, the average age for U.S. senators is 62.2 years. House members average 56.7 years. (Ironically, the Commander-in-Chief is a youngish 51.)

The current political system heavily favors incumbents with strong name recognition and well-developed followings—meaning older candidates, who are established with the public. Youthful outsiders have a tough time replicating those skills because of the crushing costs of campaigning and limited largesse.

No doubt, experience counts in many endeavors, politics included. "Domain knowledge," as it is often called, is essential in any field, and the United States can't afford to lose those legislators who are still at the top of their game. There is no guarantee that their replacements will be any better.

That said, the prevalent practice gives inordinate power to time-servers, who are often reluctant to pass the baton to younger, energized competitors. Take Senator Robert Byrd (D–West Virginia), the longest-serving member of either house in U.S. history. In his late eighties, he said, "I love the Senate. If I could live another 100 years, I'd like to continue in the Senate." Byrd died in office, aged 92.

"Next to the assumption of power is the responsibility for relinquishing it," argued British PM Benjamin Disraeli. Like others we have examined, political leaders with Potomac fever not only endanger their legacies by refusing to retire, but also deny new blood to the nation they love. An important characteristic of any institution's success is openness and fluidity. "A political class that remains open, mobile, and self-generating in successive generations is a healthy sign," says Stephen Hess, senior fellow emeritus at the Brookings Institution.

All may not be lost. As Alexis de Tocqueville observed, "The greatness of America lies in her ability to repair her faults." Many claim to have helped repair this underperforming political culture, but Tom Coburn can make the claim legitimately. Now in his second and final term, the rock-ribbed Republican senator from Oklahoma has made it his mission to break up the logjam of Beltway enablers and aging appropriators. He has thrived in Washington with a reputation for hard work, straight talk, and a relatively balanced view of complex problems.

Born on March 14, 1948, Thomas Allen Coburn forged his maverick mind-set in Wyoming's high plains. Growing up in cowboy country, he was strongly influenced by his father, a prominent optician and founder of Coburn Optical Industries. As a youngster, he moved with his family to Muskogee, Oklahoma, where he graduated from public high school in 1966. Four years later, he earned an accounting degree, with honors, from Oklahoma State University. From there, it was on to Colonial Heights, Virginia, where, at 22, he ran the family business's ophthalmic division. Under his leadership, the company blossomed, capturing 35 percent of the U.S. market.

In 1975, Coburn was diagnosed with malignant melanoma. Doctors told him he had only a 20 percent chance of surviving beyond one year. But survive he did and, at age 30, two years after Coburn Optical was sold, he made a bold leap and decided to pursue a medical career. He attended the University of Oklahoma Medical School, where the relative oldster earned the nickname "Gramps" from his classmates. He served as class president and graduated in 1983. He then interned in general surgery at Saint Anthony's Hospital in Oklahoma City, followed by a family practice residency in Fort Smith, Arkansas. With his formal training behind him, he returned to Muskogee, where he set up his medical practice and served as a deacon in the Southern Baptist Church.

Despite his strong track record in business and medicine, those who knew the straight-shooting maverick warned him not to enter politics. "You won't fit in," they said. "You don't have the right personality for Washington." But the young doctor was sick and tired of what he saw from the nation's ruling elite. "I got into politics because I thought I could make a difference that others couldn't make," said the tough-willed cancer survivor.

Voters concurred, electing the 46-year-old "Okie from Musk-ogee" to the House of Representatives in 1994, making him the first Republican to represent his district since 1921. Not wanting to become a career politician—and, still juggling his medical practice—Coburn upheld his campaign pledge to serve no more than three consecutive terms. Thus, he retired from the House in 2001, once that span elapsed.

During his first stint in Washington, the plainspoken Oklaho-man quickly became known as a staunch fiscal and social conserva-tive, famous for his opposition to deficit spending and pork-barrel shenanigans, as well as for his support of term limits, gun and pro-life rights, and the death penalty. Fiercely independent, he ruffled feathers on the right and left. He had numerous battles with fiery House Speaker Newt Gingrich, feeling that the Repub-lican caucus was moving away from the conservative "Contract With America" proposals that had swept the GOP into power in 1994. In particular, he was upset that term limits had not been implemented and that Republicans were continuing to support careerism and earmarks—in Coburn's words, "the gateway drug to spending addiction"—that they had opposed under Democrat rule.

After leaving Capitol Hill, Coburn returned to his medical practice and authored *Breach of Trust: How Washington Turns Out-siders Into Insiders*. The book detailed his long disdain for career politicians. High on the list: fellow Republicans Gingrich, J. Dennis Hastert, Dick Armey, Trent Lott, and Bob Dole.

But after three years of delivering babies, the former businessman-turned-physician decided to return to Washington. On November 2, 2004, he was easily elected to the U.S. Senate. "I got back into it this time because I was begged to," he says. "I believe in trying to achieve things. The satisfaction of being a senator will come if my children and yours get the same opportunities we have." About the same time, he also beat a reoccurrence of cancer, which caused him to lose part of his colon.

Reminded of his mortality, Colburn vowed to serve just two terms, believing that his self-imposed exit allows him to focus on what is best for the nation and not his re-election. Staying grounded as a citizen legislator, Coburn has tended to squeeze every minute out of every day. After inflicting pain in Washington, he returns home on weekends to Muskogee, where he continues to treat patients on Mondays. He still delivers an estimated 20 babies a year—more than 4,000 in his almost three-decade medical career.

"Politics are hardly ever mentioned," Coburn says of his patients. "The reason people still want to see me is that they have confidence in what I can do as far as their medical needs are concerned."

Upon returning to Washington, the rookie senator turned his attention once again to thwarting wasteful spending and reducing the size of government. In the process, the congressional lightning rod seemed indifferent to whether or not people liked him. He often attacked President George W. Bush on spending, saying that it was "immoral to spend the next generation's standard of living." He took on fellow Republican Ted Stevens, the senior senator from Alaska and attempted to divert the infamous $452 million "Bridge to Nowhere" to Louisiana's Twin Spans Bridge, which was devastated by Hurricane Katrina. In the imbroglio,

Stevens, a 40-year veteran of the Senate, threatened to resign, and Coburn's amendment was defeated in the Senate, 82–14. In a subsequent action, his "School House Pork" report showed billions in the Department of Education's budget going to "stupid stuff," including mariachi classes in Las Vegas, wine studies in central Washington, and funds for Cleveland's Rock and Roll Hall of Fame.

Pork has not been the doctor's only target. The pro-military, but antiwar, activist complained that the Bush administration's handling of budget requests for the Iraq War through "emergency" supplemental spending was a phony way to do business. Known as "Dr. No" for his willingness to make a point, he has infuriated colleagues of both parties by delaying votes. His willingness to block or neuter bills through an array of procedural measures has made him an effective nuisance.

Describing Coburn's methods as "very frustrating," Sen. Claire McCaskill (D–Missouri) concedes, "He uses the rules to their full advantage to advocate positions he believes in, and I respect him for that. I may disagree with him, but I admire and respect him for doing it in the open."

Though at times hyperbolic in his rhetoric, Coburn has forged a number of notable powwows across the aisle. The politically ambidextrous crusader joined hands with staunchly liberal Democrats: Sen. Dick Durbin on deficit issues, Sen. Carl Levin on tax-cheating stimulus contractors, and Sen. Dianne Feinstein on legislation to eliminate ethanol subsidies, as well as Independent Sen. Joseph Lieberman on a bipartisan bill to save Medicare.

But his most interesting alliance is with President Barack Obama. Their friendship was forged when they were both elected to the Senate in 2004. Two years later, the unlikely allies won enactment of a proposal to create a central database for citizens to track federal grants and contracts.

"He's fearless in his approach," says Obama, who has vocally supported Coburn's efforts in spending and lobbying reform and who, in 2010, appointed the Oklahoma Republican to his deficit reduction committee. Similarly, Coburn has considerable respect for his ideological opposite. "I love the man," he told Bloomberg TV in 2011. "I think he's neat. I disagree with him adamantly on 95 percent of the issues, but that doesn't mean I can't have a great relationship. And that's a model other people should follow." Coburn says that he still speaks regularly and writes supportive notes to the president, even while publicly ripping him for his performance.

Besides playing a central role in Medicare and healthcare debates, Sen. Coburn was part of the six-member bipartisan group, the "Gang of Six," negotiating a $4 trillion debt-reduction package. Those sessions, in part, contributed to raising the federal debt limit. Earlier, Coburn had introduced his own plan that called for $9 trillion in overall savings, including $1 trillion in new revenues. In advocating revenue hikes, the senator broke with House Republicans and many conservative leaders. Unrepentant, Coburn simply said, "I've always considered myself an opposition within the opposition." To that end, he recently penned *The Debt Bomb*, a bold plan to slash wasteful government spending. Even *The New York Times*, hardly a beacon of conservative support, huffed that Coburn "deserves credit for challenging at least some of his party's shield-and-cosset-the-rich orthodoxy."

Straight-shooting has won the doctor a core of other supporters, including famed investor Warren Buffett, who calls him "a real statesman." But along the way, he also has had his naysayers. In his first senatorial race, he was confronted with allegations that he had sterilized a 20-year-old patient without proper consent and defrauded the government by withholding information about the procedure. The 13-year-old claim was ultimately dismissed, with no finding of liability on Coburn's part.

In 1997, Congressman Coburn protested NBC's plan to air the R-rated Holocaust drama *Schindler's List* during primetime. Stating the film depicted "full-frontal nudity and irresponsible sexual behavior," Coburn was roundly criticized. He later apologized for his "error in judgment," although he still feels the graphic material was unsuitable for showing during family hours.

More recently, the senator was accused of attempting to cover up then-Senator John Ensign's extramarital affair with a staffer in 2009. The allegation suggested that Coburn tried to intervene to end the tryst prior to its becoming public. Citing legal privilege as a licensed physician and ordained deacon, Coburn refused to discuss any such involvement, simply stating that "a lot of mistakes" were made.

Such skirmishes, however, have never prevented the plain-spoken physician from challenging the powers that be on Capitol Hill. Sidestepping the torpid world of politics, the multifaceted lawmaker admits his victories are rare, and the ire from his colleagues is intense. Dogged and determined, he doesn't seem to mind. Making good on his determination not to be a Capitol Hill lifer, this Washington wise man prepares to leave on top and head back home in 2016.

Now in his second and final term, Sen. Coburn remains optimistic about the future. "America's still a great country," he tells constituents. "But we need to embrace what made the country great and return to our core values. In particular, we need to think about the next generation—not the next election."

❧

Also completing his last lap in the U.S. Senate is Daniel Akaka of Hawaii. However, the 88-year-old Democrat is taking a far different path from Sen. Coburn. For years, the Aloha State's revered junior senator had contended that age was no reason to quit politics. He portrayed his 30 years in Washington as his greatest asset, saying that his accrued seniority allowed him to enhance the economic fortunes of his small, isolated state.

In recent years, however, party leaders openly questioned Akaka's performance and even his ability to function in his advanced years. In 2011, he was removed as chairman of the Veterans Affairs Committee and given the decidedly less taxing Indian Affairs subcommittee. At the same time, one critic found that he was "so inactive . . . that staffers joke that Hawaii is the only state with one senator." In addition, Hawaii's other senator, Daniel K. Inouye, stated that he wouldn't be able to provide his colleague with the financial support of years past. He noted that Akaka's slow fundraising pace for a potential re-election—with just $66,278 in hand—was far short of the minimum $3 million he would need to mount a successful campaign.

"He'd likely get crushed in 2012," predicted political pundit Bob Jones. "Not just beaten mind you, crushed. . . . But how do you tell an icon, who'd probably like to eventually lie in state in the Capitol Rotunda as the first Native Hawaiian senator, to step aside?"

In early March 2011, Sen. Akaka reluctantly announced that he would not seek re-election after 22 years in the Senate. With a mixture of relief and regret, the only U.S. senator of Native Hawaiian ancestry (and the only current senator of Chinese ancestry) said, "I feel that the end of this Congress is the right time for me to step aside. I have always strived to serve the people of Hawaii with much love and Aloha."

Regrettably, Hawaii's "true ambassador of Aloha," as Sen. Inouye has called him, could have left office on a high note—saving face instead, as some see it, of having egg on it. As we have seen in other chapters, the gravitational pull of aging can lead to diminishing returns. Hence, there comes a time when the reins must be passed. And the beloved, but reluctant, elder statesman would have been well-advised to have followed the old social axiom: leave the party when you're still having a good time.

Daniel Kahikina Akaka was born on September 11, 1924, in Honolulu. Raised by deeply religious parents, he attended the Kamehameha School for Hawaiian and part-Hawaiian students. After graduating, he enlisted in the U.S. Army Corps of Engineers and served in Saipan and Tinian from 1943 to 1947. Upon returning home, he enrolled in the University of Hawaii on the G.I. Bill, earning a bachelor's degree in education in 1952.

Akaka taught high school from 1953 to 1960 and was promoted to principal in 1963. Six years later, Hawaii's Department of Education hired him as a chief program planner. His political career began in 1971, when Gov. John Burns appointed him to direct the state's antipoverty programs. In 1975, he served as Gov. George Ariyoshi's special assistant for human resources.

Encouraged by party elders to seek political office, he successfully ran for the U.S. House of Representatives in 1976 and won seven consecutive terms by wide margins. In 1990, Sen. Spark Matsunaga died in office, and the governor appointed Akaka to take his place, transforming him into a fully entrenched member of the state's powerful Democratic machine. A few months later, he waged his first race for the U.S. Senate, capturing 54 percent of the vote. Dependable and free of notoriety, he won his next race decisively, scoring more than 70 percent of the ballots in 1994 and 2004.

In 2006, as the third-oldest member of the Senate, Akaka faced his sternest political test in the Democratic primary from two-term Congressman Ed Case, 53, a cousin of America Online co-founder Steve Case. The contest, described by *Honolulu* magazine as "a bombshell of massive proportions," challenged the party's traditional grip on the electorate. The younger, independent-minded Case created a political bees' nest in taking on a popular, well-entrenched incumbent, who over the years had endeared himself to his constituents.

"This election raised some credible concerns about the Democratic power structure in Hawaii," wrote *The Honolulu Advertiser*. "The party, which has done little to nurture the careers of subsequent generations of leaders, seems mired in the maintenance of the status quo." Political writer Richard Borreca described the state as "the country for old men; old women, too."

Case's risky strategy, besides rankling the Democratic elite, made his veteran opponent's age the central issue. "We have two 82-year-old senators," he told *USA Today*, referring to Akaka and his elder by four days, Inouye. "They're coming to the end of their careers. What makes complete sense in an objective way is to bring in the next senator now to build up seniority while Inouye is still serving."

Not surprisingly, Case's rationale brought a sharp retort from the highly respected Inouye, who then ranked second to West Virginia Sen. Byrd among Democrats on the powerful Senate Appropriations Committee. "It sounds almost as if Mr. Case is playing God, suggesting that Sen. Akaka or I would soon be meeting our maker," the senior senator said. "Yes, Sen. Akaka and I could be hit by a car or by lightning. But so, too, could Mr. Case."

Highlighting his experience and opposition to the Iraq war, the incumbent Akaka defeated his ambitious, younger challenger with 55 percent of the vote. But the contentious campaign hurt the senator's popularity and indicated his vulnerability. Akaka went on to beat his Republican opponent in the general election with 61 percent of the vote, his lowest re-election rate ever.

Paul Douglas, the former senator from Illinois, once said he came to Washington to save the world. After a while, he decided he wanted to save the United States. A little later, he hoped to save Illinois. And when he was about to retire, he said he just wanted to save the Illinois dunes—a worthy effort, but not the world.

Over the years, Sen. Akaka has also had to moderate his goals. As a legislator, he has had two overriding missions: (1) to reverse decades of neglect and restore a sense of dignity for Native Hawaiians, including the right to form their own government and (2) to insure that the Aloha State's fragile economy gets the dollars and support it deserves.

His signature legislation, the so-called Akaka Bill, attempts to restore Hawaiian self-determination, lost in 1893 with the overthrow of the Kingdom of Hawaii, and would include giving up the ability to sue for sovereignty in federal courts in exchange for recognition by the federal government. Despite his longstanding connections on Capitol Hill, the senator's top priority of the last dozen years has been stalled indefinitely, particularly given the sway of the conservative Republicans.

On other fronts, the low-key senator has consistently voted the Democratic Party line over the course of his career. No fiscally conservative Blue Dog Democrat, Akaka's staunchly liberal, social, and economic views have secured him the endorsement of influential labor organizations, including the AFL-CIO. His list of legislative credits, though not spectacular, include significant benefits for Hawaiian veterans, public workers, and native people; protection of Social Security, healthcare, and workplace safety; and support for various Hawaii-based projects in agriculture, education, and renewable energy.

Nonetheless, the senator's detractors complain that such accomplishments are mediocre at best and that his genial demeanor has worked against him in failing to accomplish more in Washington. In 2006, *Time* magazine cited him as one of the five worst senators, calling him the "master of minor resolution" and "living proof that experience does not necessarily yield expertise." The article also chastised him for focusing on Hawaii-centric issues.

No doubt, the humble and gracious lawmaker's effectiveness is often discounted in comparison with his fellow octogenarian and Hawaii's major source of political clout, Sen. Inouye. A Medal of Honor recipient and longtime pillar of the Senate, Inouye's canny political skills have made him an institution within an institution. Declared the "king of Hawaii" by the *Washington Post*, the iconic senator has earned enormous respect at home and abroad. As president pro tempore and chairman of the Senate Appropriations Committee, he is widely recognized as a voice of reason in Washington. From his lofty perch, he has also brought billions of dollars for highways, airports, federal offices, military installations, and other projects to a state long reliant on tourism. What's more, by every indicator, Hawaii's timeless wonder—like fine wine—has gotten better with age. Cheating Father Time and Mother Nature, this über-oldster is still going strong.

Over the years, Sen. Inouye has vigorously defended the other Dan's record and understated style. "He's done well," Inouye says of his friend and ally. "The fact that someone is quiet and studious doesn't mean he's a weakling or he doesn't know what he's doing. He's been a willing and loyal partner . . . a tireless advocate for Hawaii's residents."

That said, opponents quietly argued that Sen. Akaka should be handed a gold watch rather than another stint in Congress. In early 2011, the increasingly frail lawmaker was beginning to feel the strains of his diminishing standing in the Senate and the prospects of a difficult and bruising re-election campaign. In the end, health and family trumped politics. Applauding his decision to stand down, the *Honolulu Star-Advertiser* wrote, "Now, Akaka, at age 86, has rightly decided to end his political career gracefully rather than test today's rough political waters."

For most elected officials, their entire identity is tied up in politics. To re-pot, to go from 100 to zero, is unthinkable. Yet, to his credit, Akaka bears no trace of the sadness and lack of purpose that hang over many once-powerful men in their later years. Although he hoped to go out on a high note, including passage of the Akaka Bill, he is excited about the next season of his life.

In an emotional swan song to his staff, Akaka said he was looking forward to heading home to Hawaii and spending more time with family. "I would also like to spend time documenting my life and career," he added, "and serving as a mentor to future political leaders."

Called the nation's greatest surgeon, Dr. Michael DeBakey continued to rebuild human hearts well into his nineties.

Multitalented Harry Gruber traded in a promising medical career to become an entrepreneurial dynamo in biotech and high-tech.

CHAPTER 9

CREATIVE GENIUS

"Creativity is just connecting things."

—STEVE JOBS

YOUTH, AS WE HAVE REPORTED, is almost always served. Unburdened by old habits and prejudices, creative types often come up with their brightest ideas at an early age. The so-called "inverted U curve," first introduced by 19th-century French mathematician and sociologist Adolphe Quetelet, suggests that most creativity curves up between the ages of 25 and 50, then peaks and starts to decline in later years. No doubt, as we all move toward old age, we often lose things we treasure: looks, vitality, and acumen. However, as Cicero pointed out in his brilliant essay "On Aging," "Great deeds are not done by strength or speed or physique. They are the products of thought, character and judgment. And far from diminishing, such qualities actually increase with age."

Doctors, particularly those engaged in fields that are in constant flux, often enjoy prolonged productivity. Think about it: Before a physician can invent a useful new idea, cure, or procedure, he or she must first learn a dazzling assortment of details. By focusing on a particular specialty over a prolonged period, one's skills generally sharpen, not atrophy, with age.

New York Times columnist David Brooks reported this age-defying trend: "We are living in an age of reverse-generativity," he writes. "The elderly. They are the future." In several professions—medicine, science, the law, among them—old dogs can learn new tricks and should not hang up their spurs prematurely.

Dr. Michael DeBakey made it his life's mission to demonstrate that creative renewal can spring from remaining curious and engaged throughout life. Rather than call it quits, this national treasure took his life-saving achievements to unprecedented heights well into his 80s and 90s. Described as the "greatest surgeon ever," DeBakey deployed his dexterous scalpel and needle on more than 60,000 human hearts and arteries. His patients included the rich and famous—Russian President Boris Yeltsin, film legend Marlene Dietrich, the Shah of Iran, the Duke of Windsor, comedian Jerry Lewis—as well as the uncelebrated.

Working incessantly until his fatal heart attack at 99, the Geriatric Goliath oversaw multiple surgeries, traveled the world, published in leading scientific journals, and invented scores of medical procedures and instruments. For seven decades, his hands remained steady, his hearing sharp. His personal health regimen included lopping up and down the stairs and covering his hospital's labyrinthine corridors at a brisk pace.

In awarding DeBakey the Congressional Gold Medal, the nation's highest civilian honor, in 2008, President George W. Bush said, "His legacy is holding the fragile and sacred gift of human life in his hands and returning it unbroken." Three months later, the father of modern cardiovascular surgery passed away in Houston, the city that he had transformed from a provincial backwater to a major center of leading-edge healthcare.

Michael Elias DeBakey began a life of unmatched productivity on September 7, 1908, in Lake Charles, Louisiana. His parents were Lebanese immigrants who moved to the United States to escape religious intolerance in the Middle East. Self-educated and hardworking, the couple ran a drugstore and dabbled successfully in rice farming, real estate, and construction. Young Michael was inspired to become a doctor from chats with local physicians while he worked at his father's pharmacy. Later, he credited much of his surgical success to his mother for teaching him one of his future career's most essential skills—sewing.

After finishing high school as valedictorian, DeBakey graduated from Tulane University in 1930 and its medical school just two years later. During his senior year in med school, he showed his gift as an innovator, developing a modified roller pump, a device that two decades later became a crucial component of the heart-lung machine used on patients during open-heart surgery.

While training at Charity Hospital in New Orleans, DeBakey conducted groundbreaking research that provided the first substantial evidence linking smoking to lung cancer. Although many prominent physicians derided his findings in 1964, the Surgeon General confirmed the relationship.

At the urging of his mentor, celebrated surgeon Alton Ochsner, the young doctor went to Europe for further training in cardiology at the University of Strasbourg in France and, later, the University of Heidelberg in Germany. Upon his return to Tulane in 1937, he married his first wife, Diana, a nurse he met in New Orleans. They would have four children. (Mrs. DeBakey died of a massive heart attack in 1972, while her husband was in cardiac surgery in another theater. He rushed to his wife's bedside but was unable to keep her alive. Three years later, he married Katrin Fehlhaber, a German film actress, with whom he had a daughter.)

During World War II, DeBakey volunteered for military service, working in the U.S. Surgeon General's office. His efforts led to the establishment of the Mobile Armed Surgical Hospital (MASH) units that saved countless lives in World War II and subsequent conflicts. For his contributions, the Army awarded him the Legion of Merit. In addition, Col. DeBakey first proposed systematic health services and follow-up studies of returning veterans with medical problems, which eventually evolved into the Veterans Administration.

After the war, he returned to Tulane as an associate professor of surgery. In 1948, he moved to Baylor College of Medicine in Houston as chair of surgery. Shortly after his arrival, DeBakey discovered that the school was on academic probation and out of funds. With the help of a wealthy donor and the Truman administration, however, he was able to link Houston's Navy hospital to the fledgling school and then launched the city's first surgical residency program. With the college on firm footing, DeBakey remained at Baylor for the rest of his academic career, eventually becoming the president of its College of Medicine, then chancellor, and, later, chancellor emeritus.

Today, heart disease remains the nation's Number 1 killer, with strokes fourth, just behind cancer and chronic respiratory problems. Heart disease and strokes both develop from disease of the arteries, and together account for roughly 75 percent of all U.S. deaths. These gruesome statistics, also prevalent in the '50s and '60s, prompted Dr. DeBakey to attack various arterial diseases with a vengeance. "We can't stand by and wait for final answers," *Time*'s Man of the Year said in 1965. "There are lives to be saved, and future illnesses to be prevented."

Deeply involved in forward-looking research, the Houston-based crusader launched a frontal assault on the nation's most pressing health problem. Unlike many of his colleagues, he rejected cholesterol levels and stress as major causes of heart disease. "We can find no significant relation between cholesterol levels and the extent and severity of the disease," he said. Equally dismissive of the effects of stress, he added, "Man was made to work, and work hard. I don't think it ever hurt anyone." He argued that the primary cause of atherosclerosis—the systematic disease in which fatty deposits cause damage to the arteries feeding the heart and other tissues—was "as distinct as there are different kinds of fevers." Impatient for scientific evidence to support his instincts, he turned his energies to innovative surgical strategies to confront heart disease.

With inexhaustible energy, DeBakey followed a rigorous 20-hour-day routine that would persist seven decades. Awakening each day in the predawn hours to record his research and read medical journals, he refused to waste time—a trait handed down to him by his father. He rarely drank, never smoked, ate sparingly (coffee and a banana for breakfast, no lunch, and a light salad for dinner). He arrived at 7 A.M. at the hospital, where he checked the three adjoining operating rooms that he directed with the aid of two assisting surgeons. When his surgeries were over, he retreated to his spacious, blue-carpeted office in Baylor's College of Medicine, where he kept an administrative assistant and three secretaries frantically busy.

Nicknamed "the Texas Tornado" for his furious work habits, DeBakey would return home late at night, working in his den until midnight. Despite his backbreaking schedule, he got by on only four or five hours of sleep.

The hyperkinetic M.D. applied his problem-solving skills on everything from clogged arteries to lung cancer to surgical infections. In 1952, he first repaired an aortic aneurysm—a ballooning of an artery—by cutting out the damaged segment in the abdomen and replacing it with a graft from a cadaver. The next year, in another breakthrough, he repaired a blocked carotid artery in the neck. The blockage threatened to cause a stroke by choking off blood flow to part of the brain. In the process, he went on to discover—again, in the face of professional skepticism—that knit Dacron grafts were excellent substitutes for damaged parts of arteries, allowing surgeons to repair previously inoperable aneurysms of the aorta in the chest and abdomen. In 1958, DeBakey performed the first successful patch-graft angioplasty to reverse the narrowing of an artery caused by an endarterectomy. Later, he was the first to execute artery bypass surgery, using the large vein in the leg to bypass the blocked or damaged area between the aorta and coronary arteries, a life-saving operation now used throughout the world.

In 1963, DeBakey participated in a federally funded program to design an artificial heart. At the time, he predicted that a complete artificial heart "could be ready for permanent implementation within three to five years. Today, it may be only a dream; tomorrow it will be a reality." In 1966, the innovative surgeon developed a device that helped blood move from one chamber of the heart to another and, later, he created a partial artificial heart. His left ventricular assist device (LVAD), implanted to increase blood flow and developed with NASA, was one of his proudest accomplishments. "Thank God, I lived to see it," he said in 1998.

Shortly after Dr. Christiaan Barnard performed the first human heart transplant in 1967, in Cape Town, South Africa, DeBakey followed, somewhat warily. The next year, his team of surgeons was the first to transplant four organs—a heart, two kidneys, and a lung—from one donor to different recipients. But given the limited supply of human hearts for transplants, DeBakey continued to expand the use of his LVAD.

That effort, in turn, sparked one of modern medicine's most famous feuds. Unbeknownst to DeBakey, his Baylor colleague Dr. Denton A. Cooley—without DeBakey's or the school's permission—commandeered an artificial heart from his former partner's lab and imbedded it in a patient at St. Luke's Hospital in Houston in 1969. Cooley defended the first-ever implantation as a desperate measure to keep his patient alive until he could secure a heart transplant. But others contended that Cooley had secretly been planning to use the device for several months.

After the incident, the American College of Surgeons censured Cooley, who was forced to resign from Baylor. Many contended that the incident robbed DeBakey of a Nobel Prize. For almost 40 years, the two master surgeons—each with Texas-size egos—rarely spoke, but they eventually reconciled in 2007, just eight months before DeBakey's death.

As cardiac surgery moved from its infancy, Dr. DeBakey continued to distinguish himself as a medical statesman. Despite his advanced years, his views were wide-ranging, detailed, and commanding. In the early 1960s, he urged Presidents Kennedy and Johnson to support the creation of the federal Medicare health insurance plan, bucking the American Medical Association. Later, he helped establish the National Library of Medicine, the world's largest and most prestigious repository of medical archives, housing more than 3.8 million books, journals, and technical reports.

The renowned physician, whose persistence and Southern charm transformed modern medicine, also had a reputation for terrorizing coworkers. He was a perfectionist—intolerant of incompetence, sloppy thinking, and laziness. Despite his velvety Louisiana drawl, he unleashed brutally biting criticism on seasoned surgeons, as well as first-year medical students, who failed to meet his lofty standards.

"At times, he could act like the meanest man in the world," said Dr. John L. Ochsner, whose father was DeBakey's mentor at Tulane. "The thing that made him so mad was that he was always trying to conquer the world, and every minute was important to him. He had no time for frivolity."

The famous surgeon performed his last operation at age 90. "I just felt that I'd done enough and should turn it over to my colleagues," he said at the time. One of his greatest legacies was training successive generations of surgeons. Over the years, DeBakey had a knack for recruiting many outstanding physicians who played key roles in many of his successes. Today, the Michael E.

DeBakey International Surgical Society, composed primarily of his former students and residents, conducts international medical symposiums and confers an award in his name biennially.

The demanding workaholic would outlive most of his peers. But on New Year's Eve 2005, DeBakey, then 97, experienced first-hand the trauma of heart disease. Alone at his Houston home, he felt a sharp pain ripping through his upper chest and between his shoulder blades, then moving into his neck. "The pain was so severe that I would have welcomed anything to relieve it—including death," said the physician who had saved so many lives.

When his heart kept beating, DeBakey suspected he was not suffering a heart attack, but rather a dissecting aortic aneurysm. No one was more qualified to make the diagnosis because, years before, he had devised the initial operation to repair such torn aortas, a condition almost always fatal. The oldest survivor of the procedure he invented, DeBakey made a miraculous recovery, saying he was "gratified to have been given a second life." Several weeks later, he resumed his jam-packed schedule.

To no one's surprise, the Mount Rushmore of medicine refused to go gently into the night. He viewed death as a personal enemy and a monumental waste of time. Until his final day of reckoning came, there would be no wick on his life's candle left to burn.

That candle was snuffed out on July 11, 2008, when the father of modern cardiovascular surgery died, just two months before his 100th birthday. He was buried in Arlington National Cemetery. "I can't think of anyone who's made more of a contribution to the field of medicine," says Dr. Sherwin Nuland, a retired surgeon at the Yale University School of Medicine and medicine's best-known historian.

"I'm a firm believer in the longer you live, the better you get," singer-songwriter Bob Dylan once said. Intensely curious and active well into his senior years, the rebuilder of human hearts proved that a grayer world can lead to a better world. Refusing to abandon the profession he so dearly loved, Dr. Michael DeBakey remained on a never-ending quest to improve humankind.

"A person doesn't have to be a doctor to be compassionate," he told *Esquire* magazine. "Everyone can help others, simply by being kind. If we could just remember that, our lives, our society, would be far better off."

It's hard to imagine Michael DeBakey ever leaving medicine. The traditional image of the successful doctor-cum-researcher is that of the compulsive workaholic, someone totally dedicated to the art of healing. But for every Dr. DeBakey, there is growing evidence that sticking to the practice of medicine is not the only path to happiness.

On the heels of the eleventh anniversary of September 11th, we are reminded that work and life are not mutually exclusive. As the idea of "balance" pervades the culture, more and more expertly trained doctors and scientists, eager to capitalize on their skills, are gracefully exiting medicine—shedding their workplace skin to feed their souls.

Of course, for years many adventurous physicians abandoned their stethoscopes to pursue a second life as full-time writers. More than a century ago, the Scottish physician Arthur Conan Doyle introduced the double helix of science and crime fiction in his gripping Sherlock Holmes stories. Michael Crichton quit medicine shortly after graduating from Harvard Medical School. His subsequent métiers ranged from science-fiction writing and film producing to computer-games creation. Other non-practicing doctor-writers include Robin Cook (*Coma*), Tess Gerritsen (*Harvest*), Ethan Canin (*America, America*), Deepak Chopra (*The Seven Spiritual Laws of Success*), Spencer Johnson (*Who Moved My Cheese?*), and Sanjay Gupta (*Monday Mornings*).

Given the stresses and strains of authorship, most medical defectors prefer a less risky path to a new life. Disenchanted with America's troubled healthcare system, more and more of them are transferring their unique patient skills and knowledge of healthcare analytics to commercial use. To illustrate:

- Dr. James Kuo, a holder of M.B.A. and M.D. degrees, jumped to a Wall Street job with a large healthcare venture-capital firm. Today, at 48, he is the CEO of Adeona Pharmaceuticals, based in Ann Arbor, Michigan, a company developing innovative medicines to treat various nervous diseases.
- Dr. Wendye Robbins runs Limerick BioPharma, a San Francisco start-up, which she founded with business partners seven years ago. The firm focuses on transplant-associated metabolic diseases, particularly Type 2 diabetics. Her advice to M.D.s-turned-entrepreneur: "Take a risk, step into the unknown. Don't be afraid to fail."
- Dr. Gerald Bortolazzo, after 30 years as an emergency-room physician, cofounded Atlanta-based ApolloMD, one of the nation's largest providers of emergency medicine, anesthesia, and radiology services to hospitals nationwide. After a serious cancer scare three years ago, he sold his interest in the company. Today, the former E.R. doc gets his kicks owning race horses.
- As reported in Chapter 3, after graduating from Harvard Medical School, Dr. Richard Kelley worked at hospitals in Boston and San Francisco before returning to Honolulu in 1962, where he worked as a pathologist. Eight years later, he juggled medicine with various roles in the Outrigger Enterprise Group, the hotel chain founded by his parents. Shortly thereafter, he left doctoring to oversee the privately

held company that today operates a portfolio of 45 properties in Hawaii and Asia Pacific.

"I never looked back [on leaving medicine]," Doc Kelley told *Pacific Business News*. "The whole concept of caring for others, for customers, comes from the self-reliance, responsibility, the dealings with colleagues [and] all the things you learn in a hospital that are applicable to life no matter what you're doing."

Turning their backs on their day jobs, these and other intrepid adventurers recognize that lifestyles can—and should be—elastic. Above all, they want to stretch their limits. They are on a never-ending search for higher mountains to climb.

"Physicians are bright people," explains Dr. John E. Prescott, chief academic officer at the Association of Medical Colleges, a trade group in Washington that represents more than 150 medical colleges. "They want to make a difference. Some do it one patient at a time. Others see a bigger impact [via] business applications."

Increasingly bright, ambitious doctors are on a mission to commercialize their medical training in new and exciting directions. It takes, of course, tremendous drive and confidence to leave at the top of a promising medical career and plunge into unchartered waters. Those who break the mold are optimists, convinced they can do anything. They have hungry, urgent minds and refuse to sit on the sidelines. They long to get involved in new projects, new ideas, and challenging assignments.

In 1986, Dr. Harry Gruber began his search for a new identity with his quest to start innovative businesses that could benefit both shareholders and society. At last count, the doctor-turned-serial-entrepreneur had given life to seven biotech and high-tech companies, which eventually achieved a combined value of more than $7 billion.

Growing up in West Orange, New Jersey, Gruber knew he wanted to explore new horizons after his first visit to his favorite haunt, Thomas Edison's nearby mansion and research labs. "What amazed me," he recalls, "was how many things Edison was working on at the same time." The famous inventor was intensely curious, discovering everything from the nickel-iron-alkaline battery and the gramophone to the incandescent lightbulb. The Wizard of Menlo Park's persistence also impressed the young visitor. Edison, who still holds the record for patents, came up with 1,600 versions of the lightbulb before he got one to work.

Although Gruber hasn't invented anything as earth-shattering as electricity, Edison's message of persistence and discovery had a lasting impact. In the 1970s, the future Renaissance man excelled at the University of Pennsylvania as an undergrad and medical student. After graduation from med school in 1977, he received additional qualifications in internal medicine, rheumatology, and biochemical genetics at the University of California–San Diego, where he subsequently joined the faculty. There, Gruber made his first contribution at 27, when he patented a class of compounds that regulate adenosine, a building block of DNA. The discovery helped reduce injury from heart attacks and strokes.

After failing to interest pharmaceutical companies in the breakthrough, the young doctor left the university to begin his second career as an entrepreneur. "There was no other choice," he told *USA Today*. In short order, he founded Gensia Pharmaceuticals, Inc., raising $4 million from a handful of wealthy San Diego investors and venture capitalists. The new enterprise focused on gene therapy, as well as adenosine research. Four years later, Gensia went public, with a market capitalization of $100 million. In 2003, the company, rebranded as Sicor, Inc., was acquired by Teva Pharmaceutical Industries, Ltd. for a whopping $3.4 billion.

The deal not only fattened Gruber's wallet but established him as a serious entrepreneur. His next home run: Viagene, a Gensia spinoff, also specializing in gene therapy, which went public in 1993 and was snapped up two years later by biotech giant Chiron Corp. for $150 million. Then came Aramed, Inc., a drug discovery company focusing on the central nervous system. The biotech firm achieved a public market capitalization of $600 million and was later acquired by Gensia for $750 million.

Despite the hectic pace, the 47-year-old biotech expert readied himself for more opportunities. "I thought I'd take some time off and then do another genetics project," he told *Investor's Business Daily*. However, the soft-spoken scientist had grown frustrated with biotechnology, because none of his patents had turned into FDA-approved drugs. "An invention doesn't count unless someone is using it," he complained. "Otherwise, it's just a dream. I like to see things move fast. So I needed to change fields."

Gruber had become fascinated with video delivery on the Internet. In 1995, he shifted gears again, joining the ranks of high-technology heavyweights after a conversation with a neighbor in the real estate business bemoaning the lack of software to present online listings of houses that were for sale. Immediately, he began crafting patents for the appropriate technology and raising money for his fourth start-up. It wasn't easy. "Venture capitalists kept asking, 'How does a biotech guy become a high-tech guy?'" Gruber recalls. "I met resistance."

But the resilient chameleon pressed on, turning to angel investors, who raised $10 million for InterVu, Inc. The San Diego–based firm delivered video and audio on the Internet for high-profile corporate customers such as NBC, CNN, and Bloomberg. Its success was almost immediate, prompting Microsoft Corp. to invest $30 million in the company. In 1997, Gruber took his new baby public, with a market cap of $100 million. Three years later, he hit gold again, selling InterVu to then-high-flying Akamai Technologies for $3.5 billion. The deal netted the founder a take worth $245 million.

Though Croesus-rich, Gruber set out to score another victory. His new target: online fundraising. Helping John McCain during the 2000 presidential campaign, Gruber found that through online town hall meetings people would gladly pay handsome sums to support their cause. Wealthy folks tend to be heavy Web surfers, and the Internet could allow them to interact with charitable organizations or political candidates much more personally than watching a telethon or responding to junk mail.

In 2000, he borrowed a few ideas from InterVu and founded Kintera, Inc., an Internet marketing service provider for nonprofit organizations. The venture would prove to be Gruber's greatest challenge. For starters, convincing the nonprofit world to move beyond its traditional fundraising methods was difficult. At the time, U.S. nonprofits collected only 5 percent of their donations online. In addition, many of them were reluctant to shell out fees to third parties like Kintera. "When we approached them, we got 100 percent turn-downs," Gruber said. "They often say, 'I can do it myself.'"

Undeterred, the tenacious chairman and CEO won over several blue-chip clients: the American Heart Association, the American Cancer Society, the Salvation Army, and the University of California. He also adopted an aggressive acquisition strategy to cover a broader spectrum of nonprofit, government, and corporate customers. "We're trying to build a substantial company in a short time period," Gruber told the *San Diego Business Journal*.

Thanks largely to more than a dozen acquisitions, Kintera enjoyed strong top-line growth, but profits eluded the company in the early years. To reduce nearly $30 million of debt, Gruber took the business public in 2003, raising $35 million. Despite higher revenues and significant downsizing, Kintera continued to lose money.

Although Gruber's chutzpah had fueled the firm's growth, impatient investors concluded that the business needed fresh leadership. In early 2007, several major shareholders campaigned to oust the company's founder. "It appears that Mr. Gruber runs Kintera more as a family business than as a value-maximizing public company," said one dissident.

Under shareholder pressure, Gruber bid adieu. His replacement, Richard N. LaBarbera, made it a point to defend the departing CEO and his colleagues, saying they did "an outstanding job of getting the company to the point they did."

Despite the setback, Gruber hadn't purged start-up fever from his system. In March 2007, he launched another new venture. Returning to biotechnology, he cofounded Tocagen, a company dedicated to the development and commercialization of breakthrough treatments for cancer using gene-transfer technology. The privately held, San Diego–based firm focuses on treatments for patients with advanced brain cancer. Thanks to Gruber's scientific reputation, Tocagen has attracted major grants from leading brain cancer foundations, with trial sites at some of the country's leading medical centers, including UCLA, the University of California–San Francisco, and the Cleveland Clinic. The end game, says CEO Gruber, is "to deliver cancer-killing drugs to tumors without systematic side effects."

Of course, there's no guarantee that the peripatetic entrepreneur, now 60, will end his career at Tocagen. But the former physician and medical researcher remains committed to personal and scientific rediscovery. With 33 patents to his credit, Gruber wants to see more and more of his ideas commercialized to everyone's benefit. "To me, that's the best of both worlds," he says. "Starting another business and saving the world." Yet, he acknowledges that breakthroughs in business or the lab never come easily. "I remember Edison and how much he did," he says, "but I never recognized how hard it was to do."

Golden Girl *Betty White, 90, never got off the entertainment bus. When, if ever, will her showbiz run end?*

Country music legend Jimmy Dean crafted a successful second life as a sausage-maker.

CHAPTER 10

THE ENTERTAINER: A SURVIVOR'S GUIDE

"The hell with critics—I know when I'm good."

—SINGER ETHEL MERMAN

AGING IS A SENSITIVE, uncomfortable subject. Many seniors are still envisaged as harmless duffers or placidly smiling grannies. In Hollywood especially, it's rarely accepted that older folks might actually be better at doing certain things than younger people—let alone that they might impose a threat to them. Legendary actor Jimmy Stewart once said that the secret to longevity in show business was all about staying on the bus. If you get on at the start, you might sit up front. Then, as time passes, you shift to the middle. Later, you might move to the back. The key, Stewart said, is to never get off the bus.

For 64 years, Betty White never got off the bus. Described by *The Wall Street Journal* as "television's longest-working actress," the 90-year-old diva got her first TV gig in 1949 and became a fan favorite in middle age when she landed her comedic roles on *The Mary Tyler Moore Show* and *The Golden Girls*. These days, she's enjoying a glorious late career, with a huge resurgence in popularity. She has a spicy sitcom on TV Land's *Hot in Cleveland*; NBC's new reality show, *Betty White's Off Their Rockers*; a new book, *Betty & Friends: My Life at the Zoo*; and an ad campaign for AARP. The message: get over your age.

Old age hasn't diminished Ms. White. It's given her a second, a third, a fourth wind. "It's ridiculous at my age to have all this going on," she admits. "I'm not fighting it—I'm loving it. When I'm asked to do something, I always say 'Yes'." The amazing, multiple Emmy–winning Academy Hall of Famer remains on Hollywood's A-list—with no plans to step down. Facing age with a saucy wink, she insists, "Retirement is not in my vocabulary! I'm having too much fun working."

What's the secret to the Golden Girl's longevity? What has she done right? And when, if ever, will her showbiz run end?

Born in Oak Park, Illinois, in 1922, White moved to California with her family during the Great Depression. At Beverly Hills High School (attended also by Jackie Cooper, Rhonda Fleming, Nicolas Cage, Angelina Jolie, and many other luminaries), she discovered her interest in performing. Just three months after graduation in 1939, she debuted on an experimental Los Angeles TV channel. White and a classmate sang songs from *The Merry Widow* in a cramped, sixth-floor studio, in the old Packard Building, while the viewing audience gathered in the ground-floor automobile showroom.

After World War II, she worked in radio and starred in *The Betty White Show*. In 1949, she was spotted by the top disc jockey in Los Angeles, Al Jarvis, who was transferring his hit radio program to television. Playing his Girl Friday, White took to the airwaves five and a half hours a day, six days a week, for $50 a week. "I was in heaven!" she recalls. After Jarvis's departure in 1952, White began hosting *Hollywood on Television*—the first female to headline a daytime chat show.

Like the traveler in Aesop's fable *The North Wind and the Sun*, most entertainers are afraid to take off their overcoats—refusing to diversify and, consequently, getting typecast or pigeonholed. By contrast, Betty White, at the tender age of 28, knew that just performing had its drawbacks; power went to the producers. Breaking convention, she cofounded Bandy Productions in 1952 with two male partners, creating her own self-starring sitcom, *Life with Elizabeth*.

She was the first female television producer in the industry, and *Elizabeth* became one of the classic shows of the 1950s. Not only was it syndicated nationally to 104 stations, but it gained the funny lady her first Emmy. While *Elizabeth* was still in production, Bandy Productions also launched *The Betty White Show* for NBC in 1954.

The following year, the network pulled the daytime variety show, primarily for scheduling reasons. "I was convinced it was the end of the world," she says in her autobiography, *Here We Go Again*. "I would never work again. It was my first brush with the classic rejection syndrome. But it certainly wasn't the last."

Licking her wounds out of the spotlight, White began planning a new sitcom. In 1957, she co-created and produced *Date with the Angels*, based on a pair of newlyweds fumbling through their first year of marital bliss. For fodder, White could draw on her own two failed marriages. Her first, to an Army Air Corps pilot, was short-lived. "It lasted six months, and we were in bed for six months," she recalls. The second, to a Hollywood agent, dragged on for a couple of years. "I was deeply in love," she says. "But he wanted me to get out of show business—a deal breaker." Lackluster ratings caused *Angels'* demise the next year.

As the 1950s came to a close, White was in limbo. She had expected some dry spells, but refused to equate the occasional setback with defeat. Once again, the confident actress plotted another comeback.

For the next several years, Betty White—pretty, pert, charming—reintroduced herself to American audiences on talk shows and game shows. However, it was only in middle age that she landed her two most famous roles, both of which reconfirmed her as a funny, unusually nimble actress who could quicken the chemistry of any sitcom ensemble.

It was in 1961 on *Password*, the country's hottest daytime show, that White met, and later married, the show's host, Allen Ludden. The couple were good friends of actress Mary Tyler Moore and her producer husband, Grant Tinker, powerhouses behind *The Mary Tyler Moore Show*. After a guest appearance in season four of the series, White landed a role as TV personality Sue Ann Nivens, aka The Happy Homemaker, a woman as sweet as angel cake on the outside but, under the surface, much more diabolical. Satirizing the neighborhood nymphomaniac, she quickly became an integral part of the hugely popular program's success. For her efforts, White won two consecutive Emmys as best supporting actress.

After the end of *The Mary Tyler Moore Show* in 1977, she premiered on CBS in her own sitcom, *The Betty White Show*. Critically acclaimed and costarring John Hillerman and Georgia Engle, the program faced tough competition on Monday nights and was canceled after one season. Rejection again. For the next several years, White returned to the game-show world, while guest-starring in numerous TV shows (including Johnny Carson's *Tonight Show*) and doing summer-stock musicals as well as the occasional movie.

In 1985, at age 63, White landed a role on *The Golden Girls*, a sitcom that defied conventional programming wisdom. It was about a bunch of saucy old broads in which Betty played a Minnesotan native, naïve Rose Nylund. Innocent and adorable Rose, whose nature bespoke of a more optimistic and trusty time, was joined by oversexed Blanche Devereaux (played by Rue McClanahan), hard-bitten Dorothy Petrillo Zbornak (Beatrice Arthur), and Dorothy's brutally frank mother, Sophia Petrillo (Estelle Getty). The show chronicled how these four widowed or divorced women in their "golden years" coexisted in their Miami home. The smashing series, which ran from 1985 to 1992, earned White an Emmy for the first season and nominations every subsequent year (the only cast member to receive such distinction).

After *Golden Girls* ended, CBS reintroduced White, McClanahan, and Getty as co-managers of a South Florida hotel. *Golden Palace* aired for only one year. "It was a moderately pleasing show—not a grabber," White admits. The cancellation "was disappointing, but by no means as heart-wrenching as other times." So it was back again to guest-starring, TV commercials, and voice-overs for animated shows.

A few years ago, White's career began a remarkable renaissance. With wrinkles and randy remarks, the irreverent entertainer forged her most impressive comeback. It all began with a wildly popular Super Bowl ad for Snickers in which she played tackle football with a group of grisly young men. Suddenly, the sassy actress was everywhere: jumping into the shower with Hugh Jackman on *The Tonight Show*, gyrating with Chippendales dancers on *Ellen*, shooting a Hallmark Hall of Fame movie, and, by popular demand via Facebook, hosting, at age 88—by far the oldest person to do so—*Saturday Night Live*. That performance notched her seventh Emmy. She also received the Screen Actors Guild's Lifetime Achievement Award.

The dame still had game. Nothing, it seemed, could cool down the super-celeb. In 2010, White took on the role of Elka Ostrovsky, the house caretaker on TV Land's sitcom *Hot in Cleveland*, now in its third season. "If you have one good series, it's a blessing," she reflects today. "Two is unusual. Three is phenomenal. Where do you get privileges like that? I owe Someone, big time."

She says the actors she's worked with on all three shows have been like family. And she has felt their love and loss as she gets older. She particularly mourned the recent death of her good friend Rue McClanahan. White is now the only one of the four "Golden Girls" living. "I was the oldest," she explains. "The fact that I'm still around doesn't seem fair."

Nor is the void filled by family. Early on, she committed to career over kids. "I'm an incurable workaholic," she admits. "I just knew I couldn't juggle being a career woman with being a great mother. So I opted not to have children."

It's also been 30 years since the actress-comedienne lost the love of her life, Allen Ludden, after 18 years of marriage. She's been going solo ever since. "When you've had the best, who needs the rest?" she says—adding with a twinkle, "Then, Robert Redford never calls."

A lifetime pet enthusiast and tireless animal-health advocate, White says, "Animals are my real life," conceding that she prefers them to people. Her most treasured possession? Her golden retriever, Pontiac. White's latest book, part of a seven-figure advance from G. P. Putnam's Sons, is devoted entirely to her love of zoos, which she believes play a crucial role in preserving biodiversity. She also has served on the board of directors of the Los Angeles Zoo since 1974 and considers the zoo her home away from home.

When she's not caring for her animal kingdom, the timeless wonder remains the hottest thing in showbiz. The gal who looks like everyone's kindly old grandmother continues to dish out her bawdy double entendres to an ever-expanding audience. If people like her ribald sense of humor, White says, it's because she tries not to overthink a joke. "You can't think about comedy too much and keep it funny," she explains. "You just have to let it pop out."

As for her incredible staying power, she credits her old-school, Midwestern work ethic. The Illinois-born star says she's blessed with good health and she has never needed much sleep. "I go to bed late and get up early," she adds. "I'm rarely in bed before midnight, and then I'm up again at 6:30. If I get four or five hours sleep, I'm all right." Arriving fresh, prepared, and raring to go has made her one of the hardest-working actresses of any era, "a sort of a fixture," in her words.

It has been a long, highly diverse career: from early television star to producer/actress to game-show regular to Emmy-winning Golden Girl, and beyond. Generations of audiences have discovered her—like a bright, new penny—along the way. Each incarnation has brought with it a new set of devotees. "Many of my fans grew up with me, and their moms and dads—and, in some cases, their grandmothers and grandfathers—grew up with me," White beams proudly.

Taking life one wrinkle at a time, she remains convinced that old age has its benefits. "You've seen enough to be interested in many different things and make time for them," she points out. "You can't do that as a youngster because you're so into yourself."

"I'm not scared of dying, I just don't want to be there when it happens," Woody Allen once quipped. Betty White, now in her ninth decade, "doesn't fear death. To some, it is such a bête noire that it ruins some of the good time they have left." Not her. The shadow of mortality continues to inspire the beloved actress not to play it safe—to go for broke, instead. Nor is she in any hurry to bow out, continuing to connect with audiences with her effortless charm and long-lasting authenticity.

"I'm just very grateful not only to be busy, but enjoying all of it," she says. "I've really never gone away." Or, as Jimmy Stewart would put it, Betty White never got off the bus.

∽

Following a road less traveled, Jimmy Dean not only got off the bus—he changed stations. Over the years, he mastered the art of making himself up as he went along. In fact, he liked to say he had ad-libbed his life. From country and western singer/songwriter to

television host to actor, the popular entertainer parlayed his musical skills, folksy integrity, and aw-shucks Texas charm to the max
during the 1950s and '6os. Then, in his early forties, he plunged
into unchartered waters, exiting showbiz for his most remarkable
role: founder, chief executive, and spokesman for the Jimmy Dean
Meat Company. "I'm Jimmy Dean and I'd like you to try my
Pure Pork Sausages," he asked America. For the next three
decades, his entrepreneurial talents not only eclipsed his earlier accomplishments, but they also made the legendary singer a
wealthy man.

Jimmy Ray Dean, a distant cousin of the actor James Dean,
was born just outside Plainview, a farming town in the Texas
Panhandle, on August 10, 1928. He was raised by his mother,
Ruth, on an impoverished farm. Mrs. Dean ran a barbershop out
of their home to make ends meet. From this petite fireball ("the
toughest lady I've ever known"), Jimmy got his drive, his grit.
Early on, his father, G. O. Dean, disappeared, leaving Jimmy, the
older of two sons, as the male head of the household. During the
Depression, he went to work at age six, pulling cotton balls at 50
cents per 100 pounds. Later, it was driving combines, tidying up
chicken houses, and cleaning septic tanks. "I was a hard-workin'
little boy," he told *TV Guide* in 1964.

Every fall, he and his grandfather made sausage in a washtub
from one of their hogs so they could have meat in winter. The
scrawny kid, who wore discarded sugar sacks fashioned into shirts
under his bib overalls, dreamed of indoor plumbing and ice cream.
"That's as rich as I wanted to be," he recalled. The fear of poverty
would always motivate him more than anything else.

His mother taught him how to play the piano at age 10 and,
along the way, he picked up the guitar, harmonica, and accordion.
Dropping out of high school at 16, Dean hopped a Greyhound
bus for Dallas and enlisted in the manpower-starved Merchant
Marine. Two years later, he joined the Air Force and was sent to

Bolling Air Force Base in Washington, D.C. While stationed there in the late 1940s, he and three other airmen formed their first band, the Tennessee Haymakers, and played seedy honkytonks.

After his discharge in 1948, Dean extended his musical reputation with his new band, the Texas Wildcats, which featured Roy Clark as lead guitarist. The quartet developed a strong local draw in the D.C. area and earned their first country top 10 hit in 1953 with "Bummin' Around," which sold close to a million copies.

The next year, Dean hosted a popular radio program, *Town and Country Time*, in Arlington, Virginia. The syndicated variety show helped bring country music into the American mainstream, popularizing a number of future stars, including Clark, Patsy Cline, and Roger Miller. In 1957, the program moved to television and was carried regionally. That same year, Dean and the Wildcats were hired by CBS to appear on national television each morning opposite NBC's opening hour of *Today*, hosted by Dave Garroway. The show eventually moved to other time slots until it was pulled in 1959. Nonetheless, he was by then a hero back in the Lone Star State.

In the innocent '50s and early '60s, America was ready for the honest, homespun quality of country music, with its inspirational lyrics about heartbreak and salvation. This period marked Dean's heyday, when the down-home singer recorded his greatest tunes. His breakthrough moment occurred in 1961, with his spoken-narrative song about a heroic coal miner—"a giant of a man"—who saves 20 men from a would-be grave after their mine collapsed. It ended with the words "at the bottom of this mine lies one hell of a man."

"Big Bad John," which Dean wrote on a 90-minute flight from New York to Nashville, went to No. 1 on the *Billboard* charts and won him a Grammy Award for Best Country & Western Recording. At last count, over eight million copies had been sold. The signature song led to several subsequent hits, most notably "P.T.

109," a ballad lionizing young torpedo-boat commander John F. Kennedy, as well as "Little Black Book," "Sam Hill," and "I.O.U.," a spoken-word song dedicated to his mother, which sold a million records in just two weeks.

By the 1960s, Dean was justly celebrated as a powerhouse performer. His string of hit records caused ABC to offer him his own hour-long TV variety show in 1963, which ran for three years and served as another platform featuring traditional country music themes: lyin', cheatin', and drinkin'. George Jones, Charlie Rich, and Buck Owens got their start on *The Jimmy Dean Show*. Among the more interesting guests was the early Muppet character Rowlf, a piano-playing dog cooked up by master puppeteer Jim Henson. Dean, in fact, was offered 40 percent ownership in the Muppets, Inc., but he declined because he felt he hadn't contributed to Henson's clever creation.

Because of his affability and burgeoning popularity, he followed Betty White's lead—appearing as an occasional guest and host of *The Tonight Show* and *The Mike Douglas Show*, where his laid-back country wit stood up surprisingly well, as well as on several variety shows, including *The Ed Sullivan Show*, *The Steve Allen Show*, *Rowan & Martin*, *The Pat Boone Chevy Showroom*, and *The Hollywood Palace*. His singing career also remained strong into the mid-1960s. In 1965, he recorded his second Number 1 hit, "The First Thing Ev'ry Morning (and the Last Thing Ev'ry Night)"; "Stand Beside Me" also cracked the Top 40. On off days, Dean became the first country singer to headline in Las Vegas, besides performing in such diverse venues as Carnegie Hall, The Grand Ole Opry, Hollywood Bowl, and the London Palladium.

"Music is spiritual. The music business is not," warned singer-songwriter Van Morrison. As the '60s evolved, Dean sensed that the times were a-changin'. America had lost its innocence. With the Vietnam War in full swing, the homey, often heroic, lyrics of country ballads failed to curry favor. Suddenly, he started to sense new currents in music, most notably "the British invasion" and Beatlemania.

To protect himself from the vagaries of showbiz and with his reputation still intact, Dean began to gracefully exit the music business—and diversify. In the late 1960s, he turned to acting and landed a recurring role in the television series *Daniel Boone* and, later, in *J.J. Starbuck*. He also played the reclusive Las Vegas billionaire Willard Whyte in the James Bond suspense thriller *Diamonds Are Forever*. Between infrequent acting jobs, he began investing in Christmas tree farms, limousine companies, lime groves, and racehorses.

Happy lives often include happy accidents. Serendipity favored the country boy back home in Plainview. While eating a breakfast sausage, he bit into a piece of gristle about the size of the tip of his little finger, which got lodged between his teeth. Infuriated, he vowed to produce a high-quality product. And with hog prices dropping, the timing couldn't have been better.

In 1965, he bought a pig farm in Plainview and, later, started the Jimmy Dean Meat Company with his brother, Don, using a family recipe. The operation was "the biggest thing to hit the Panhandle since irrigation," Fryar Calhoun reported in *Texas Monthly*. Eventually the plant employed 150 people and had an annual payroll of more than $3 million—sizeable figures for the dwindling farm town of 18,000 people. It wasn't long before the company expanded throughout Texas, Louisiana, and Oklahoma.

The Dean of Country Music sensed that his new venture in the sausage business could add zest to his life—and his pocketbook. Following his bliss, as scholar Joseph Campbell might put it, he leveraged his down-home appeal and kind face into a series of extemporized, humor-filled TV commercials. "Sausage is a great deal like life," he said in one. "You get out of it about what you put into it."

No Southern entertainer this side of Dolly Parton was more successful in marketing himself or his wares. Dean emerged as a shrewd entrepreneur who understood that straightforwardness and unfiltered sincerity would sell his crumbly, spicy-sweet sausage. Besides his television ads, he appeared at state fairs and rodeos. "State fairs are a very big business," he once said. "They make Vegas look like Sharecroppers' Row." The so-called "King of Country Fairs" and his second wife, former singer Donna Meade Dean, also made it a point to serve Jimmy Dean Sausage pinwheels with cocktails at home, with his breakfast favorites to overnight guests. "When people come to our house, they expect us to serve sausage," Mrs. Dean said.

By every measure, the crossover artist lived high on the hog. The Jimmy Dean Meat Company was almost instantly profitable and quickly became No. 1 in its product category. The brothers, however, fought over who would control the business. Dean prevailed; he and Don never reconciled. During an appearance on *The Mike Douglas Show* in 1977, Jimmy read a caustic poem that concluded, "When you make your brother a partner, you start ills for which there are no cures. You'll find he'll develop eye trouble, and he can't tell his money from yours."

Although the company's processed meats became the bane of health-conscious critics, its rapid commercial success caused Chicago-based Sara Lee Corporation to acquire the business in 1984 for a reported $15 million. Dean stayed on as chairman and lead pitchman.

Then, in 2003, Sara Lee phased him out of the commercials in favor of a man in a sun costume, saying the brand was moving in a different direction. Dean's wife claimed that he was dropped because of his age. Livid and living in semiretirement, Dean suffered a ministroke, perhaps from the stress of not working. Disenfranchised from the business, he sold all his stock except one share, which he held so he could attend the annual meeting. He also stopped eating the product that bears his name and removed his license plates that once read SSG KING.

In 2004, the country music legend vetted his frustrations in *Thirty Years of Sausage, Fifty Years of Ham*, a blunt, straight-talking autobiography, coauthored with Donna Meade Dean, whom he married in 1991. The couple lived on a magnificent 200-acre property in Varina, Virginia, just outside Richmond. In 2009, the main house was gutted by fire, although the Deans escaped injury. They rebuilt the home on the same foundation and returned the following year.

During his final years, the folksy singer continued to build his fortune, estimated at $75 million. He assisted the State of Virginia in its wildlife and boating activities. He also dabbled in philanthropy, donating $1 million to Wayland Baptist University in Plainview, the biggest gift ever offered the small school. Like many a poor boy who left home and made it big, Dean wanted to do something for his hometown. "I've been so blessed," Dean said at the time. "It makes me proud to give back."

Elected to the Hall of Fame for both Country Music and the Meat Industry, the Texas-born entertainer who made his fortune with sausage passed away peacefully, at 81, at his Varina home. The man who followed two separate paths to celebrity believed, as John F. Kennedy once noted, that "success has many fathers." Always haunted by the fear of poverty, he understood fully the quirks and foibles of the music business—and the need to exit gracefully and pursue new challenges. His willingness to take significant risks and to reinvent himself ultimately led to the financial security he so desperately longed for.

At his memorial service, Dean was entombed in a $350,000, piano-shaped granite mausoleum overlooking the James River on the grounds of his Virginia estate. His epitaph reads, Here Lies One Hell of a Man.

Preferring seclusion to celebrity, Johnny Carson (right) mastered the art of leaving on top. His second banana, Ed McMahon, did not.

CHAPTER 11

EXIT LAUGHING

"Don't confuse fame with success.
Madonna is one, Helen Keller is the other."

—ERMA BOMBECK

I N THE 1950S, A NEW KIND of entertainment hero emerged on the American scene. Pioneered by Steve Allen, Jerry Lester, and Morey Amsterdam came an edgy mix of stand-up comic and social commentator: the late-night talk-show host. Appealing to television audiences looking more for personality than intellectual heft, these multitalented performers began to take the country by storm. When the dust settled, Johnny Carson was the "King of the Night."

For the better part of three decades, this Conversational Everyman ruled the late night, inducing people to laugh. As the enormously popular host of *The Tonight Show*, Carson welcomed more than 20 million viewers to his entertainment sandbox every night. No one offered by competing programs—including Joey Bishop, Merv Griffin, Mike Douglas, David Frost, Dick Cavett, and Joan Rivers—came close to him in ratings or popularity. With a fan base that spanned multiple generations, the most successful performer in the history of television became a fixture of American life, an integral part of our cultural foundation.

But on May 22, 1992, the country's chatter icon abandoned his hammerlock on late-night TV—stepping down from his throne and stepping back into private life. Asked "Why are you leaving one of the best-paying gigs in television history?" Carson simply replied, "You've got to know when to get off the stage and the timing was right for me."

The toast of a nation made his exit a graceful and classy one. After more than 4,500 shows, the 66-year-old showbiz legend choked back tears and told his final audience, "I bid you a very heartfelt good night." Walking off the set, he met his wife, Alexis, who was waiting in the wings, and took a helicopter to their Malibu home.

In his quiet retirement of nearly 13 years, the six-time Emmy winner received numerous offers to return to center stage. Other than hosting Academy Awards ceremonies and the occasional nightclub appearance, he preferred seclusion to celebrity. *The Tonight Show* would remain his creative legacy. "I have an ego like anybody else," he told the *Washington Post* in 1993. "But I don't need it to be stroked by going before the public."

"We can do as partners what we cannot do as singles," Daniel Webster once said. Early on, the talented Carson knew that to be successful, you also need a little help from your friends. You can't do it alone. Enter Ed McMahon.

During their time together, "Big Ed" became America's most famous second banana. Beginning in 1957, this entertainment duo fed off each other's unique skills. Widely different in background and personality, Carson and McMahon made contributions together that would have been unimaginable for either of them independently. Theirs was truly a great partnership.

But dependency had its costs. When their last show concluded in 1992, McMahon's career would take a much different trajectory. In his later years, he encountered a litany of serious legal, financial, and health problems that would tarnish his legacy. It's instructive to compare Carson's graceful exit and peaceful retirement with the troubled afterlife of his longtime sidekick.

John William Carson was born on October 23, 1925, in Corning, Iowa, but moved with his family to nearby Norfolk, Nebraska, when he was eight years old. Four years later, he stumbled across a book of magic and quickly purchased a mail-order magician's kit. Dubbed "The Great Carsoni," he soon began appearing at local venues for the grand sum of $3. His ability to perform skillfully, somehow overcoming an innate shyness, made him an instant hit.

At Norfolk High School he continued to entertain—appearing in student productions and writing a humor column for the school newspaper. To pay for his magic tricks, he ushered at the Granada Theatre and sold *Saturday Evening Post* subscriptions door-to-door. In 1943, at the height of World War II, he joined the Navy, where he continued to perform magic and entertain the troops.

After his military service, he enrolled at the University of Nebraska. His senior thesis, *Comedy Writing*, explained the techniques of the major radio comedians of the time—Jack Benny, Bob Hope, and Fred Allen, all of whom he would work with later in his career. Just prior to graduation, he received his first radio job with KRAB in Lincoln, Nebraska, followed by a stint at WOW in Omaha, where he wrote comedy and did commercials.

Deciding that his entertainment future was in California, he landed a job at KNXT-TV in Los Angeles in 1950. His low-budget comedy show, *Carson's Cellar*, aired for 15 minutes on Sunday afternoons. Despite its terrible time slot, the program ran for three years, winning over a growing audience, including comedian Red Skelton, then a huge film and television star. That led to a writing job on Skelton's TV show.

In 1954, Skelton injured himself an hour before his live show began, and Carson successfully filled in for him. As a result, CBS gambled on the up-and-coming comic, giving him a self-titled, prime-time variety show.

At 29, the rail-thin, wisecracking Carson began to develop the pointed, yet pleasantly silly, characters that would later populate *Tonight*, including Carnac the Magnificent and others. From the beginning, his unshakable poise was evident. In his opening greeting to the studio audience and the sketches that followed, elements of the wry Carson charm gave hints of a late-night legend in the making. Poor ratings, however, led to the show's cancellation after 39 weeks.

With borrowed money, Carson moved to New York in 1956 to revive his career. He appeared on Broadway and television, including a role in a *Playhouse 90* production. The following year, he was hired to host the ABC-TV daytime game show *Who Do You Trust?* It was the first opportunity where he could ad lib and interview guests. Because of his on-camera wit, the show lasted for five years and was tabbed "the hottest item on daytime television." It was here that Carson met his future sidekick, Ed McMahon.

After *Who Do You Trust?* had been on the air for four years, NBC began looking for a replacement for the popular but prickly Jack Paar. When his ratings began to fall, NBC invited Carson to join *Tonight*. Initially, he declined, fearing the difficulty of interviewing celebrities for 105 minutes every day. But eventually he agreed to join the show as soon as his ABC contract expired.

On October 1, 1962, Groucho Marx introduced Carson to the nation's late-night television audience as the new host of *The Tonight Show*. Also on that first program were Joan Crawford and Rudy Vallee, people who enriched the meaning of the word *ego*. For 90 minutes, they were gently manipulated by the Iowa-born master.

"When the show was over, I sensed we had a hit, but I wasn't sure," said McMahon, who had followed Carson from *Who Do You Trust?* "But I soon learned Johnny was America's newest star when the next day, one person after another came up to me and said, 'Heeeere's Johnny!'"

From the first show on, Carson custom fit the program to his tastes. Announcer McMahon's famous introduction became a national catch phrase. The jaunty, brassy, and recognizable theme music, written by Paul Anka, was rendered by bandleader Skitch Henderson and, later, Doc Severinsen. It cued Carson to appear from behind a curtain and warm up the audience with jokes. His obvious knowledge of comedy (Jack Benny, Groucho Marx, and Jonathan Winters were just a few of the masters you could hear in his delivery) made his opening monologue the centerpiece of the show.

Aided by a polished platoon of spicy writers, Carson delivered a nightly barrage of topical ditties with self-deprecating pauses and Midwestern modesty. It didn't take long for his genius to be revealed. His greatest skill, wrote *Time*'s Richard Zoglin, "was his perfection of the 'saver': the snappy comeback to 'save' a joke that bombs. When a joke would draw a disappointing titter or dead silence from the studio audience, Carson would always react: a sarcastic or belittling wisecrack, a panicked double take or maybe just a pained Jack Benny look of exasperation." He always found a way to counteract a slow moment.

"One night, he began to read about six pages of jokes and it didn't take long for us to know they were going nowhere. . . . It was bombs away," McMahon recalled. "Suddenly, while Johnny still had a couple of pages in his hand, I picked up a lighter and set fire to them. He looked at the audience with his steely blue eyes and said, 'You're absolutely right.' And then he threw the burning pages in the wastebasket while Doc Severinsen played *Taps*."

Straightening his tie or craning his neck, Carson and his brand of inspired nonsense soon began to rule late-night TV. Tanned, dapper, and relaxed, he welcomed thousands of guests to *Tonight*—from authors to astronauts, from Ronald Reagan to Andy Rooney. But showbiz insiders were his biggest fans. For comedians, in particular, appearing on the show was the Holy Grail. "If you made it, if Johnny passed his blessing on you, you were made," wrote biographer Laurence Leamer.

Unlike many other hosts, Carson never tried to upstage his guests, often serving as a self-effacing straight man. "He was so

secure in himself that he never had a problem laughing his ass off
when somebody was funny," said Jeff Wald, George Carlin's former manager. The legendary George Burns, who often appeared
on *Tonight*, agreed: "Nobody ever listened as good as Johnny. He
laughed at my jokes like he never heard them." Small wonder that
a stream of aspiring comics—from Bill Cosby and Woody Allen
to Jay Leno and David Letterman—considered time on Carson's
stage as a vital rite of passage.

Drew Carey remembers when it happened to him. "I felt like I
was in a dream. It was like being called by Jesus," he told a recent
press gathering. "It's something I'll never forget."

Aside from his banter with celebrities, Carson established
absurd comic roles familiar to generations of Americans. As
the turbaned psychic, Carnac the Magnificent, he would divine
answers to silly questions fed to him by McMahon before seeing
them. (Question: "What did it say in the beaver's will?" Answer: "I
don't give a damn.") His Art Fern, the Tea Time Movie announcer,
jokingly reminded viewers they were watching a favorite film.
The stereotypical redneck, Floyd R. Turbo, offered cantankerous
responses to left-leaning causes or news events. A frizzy-haired
holy man, The Maharishi, spoke in a high-pitched, tranquil tone—
answering zany philosophical questions. And so on.

In a memorable 1965 skit, Ed Ames, who played Mingo on
the *Daniel Boone* TV series, threw a tomahawk at a board that
had a human outline on it. When the tomahawk smacked into
the crotch, Carson—after a long, quizzical look—ad-libbed a
circumcision joke: "I didn't even know you were Jewish." But there
was also a serious side to the clever host.

"Once you take the anchor chair," David Letterman told *The
New York Times*, "that's what you do." It's a lifetime commitment,
and Carson's devotion to *Tonight* never wavered. Not only did he
want his show to be the very best, but he demanded excellence
from every cast member, driving them at warp speed. The seemingly laid-back farm boy was an unusually tough taskmaster off

camera. A demanding perfectionist, he was incapable of praising his subordinates. "Silence was the highest accolade," Leamer wrote in *King of the Night*. "He wanted no family of regulars around him. He gave out no tenure."

In the public arena of *Tonight*, Carson put a private wall around his life. Socially insecure and exceptionally secretive, he was a recluse who had few friends and rarely invited anyone to his home. "I live my life, especially my personal life, strictly for myself," he told *Playboy* in 1967. "What you do is your own business." In another profile, critic Kenneth Tynan wrote that attempting a man-to-man chat with him was like "addressing an elaborately wired security system." Almost every aspect of America's supposedly trusted companion was very different from what he appeared to be on television.

To network moguls, though, Carson was their golden boy. At times, *Tonight* generated 15 percent of NBC's annual revenues. Accordingly, he was given carte blanche, including creative control of the show. In addition, the network provided the $12 million to launch Carson Productions, a cash cow that eventually produced *Late Night with David Letterman*.

By the late '60s, the center of the entertainment world had shifted away from New York. With fresh winds blowing from the West, Carson and NBC bigwigs knew that you had to be in Los Angeles, where most celebrities lived. In 1972, the show moved from the Big Apple to Burbank, California, allowing Carson to trump other hosts in scheduling hot properties.

The entertainer always fretted about the dangers of burnout and overexposure. In 1971, he negotiated to reduce his appearances to four shows a week, with a guest host handling Monday nights. Later, he extracted a hard-won provision to cut *Tonight*'s 90-minute format to 60 minutes, with just three appearances a week. Though the star's workload reduced, his compensation skyrocketed—from $100,000 in 1962 to $5 million in the 1980s, making him the highest-paid performer in television history.

There were other perks. Sex and booze were plentiful. TV hosts, with their on-air swagger and macho monologues, were as hot as rock stars. For the introverted Carson, not far removed from his heartland roots, this was heady stuff. He launched into an almost uninterrupted string of late-night drinking and debauchery that began in New York and ventured westward. These indiscretions, coupled with his intense obsession with work, produced a string of unhappy marriages and expensive divorces. His first wife, Jody Wolcott, was a childhood sweetheart and mother of his three sons. Then came airline stewardess Joanne Copeland Carson, followed by model Joanna Holland Carson, who reportedly received a settlement of more than $20 million. In 1987 he married Alexis Maas, a woman 26 years his junior, whom he met on a Malibu beach. (At the time, she was wearing a bikini and carrying an empty wine glass.)

Although he refused to discuss his volatile love life, the ultra-private comic once quipped, "Married men live longer than single men. But married men are a lot more willing to die." Later, he added, "If variety is the spice of life, marriage is a big can of left-over Spam."

Wisecracks aside, Carson was always on the prowl for additional income to pay for his unhappy marriages. He had also made foolish investments in a failed restaurant franchise, the ill-fated DeLorean Motor Company, and ragtag TV stations in Nevada and New Mexico. Fortunately, *Tonight* saved the day, providing him with $20 million in annual salary in his final years. Add to this, big bucks from his Santa Monica production company, with its lucrative contract with NBC. Net net, the entertainer did very well financially. In 2010, Carson's foundation—allegedly one of Hollywood's biggest charities—reported receiving $156 million from his personal trust.

Though earning mega bucks, the cool, elegant entertainer had an acute appreciation of his mortality. "Johnny was not going to end up like most entertainers or athletes, playing a season too long, going after one too many passes, or speaking too many times," reported Leamer. Rather than cling to a fading career, Carson insisted on leaving on top.

"It's been a marvelous trip," the comic said of his career. That career led to the Presidential Medal of Freedom—the nation's highest honor—and the Kennedy Center Honor for lifetime achievements. After his retirement, offers came his way for various engagements, but he steadfastly declined, preferring to "let my work speak for itself."

On January 23, 2005, 79-year-old Johnny Carson died of emphysema at his Malibu home. He left a void that only a special personality could fill. "We're all pretenders to the throne," said Jay Leno, who succeeded him as host of *The Tonight Show*. But perhaps Steve Martin put it best: "Because you retreated into retirement so completely, let me thank you, in death, for the things I could not say in life. Thank you for the opportunity you gave me and others . . . for the one hour a night across 30 years of American life when we were entertained purely, delightfully and wisely."

⁓

"The most difficult instrument to play in the orchestra is second fiddle," said famed conductor Leonard Bernstein. Second fiddlers, second bananas, straight men—whatever the moniker—need flameproof egos. That's a paradox, really, because it would seem that they would need less ego strength than their highly acclaimed stars. But especially in a society as obsessed as ours with celebrity, it takes enormous confidence to be No. 2. No matter how great a contribution a second banana makes, the majority of the credit is going to go to No. 1.

Writer Roger Rosenblatt captured the spirit of the great second banana in a wonderful tribute to the late George Burns. The cigar-smoking comic made a career of working in the shadow of his marvelously ditzy wife, Gracie Allen. Like other great partners, Burns understood the personal and professional rewards that come only as a result of collaboration.

As Rosenblatt writes, "The essence of the straight man is that he gives the best lines, the stage, the spotlight. By giving, he creates the show—the entire show, including all the performance. . . . And he gets by giving. It takes a certain person to do that—one who is willing to diminish his part for the good of the whole."

For three decades, Ed McMahon fully understood his role. As the loyal No. 2, he didn't care about the credit. He was having too much fun doing *Tonight*. "I've got the greatest job in the world," he often said. In a great partnership, McMahon knew, everybody wins.

Indeed, when everything's clicking, the relationship between the top banana and second banana is like a good marriage. As Carson later put it, "[Ed and I] developed a unique relationship—similar to that which married couples often experience—an unspoken method of communication. When it was working well, it was euphoria. When it wasn't, there was always the next night."

Yet, egos often run amok in Hollywood. Abbott and Costello, Dean Martin and Jerry Lewis, and the Marx Brothers all crashed and burned because of personality differences. Fueled by ego, warring partners routinely forget that their collective talents far outstrip their individual abilities, and that their professional fortunes are married together.

Despite the occasional flare-up, relations between the tightly wound Carson and the easygoing McMahon endured. Labor was divided easily, according to the gifts of both men. Disagreements were resolved without acrimony and without loss of mutual respect. But credit for the partnership goes largely to Carson's gifted adjunct.

Edward Leo Peter McMahon Jr. was born in Detroit on March 6, 1923. In his early years, he led a nomadic and somewhat unhappy childhood. His father, a part-time entrepreneur and full-time promoter, traveled all over the country pursuing various ventures, including carnival jobs and bingo games. His career was so erratic that, in good times, the family camped out in the Mark Hopkins Hotel, atop Nob Hill in San Francisco; in bad times, they made do in a cold-water flat in Báyonne, New Jersey.

When he was 10 years old, McMahon decided he wanted to be an announcer. "While other kids played baseball or football or cowboys and Indians, I played broadcaster," he said. "I desperately wanted to be in the business." At 15, he got his first gig broadcasting for a local circus. Later, McMahon pitched everything from fountain pens to vegetable slicers on the Atlantic City Boardwalk and in Times Square.

After graduating from high school, McMahon enlisted in the Marine Corps toward the end of World War II. He became a fighter pilot but did not see action. Following his discharge, he enrolled in Catholic University in Washington on the G.I. Bill, receiving a bachelor's degree in 1949. He then landed a job with WCAU in Philadelphia for $75 a week. Within two years, he had become a television star, hosting a dozen programs and appearing on the first cover of *TV Digest* (later known as *TV Guide*).

In 1952, Philadelphia's "Mr. Television" was recalled to the Marines due to the Korean War, where he flew 85 combat missions, earning six Air Medals. After the war, he remained active in the Marine Reserves, retiring as a colonel in 1966. (McMahon often said that he wanted his epitaph to read, "He was a good broadcaster, but a great Marine.")

Returning from the war, McMahon expected a heartwarming welcome in Philadelphia. But all of his WCAU shows had been canceled. Although he managed to rescue a five-minute spot at the end of the nightly news, McMahon traveled to New York every day hoping to break into network TV. At the same time, he began to test his entrepreneurial bent, acquiring, among other things, a stationery company and a knickknacks manufacturer. Even when he got his big break with Carson, he never divested his business interests.

Living in Drexel Hill, just outside Philadelphia, McMahon befriended neighbor Dick Clark, whose *American Bandstand* was the hottest show on television. Clark's network contacts, in turn, led to McMahon's six-minute interview in New York with Carson, then star of *Who Do You Trust?* The producers immediately liked the contrast between the skinny, five-foot-ten Midwestern WASP and the six-feet-four, 220-pound Irish Catholic, and felt they would work well together.

On October 13, 1958, the partnership began. As announcer, McMahon would introduce contestants, do the commercials, and conduct a brief conversation with the star at the beginning of each show. "I understood my job was to support Johnny Carson," he later wrote. "I didn't tell the jokes, I set up the jokes. I didn't get the laughs, I helped him get the laughs. After a few weeks, I slipped quite comfortably into the role of his straight man, his second banana . . . (and) loved it."

McMahon existed to reflect glory on the host and the guests, to be the buffoon and the butt of jokes when necessary. Through it all, he offered bluff good humor, something that must have taken considerable effort to seem as effortless as it did.

When Carson moved to *Tonight* in 1962, McMahon went along in his familiar role as the host's foil. Riding what he called a "whiskey baritone" voice, he became the most famous sidekick in television history. Although he was nominally Carson's announcer, he was really Johnny's audience. Remaining true to his modest roots, McMahon was "the in-studio representative for all those people in Oklahoma, San Diego and New Haven who closed out the day with some friendly banter and a few of Johnny's laughs," wrote David Hinckley, *New York Daily News* television critic.

Off camera, he and Carson were friends and occasional drinking buddies. But Big Ed always seemed on guard in his personal dealings with the antisocial, often surly, Carson. "He packs a tight suitcase," McMahon explained. "He doesn't give friendship easily or need it."

Although flare-ups were rare, McMahon took great care not to upstage the boss. One evening, though, Carson talked about a new report on mosquitoes that preferred to bite "warm-blooded, passionate" people. Before he could deliver the punch line, McMahon slapped his arm. The audience roared, but Carson was infuriated. The next day, he told the show's producer, "Get rid of Ed!"

Eventually, things quieted down as the star came to realize that sacking his announcer would be suicide. McMahon, for his part, swallowed his pride. He understood Carson's fragile ego. "Never for a moment in thirty years did I forget that it was Johnny's show," he later wrote in his autobiography, *For Laughing Out Loud*.

Nor did McMahon forget to seek Carson's approval for every offer he received for outside work. *The Tonight Show* had become a beacon for many delicious opportunities. Over the years, McMahon emerged as a natural to hawk products from Budweiser beer to Breck shampoo and Chris-Craft boats to Mercedes-Benz cars. He is less fondly remembered for the notorious American Family Publishers sweepstakes promotions that flooded millions of mailboxes in the 1990s.

Big Ed's visibility jumped again when he hosted daily afternoon quiz shows, such as *Snap Judgment* and *Missing Links*, before trundling off to work on *Tonight*. As if that weren't glitter enough, he made cameos in numerous TV productions—from *Hee Haw* to *The Simpsons*. That led to minor roles in films, including *The Incident*, *Fun with Dick and Jane*, and *Butterfly*. To augment his announcing chores, he also toured the Las Vegas nightclub scene and appeared briefly on Broadway. And for decades, he co-hosted the *Jerry Lewis Muscular Dystrophy Telethon*.

Over the years, McMahon morphed into a ubiquitous, highly effective pitchman—on *The Tonight Show* and off. He never denied his salesmanship, never apologized for it, and never had reason to. For his efforts on *Tonight* alone, the beefy former Marine earned $5 million a year.

"There's a time for work and a time for love," Coco Chanel once said. "That leaves us little other time." Like his celebrated boss, McMahon neglected his family. Consequently, his married life was almost as tumultuous as Carson's. In 1976, he and his wife of 27 years, the former Alyce Ferrell, divorced. They had four children. That same year, he married Victoria Valentine, and the couple adopted a daughter. That marriage ended in 1989. Three years later, he tied the knot with fashion designer Pamela Hurn, 32 years his junior.

After leaving *The Tonight Show*, McMahon brought his good-guy persona to *Star Search*, which spotlighted many up-and-coming entertainers, including Justin Timberlake, Christina Aguilera, Britney Spears, Rosie O'Donnell, and Drew Carey. As the gregarious host, he kept the show moving, the mood upbeat, and never did anything to call attention to himself. Contrast that style of hosting with current ratings champ *American Idol*, which is basically the same show with a highly tarted-up demeanor.

Star Search became one of the most successful syndicated TV programs, reaching almost 200 stations across the country. It enjoyed a 12-year run, from 1983 to 1995. Big Ed then joined Dick Clark on *TV Bloopers & Practical Jokes*. Next came a brief run as Tom Arnold's sidekick on *The Tom Show*. In a final, relatively nondescript role, he returned to radio, broadcasting *Lifestyles Live* from his home.

In his 70s, McMahon found himself cast adrift: out of work with essentially nothing to do. "My passion was broadcasting," he lamented. "And the one thing you can't do when you retire is work."

Devoid of hobbies and relegated to obscurity, McMahon had great difficulty dealing with retirement. He attempted to rein-vigorate his various business interests—with no success. His life became a soap opera, featuring a string of well-publicized legal, financial, and health problems. In 2003, he won a $7 million insurance settlement for mold that had infested his six-bedroom, five-bathroom, Beverly Hills abode. His health deteriorated rapidly after breaking his neck in a fall at a friend's house in 2007. That led to two botched spinal surgeries, leaving him unable to work. Again, more litigation.

The real shocker came in 2008, when McMahon was served a foreclosure notice for falling $644,000 behind in mortgage payments on his multimillion-dollar mansion. Real estate mogul Donald Trump tried to purchase the home and lease it back to the entertainer. That deal fell through, but—at the last hour—McMahon found a buyer to avoid foreclosure.

But there were more legal hassles. Among them, a suit for $275,168 for attorney fees in connection with a "matrimonial matter" involving his daughter from another relationship.

Appearing with his wife, Pam, on *Larry King Live* in 2008, the financially strapped former TV star acknowledged spending more money than he made. "I made a lot of money, but you can spend a lot of money," he explained. He blamed his financial woes on two expensive divorces, bad money management, and ill-advised investments. "We didn't keep our eye on the ball," his wife added. "We made mistakes."

Despite all his difficulties, the jocular Irishman was still willing to poke fun at himself, spoofing his troubles in a 2009 Super Bowl ad for Cash4Gold.com. ("I thought nothing could touch me/ until my credit went south, and debt started to crunch me.") Big Ed's enduring message: you gotta laugh—in good times and bad. This might not seem like a graceful exit for one of the most beloved figures on television, but humility remained one of McMahon's special virtues.

On June 23, 2009, TV's most famous second banana died in a Los Angeles hospital, 86 years old, following a battle with bone cancer and pneumonia. "He had a great gift," Don Rickles told *Entertainment Weekly*. "He was a magnificent straight man. People like him don't exist anymore. Another giant is gone."

CHAPTER 12

LEAVING ON TOP

"Everything has an end, only a sausage has two."

GERMAN PROVERB

DIFFICULTIES ASIDE, MOST people come to grips with bidding adieu. Brazil's popular president Luiz Inácio "Lula" da Silva, TV cohost Regis Philbin, IBM CEO Samuel Palmisano, and hotel icon J. W. Marriott Jr. all quit when they were ahead. Contrast their graceful exits with those of scandal-plagued Italian PM Silvio Berlusconi and German president Christian Wulff—as well as Republican presidential candidate Herman Cain's spectacular flameout, Penn State coach Joe Paterno's sad demise, or Brett Favre's prolonged departure from pro football.

Head first or feet first? That's the choice we are left with when contemplating when and how to leave on top. The central question, raised in the introductory chapter, remains: *Will you enjoy more— and contribute more—today and tomorrow than yesterday?* With this in mind, what have we learned about graceful exits? Here are 10 lessons, exemplified by the individuals profiled in this book.

1. KNOW THYSELF

What matters most to you? Fame? Fortune? Family? Friends? Helping others? Listen to your heart. Look at yourself as objectively as possible and analyze what's truly important.

"All truths are easy to understand once they are discovered," reasoned astronomer Galileo. "The point is to discover them." In your self-assessment, encourage full and frank feedback from others. "Honest critics can play an important role," says former Xerox CEO Anne Mulcahy. Be open and responsive to their inputs, especially the younger generation. At Infosys Technologies, India's leading IT company, chairman N. R. Narayana Murthy created brainstorming sessions called Ideation Days, led by employees under 30. Every topic—from leadership style to succession—is fair game.

Recognize, too, that it's painful calling it quits. After his years in the White House, President Franklin Pierce lamented (before dying of cirrhosis of the liver), "What is there to do but drink?" For him, everything else was anticlimactic. The single, irrefutable truth is that there comes a time when the door will close on everyone, even holders of the nation's highest office.

Think you're ready to say goodbye? Ask yourself the following hot-button questions:

- Is your heart really set on leaving, or do you want to remain in the saddle?
- Can you overcome the Superman complex, or are you too self-centered to subordinate your ego? Do you insist on being out front on every issue?
- Can you cut yourself loose from day-to-day duties and the trappings of the power—and cede responsibility to someone else?

- Can you identify and nurture potential successors, and are you willing to delegate significant responsibilities to others? What role, if any, will you play in the handover?
- Will your family, friends, and the rest of the enterprise accept your departure—and can you afford it?
- For individual contributors—athletes, entertainers, professionals—do you still have the skills and stamina to attract and retain your fan or client base?
- How excited are you about the next season of life, and have you properly prepared for it? What are your other options?
- Finally, are your goals in sync with your spouse's or partner's? Can you meld your collective needs in a new life?

If you answered yes to most of these questions, you're probably ready to leave on top. If, on the other hand, many of your answers were negatives, you should probably stay put.

2. KNOW THY SITUATION

When everything's clicking, it's easy to overstay your welcome. As we have seen, for those in entertainment and sports, yielding center stage can be especially difficult. At 71, singer-songwriter Neil Diamond has no plans of ending a 45-year marathon. "I don't think I'm ever going to stop," he admits. "It's the only challenge I have left in my life."

To be sure, many successful musicians, writers, actors, and athletes find lasting satisfaction in seeing others moved by their work. "Work is more fun than fun," Noël Coward concluded. No doubt the limos, private jets, and V.I.P. seating also can be addictive. But fame can eat its own. As Alexander Pope warned, "Walk sober off before the sprightlier age comes titt'ring on and shoves you from the stage."

After several setbacks, heavyweight champion George Foreman finally realized that bad news doesn't improve with age. Fortunately, he forged an identity independent of boxing that restored his finances and made him a rich man. Conversely, an over-the-hill Mike Tyson remained in the ring in search of just one more payday—with tragic consequences.

Situations change, and wise souls know when the magic that once underscored a great career has fizzled. Johnny Carson, faced with stage fatigue and potential burnout, knew when to call it quits. So, too, did John Calley, who after turning around Warner Bros. left the entertainment business to recharge his batteries. Wise people realize that having fun is one of the litmus tests of a meaningful career. When it evaporates, they walk away.

Those in organizational life often misread their situation. "Given the collision of pressures and challenges in business today, you'll never be on top all the time," cautions professor and senior associate dean Jeffrey Sonnenfeld of the Yale School of Management. High-flying Andrea Jung, once the longest-serving female CEO in the *Fortune* 500, saw her run as Avon chief abruptly end this year as a result of the company's lackluster growth, financial and regulatory problems, and wilting share price.

Staying power is elusive at best. Therefore, reassess the situation as conditions change. Know where you stand, and don't wait for the annual review. Even the most accomplished executives can't always be in control. They often have gone as far as ambition and ability can propel them. However, a move out of the C-suite needn't lead to misery. Look at Anne Mulcahy's joy in leading nonprofit Save the Children. Graceful exiters like Mulcahy leave on their own terms. Instead of moving away from something, they move on.

3. TAKE RISKS

Too often we're unwilling to try something new because we fear the outcome. Abandoning a lifelong calling can be downright scary. During this psychological drama, you don't need cynics and second-guessers questioning your exit strategy.

"Contrary to what you might think, preparing for the unexpected involves a little bit more than being radically open to whatever the universe sends your way," says my Honolulu neighbor and eBay founder, Pierre Omidyar. "You've got to position yourself—so when the door opens, you're close enough to squeeze through."

Don't shackle yourself to the past. Don't confine yourself to the narrow corridors of your current career. Accept change as a natural part of your transition. Life is a never-ending search for new mountains to scale. This takes courage—the courage to leave on top. As Walt Disney pointed out, "Courage is the main quality of leadership—it implies some risk, especially in new undertakings."

We have profiled several individuals who were undaunted in their willingness to break with the past. Howard Schultz, *Fortune*'s Business Person of the Year in 2011, is the consummate risk-taker. Abandoning a comfortable sales career, he acquired and transformed a neighborhood coffee shop into a global food empire. Oftentimes, though, he found it necessary to recalibrate his plans. When Starbucks began to spiral downward, he scrapped his early retirement to rescue the ubiquitous brand—and his legacy.

In similar fashion, Dr. Harry Gruber cultivated the art of making himself up as he went along. Early on, he jettisoned a promising career as a doctor and medical school professor, founding the first in a series of high-risk startups in bioscience and high-tech. Another M.D. who hung up his stethoscope was Richard

Kelley. The Harvard-trained doctor exited medicine to provide affordable hospitality for travelers from around the world.

How about Jimmy Dean, the country singer turned sausage king? He liked to say he ad-libbed his life. In his 40s he left a successful musical career to launch the Jimmy Dean Meat Company. His willingness to take significant risks and reinvent himself made the Texas poor boy a wealthy man.

Therefore, push your comfort zone. Don't be a prisoner to your current vocation. Rediscovery will expand your world. But strike out anew while you are still hardy enough to face new challenges.

4. KEEP GOOD COMPANY

To repeat, choreographing a graceful exit takes courage. It may mean sacrificing money, status, and security for a new life. It's a bit like swinging between trapezes, when you've let go of one rope but haven't yet grabbed on to the next. The space is scary—but thrilling.

You don't have to take the plunge by yourself. Reach out. Build alliances. Create a brain trust: a cadre of mentors, peers, and friends you can consult in planning your exit strategy.

"Lean on someone you can trust," wrote management expert Stephen Covey. "Good colleagues and mentors give you honest feedback. If you don't see the big picture, they can help your frame it." Red Barber, the folksy Southern gentleman, mentored broadcaster Vin Scully. To this day, Scully calls the Old Redhead "the most influential person in my life."

Stay connected. Cast a wide net, including people inside and outside your fields of interest. In plotting his return to Starbucks, Howard Schultz initially leaned on long-time friend Michael Dell, founder of the legendary PC maker. Later, he tapped a number of non-food experts to fashion the coffee-maker's resurgence.

To stretch her remarkable career, Olympic swimmer Dara Torres employed an entourage of tough taskmasters—swimming and sprint coaches, physical therapists, massage therapists, and stretchers. Her expensive, but talented, retinue had allowed the Wonder Woman of Swimming to remain competitive at the highest level.

In the movie industry, John Calley developed concentric circles of agents, filmmakers, directors, and screenwriters. Among them: Mike Nichols, Stanley Kubrick, Clint Eastwood, and Sydney Pollack. When he decided to take periodic breaks from the silver screen, he had a trusted network of advisers to call upon.

Ignore the naysayers. Keep the company of sunny characters, those with an upbeat disposition. Avoid humorless people—and, for God's sake, don't marry one. A day without laughter is a day wasted.

5. CHECK YOUR EGO AT THE DOOR

Ours is a society obsessed with celebrity, and so we have made superstars of Bill Gates, Warren Buffett, and other fascinating leaders, just as we have made legends of favored athletes, rock stars, and screen actors. While we still treat some personalities like royalty, a more egalitarian view of leadership is increasingly beginning to see them more as stewards than kings.

In this new climate, savvy leaders are abandoning the notion that the credit for every significant achievement is solely attributable to the person at the top. They understand that those fortunate enough to star or command are not gods, but the first among many contributors. Egoless people, like movie mogul Calley and hotelier Kelley, foster first-rate co-leaders, including their replacements, at every level of the organization. To them, egalitarianism isn't just a matter of style. It's a question of survival.

In addition to muffling hubris, graceful exiters function as talent spotters, always on the lookout (as Anne Mulcahy and Howard Schultz were) for able individuals who can become outstanding members of the team. As a result, trust flourished in Xerox and Starbucks. With everyone busy advancing the organization's goals, there was little time for the constant intrigue that breeds mistrust and undermines the transition process.

Mulcahy and Schultz understood the frustrations of the workplace and the strain on their once-great companies. As outstanding mentors, they made sure that good work was recognized and found ways to remove the impediments to organizational effectiveness. In the process, they developed deep cadres of potential successors that made the prospects of stepping down possible.

6. KEEP LEARNING

"Curiosity is one of the most permanent and certain characteristics of a vigorous intellect," said Samuel Johnson. Graceful exiters remain curious. They are intellectually interested, alert, and adaptable. They read, explore new places, and engage their senses. The more diverse your experiences, the better the prospects for forging a new chapter in your life.

"Educate all your parts," advises filmmaker Ken Burns. "Travel. Don't get stuck in one place. Give up addictions. Read: The book is still the greatest manmade machine of all—not the car, not the TV." You can teach old dogs new tricks—but only if they're willing to learn.

For all their shortcomings, Johnny Carson and Ed McMahon often left the comfortable nest of *Tonight*. Carson dabbled in a variety of outside ventures, from restaurants to TV stations, as well as his own post-*Tonight* production company. Second banana McMahon, for his part, not only flogged everything from

Budweiser beer to Breck shampoo, but he also hosted game shows, hit the Las Vegas nightclub scene, and appeared on Broadway. Both men got a chance to experience new pursuits—in effect, to prepare for a life after *Tonight*.

Timeless wonder Betty White also extended her career by continuously learning. Recognizing the foibles of the entertainment business, she secured her future early on as a producer, the first female to do so. Later, if one of her TV shows got axed, she refused to be demoralized—immediately reengaging in talk shows, game shows, summer-stock musicals, movies, or commercials. By continually reinventing herself, White supercharged her marvelous career.

Working virtually 24/7, Michael DeBakey also engaged in the process of continuous learning. "If creativity is just connecting things," as Steve Jobs suggested, DeBakey was unequalled in his ability to see the connections between disease and cure. For seven decades, he put his talents on display—performing multiple surgeries, publishing countless scientific articles, and inventing scores of medical procedures and instruments.

Keep your technical skills sharp. Continue to build your brand—your competitive advantage. But broaden your knowledge base. Explore new horizons. Remember it's not the road *always* traveled. It's the road *never* traveled that you have to find.

7. STAGE YOUR EXIT

The transition to what's next may take a while. Back into it. In the broadcast booth, Vin Scully and Bob Uecker got the message. Rather than fall prey to the whims of often fickle baseball owners, they slowly diversified. In the 1970s, Scully honed his credentials in a variety of other sports, from bowling to billiards and skydiving to swimming. Similarly, Uecker branched out in comedy clubs, sitcoms, movies, even beer ads. In their later years, though, both men scaled back their on-air appearances as prelude to a graceful exit. In effect, they adopted what lifestyle expert Tamara Erickson calls "decelerating roles"—scheduling work around their lives, not the other way around.

Keep in mind the Chinese proverb "A journey of a thousand miles begins with a single step." Live life incrementally. Break your departure into manageable steps. Take things bit by bit. By carefully staging your departure, you'll build confidence and create momentum for your new life.

Beware the comeback. Some strong-willed personalities have a hard time making retirement stick. For them, one goodbye is not enough. Witness Vladimir Putin's relentless crusade to regain Russia's presidency.

"What isn't yet can still become," goes an old German proverb. People seeking a return engagement try to boomerang back to their former lives. But second acts usually don't work. For every Howard Schultz, there's a Jerry Yang, Yahoo's cofounder and former CEO.

"Don't build a new ship out of old wood," Confucius said. Many comebackers get stymied by once tried-and-true strategies, when what's needed is a fresh break from the past. Recall Hall of Fame coach Joe Gibbs's modest results in his second stint with the Washington Redskins.

More often than not, encores fail, and pipe dreams can lead to disappointments. My advice: tread carefully if you're contemplating a comeback.

8. KNOW WHEN TO WALK AWAY

"In the long run, we are all dead," observed John Maynard Keynes. There is no happy ending earning a trip to a cold grave. Yet, far too often, obsessively ambitious folks make a Faustian bargain.

They give up everything else in pursuit of staying in the saddle. They lose touch with their spouses. They become strangers to their families. They turn their backs on avocations that might bring them satisfaction. Friends drop away. In extreme cases, parents are lost and barely mourned.

While many seemingly successful leaders live this way for long periods of time, they ultimately pay a terrible price. The community that supports and cares for them begins to shrink. As their legacy erodes, they fail to prepare for the next season of their lives. However brilliant they may once have been, their unbridled egos cost them soul and substance.

"Don't let making a living prevent you from having a life," warned Hall of Fame basketball coach John Wooden. Producer Calley understood this. At various stages in his career, he took sabbaticals from Hollywood's hectic pace. On one occasion, he crafted a 12-year break from the entertainment industry to reset his priorities. Similarly, to avoid burnout and the onset of diabetes, Washington Redskins coach Gibbs carefully plotted his escape from pro football to motor sports.

Certain careers, of course, are worthy of extraordinary sacrifices. Dr. DeBakey, the "Texas Tornado," worked so hard that he damaged his already precarious health in the course of trying to reduce heart disease. But in less important situations, when a profession or job becomes so demanding that it becomes a velvet coffin, it's time to say, "No More."

For example, subordinates who discover that their leader is involved in illegal or unusual behavior must counsel the chief and, if that fails, walk away. Unfortunately, in the wake of today's growing scandals, there are more and more instances of superiors who are unworthy of a decent person's loyalty.

Blind devotion often backfires. People soon discover that befriending the wrong cause—or boss—can be hazardous to one's career. Take the recent Penn State sex scandal. Mike McQueary testified that as a 28-year-old graduate assistant, he reported to head coach Paterno a possible sodomy being performed on a young boy. Then, he waited silently for retribution, which never came. In retrospect, McQueary should have blown the whistle to higher-ups and bailed. Instead, his lapse in judgment could very well taint a promising career.

Don't bend the rules to play the game. Character counts, and graceful exiters don't wimp out. In speaking truth to power, Republican deficit hawk Tom Coburn has effectively balanced personal and national interests. Using self-imposed term limits, he roils against those politicians infected with Potomac fever—and the next election.

"Go confidently in the direction of your dreams," counseled Henry David Thoreau. "Live the life you've imagined." Another common reason for leaving is a person's desire to start the next stage of life, instead of remaining in a situation that has lost its appeal. With a cache of Olympic gold safely secured, skater Eric Heiden gladly traded in the uncomfortable glare of the spotlight for a promising, but low-profile, career in sports medicine.

9. KNOW WHEN TO STAY PUT

Not everyone has to pack it in. As we mentioned in the introductory chapter, it can equally be foolish—as well as self-defeating—to leave a beloved calling prematurely. Creative output does not crest and ebb at any predetermined time. Timeless wonders like Michael DeBakey, Betty White, and John Gagliardi are cases in point. In addition, technology and genetic enhancements are propelling individuals toward the upper range of our life span. A long, healthy, and productive life awaits those who prepare for it.

If you are happy and productive, stick with your day job—the one you love. Give it your all. Remain passionate about it. Staying on "is not immoral, illegal or unethical," says leadership coach Marshall Goldsmith. "If you want to stay, and the company or any enterprise can benefit from your staying, knock yourself out! Go for it as long as you can."

10. START NOW!

"Consider what you want to do later in life while you are still young," advised anthropologist Margaret Mead. "If you associate enough with older people who enjoy their lives, who are not stored away in any golden ghettos, you will gain a sense of continuity and the possibility for a full life."

Life's prolonged course offers everyone the opportunity to chart new horizons. As Mother Teresa put it, "Life is a promise. Fulfill it!" This means setting your priorities early and putting in place the building blocks to achieve them. Don't dillydally or let procrastination steal your dreams. But dreams are nothing without action. Start now: you may not have a chance later.

Leaving on top begins when you recognize that a job, a life stage, or a relationship is over. Remember poet William Ernest Henley's words in *Invictus*:

> It matters not how strait the gate,
> How charged with punishments the scroll,
> I am master of my fate;
> I am captain of my soul.

Of course, there is no magic formula. Confronting the next chapter of a successful career represents a journey into unknown territory. Leaving on top is never easy, so get started. Don't live a deferred life plan. As Willy Loman, the joyless soul in *Death of a Salesman*, put it, "A man can't go out the way he came in. He's got to add up to something."

NOTES

Unless otherwise indicated, quotations are from interviews with the author. The following references, in chapter sequence, complement those interviews.

FOREWORD

v Winfrey is quoted in Alessandra Stanley, "The Fine Art of Quitting While She's Ahead," *New York Times*, November 21, 2009, p. C1. See too Patricia Sellers, "Oprah's Next Act," *Fortune*, October 18, 2010, p. 66; Gary Levin, "Oprah isn't quite holding her OWN," *USA Today*, March 21, 2012, p. D1, and Christopher S. Stewart, "Oprah Stuggles to Build News Network," *Wall Street Journal*, May 12, 2012, p. A1.

vi For Hemingway's sentiments, see www.write-out-loud.com.

CHAPTER 1. TIME'S UP

2 Lance Armstrong's remarks are from Christopher Clarey, "Armstrong Retires, Saying He Means It," *The International Herald Tribune*, February 17, 2011, p. 14. See too, John W. Miller, "Armstrong Crashes All But End His Tour," *Wall Street Journal*, July 12, 2010, p. D4.

3 Samuel Johnson's quote on youth is cited in Jonah Lehrer, "Fleeting Youth, Fading Creativity," *Wall Street Journal*, February 20–21, 2010, p. 13.

3 Updike's "memories impressions . . ." are from his "The Writer in Winter," *AARP The Magazine*, November/December 2008, p. 40.

3 For more on peaking early, see Jonah Lehrer, "Fleeting Youth, Fading Creativity," *Wall Street Journal*, February 20–21, 2010, p. W3. Also George Anders, "Companies Try to Extend Researchers' Productivity," *Wall Street Journal*, August 18, 2008, and Timothy Egan, "Some Peak Early, But Some Bloom Late," *The International Herald Tribune*, July 2, 2010, p. 8.

4 Ms. Bette Davis's quote is found in www.quoteshut.com.

4 Ms. Hanna's remarks on aging are from Jamie Katz, "Unleash Your Inner Genius!" *AARP The Magazine*, September/October 2010, p. 62. See too Melissa Gotthardt, "Because older brains have new strengths," *AARP The Magazine*, October 2008, p. 55, and Denise Grady, "How to Teach an Old Brain New Tricks," *New York Times*, March 8, 2012, p. F1, and Steven Greenhouse "Working Late, by Choice or Not," *The New York Times*, May 10, 2012, P. F1.

4 The Updike quote is from his "The Writer in Winter," *AARP The Magazine*, November/December 2008, p. 40. See too Terry Teachout, "When Artists Dry Up," *Wall Street Journal*, November 28–29, 2003, p. W11. Also, Malcolm Gladwell, "Late Bloomers," *The New Yorker*, October 20, 2008, pp. 1–5, and Timothy Egan, "Some Peak Early, But Some Bloom Late," *The International Herald Tribune*, July 2, 2010, p. 8.

5 Warren Bennis is cited in his *An Invented Life* (Reading, MA: Addison-Wesley, 1993), p. 154. See too Mimi Avins, "For Men, Aging's a Type-A War Zone," *Los Angeles Times*, October 3, 2005.

5 Sen. Long is cited in "Thoughts On the Business of Life," *Forbes*, February 3, 2003, p. 132.

5 Judge Holmes's quote is from Teachout, p. W11 "When an Artist Retires," *Wall Street Journal*, January 5–6, 2008.

5 Bennis's "sugarcoating" remarks are from his *An Invented Life*, p. 154.

6 Ellen Goodman's remarks may be found in her "Columnist Lets Herself Make a Graceful Exit," *Honolulu Star-Advertiser*, January

1, 2010, p. A12. See too Alina Tugend, "Fears, and Opportunities, On the Road to Retirement," *New York Times*, June 4, 2011, p. B5.

6 Mr. Otterbourg is cited in his "Time to Retread," *Kiplinger's*, April 2001, p. 102. See too his *Retire & Thrive* (Washington, DC: Kiplinger Publishing, 1999).

6 Mayor Koch's quote is from Otterbourg, "Time to Retread," p. 103. See also Edward Koch, "Why I'll Never Retire," *Bottom Line*, February 15, 2007, p. 1, and Edward Koch (with Daniel Paisner), *I'm Not Done Yet!* (New York: William Morrow and Company, 1999).

7 Paul Bowles is quoted in Christopher Sawyer-Laucanno, *An Invisible Spectator: A Biography of Paul Bowles* (New York: Weidenfeld & Nicolson, 1989), p. 62.

7 Neal Rogers's comment on Armstrong may be found in Jon Brand, "Lance Armstrong's Teflon Brand," *Christian Science Monitor*, July 19, 2010, p. 15.

7 Professor Zaleznik is cited in Myron Magnet, "You Don't Have to Be a Workaholic," *Fortune*, August 9, 1993, pp. 66–67.

8 J. B. Fuqua's remarks are from his "What's Wrong with Today's CEO?" *Chief Executive*, Spring 1987, p. 22. See also J. B. Fuqua, *How I Made My Fortune Using Other People's Money* (Atlanta, GA: Longstreet Press, 2001).

8 Churchill's remarks are from his *Thoughts and Adventures* (London: Thornton Butterworth, 1932), p. 298. For more on Churchill, including many quotes, visit www.winstonchurchill.org. See also James C. Humes, *The Wit & Wisdom of Winston Churchill: A Treasury of More Than 1,000 Quotations and Anecdotes* (New York: HarperCollins, 1994). See too William Manchester, *The Last Lion: Winston Spencer Churchill; Visions of Glory: 1874–1932* (Boston: Little, Brown, 1983), and *The Last Lion: Winston Spencer Churchill; Alone: 1932–1940* (Boston: Little, Brown, 1988).

8 Mr. Medved's comments are from his "A Question for Grads: How Do You Want Your Career to End?" *USA Today*, June 2, 2010, p. 9A.

9 George Foreman's "billion-dollar paycheck" is from his interview with Tim Dahlberg: "For Many Athletes, Retirement Is

an Uneasy, Unwanted Change," *Honolulu Star-Bulletin*, July 16, 2008, p. C2. See too David Wallis, "Help for Pro Athletes When the Cheering Stops," *The New York Times*, May 10, 2012, p. F1.

9   Martin Groder, "For Ages . . . Humans Lived 40 to 50 Years, Science Has Added Another 30 to 50 Years," *Bottom Line*, July 1, 2000, p. 9.

10 For more on Sally Ride, see my *Double Lives* (Palo Alto, CA: Davies-Black Publishing, 2002), chapter 4.

10 Ron Bass's discussion of "the business in living" is from Michael J. Bandler, "Ron Bass," *America West*, February 1999, p. 122.

10 Steve Allen is quoted in his "Blessings in Disguise," *Creative Living*, Summer 1997, p. 12.

11 Shakespeare's quote was cited in "On Leadership," *Washington Post*, November 14, 2010.

11 Del Jones's quote is from his "What Is a CEO's Secret to Longevity?" *USA Today*, December 28, 2009, p. B1.

12 Adrian King is quoted in Jeffrey Young, "The George S. Patton of Software," *Forbes*, January 27 , 1997, p. 88. See too John Marroff, "Exit, Pursued by 1,000 Bears," *New York Times*, July 30, 2001, p. C1.

14 Lee Kuan Yew is quoted in Seth Mydans, "Days of Reflection for the Man Who Defined Singapore," *New York Times*, September 11, 2010, p. A12.

14 Buffett's "love" is from Scott Patterson, "For Buffett, It Was a Very Bad Year," *Wall Street Journal*, March 2, 2009, p. C3. See too Andrew Ross Sorkin, "Delegator in Chief," *New York Times*, April 24, 2011, p. 4.

15 Charlie Chan's quote may be found in www.quoteshut.com.

15 Henry Ford is quoted in *Bottom Line*, January 1, 1998, p. 2.

16 See Tamara Erickson, *Retire Retirement* (Boston: Harvard Business School Press, 2008), and Richard J. Leider and David A. Shapiro, *Something to Live For* (San Francisco: Berrett-Koehler Publishers, 2008).

16 David Murdock's "enemy of longevity" discussion is found in Tim Talevich, "Mister Murdock's Mission," *The Costco Connection*, January 2009, p. 33. See too Frank Bruni, "Death Takes a Rain Check," *New York Times Magazine*, March 6, 2011, p. 20.

16 Disraeli's "delight" quote may be found in www.freepaperz.com.

CHAPTER 2. LETTING GO

19 The John Locke quote may be found in P. Nidditch, *An Essay Concerning Human Understanding* (Oxford, UK: Clarendon Press, 1975), p. 17.

20 John Updike's "celebrity" quote is from "The Writer in Winter," *AARP The Magazine*, November/December 2008, p. 42. See too Sam Tanenhaus, "Following John Updike's 'Paper Trail,'" *Global Issue of The New York Times*, June 23, 2010, p. 9.

20 Peter Drucker is quoted in Keith Bradsher, "A Different Sort of Scion," *New York Times*, September 20, 1998, p. B6, and Peter Drucker with Brent Schlender, "Peter Drucker Sets Us Straight," *Fortune*, January 12, 2004, p. 118.

20 Confirmation bias is discussed in Jeffrey Zaslow, "When It's Time to Pass the Baton," *Wall Street Journal*, December 2, 2009, p. D1. See too Robert Sutton, "On Stepping Down Gracefully," *Harvard Business Review*, June 2011, p. 40, and Jeffrey Hollender, "Giving Up the CEO Seat," *Harvard Business Review*, March 2010, pp. 105–109.

21 Executive turnover is variously discussed. See, for example, Jeremy Lemer, "Stress in the Executive Suite," *Financial Times*, January 4, 2011, p. 13. Also, "The Shackled Boss," *The Economist*, January 21, 2012, p. 76; Richard Hooper, "After X Years, the CEO Should Go," *The Korn/Ferry Institute Briefings*, Q3. 2012, p. 66; and Gary M. Stern, "When to Show a CEO the Door," *Investor's Business Daily*, June 11, 2012, p. A8.

21 Stanley Bing, "It Stinks to Be CEO," *Fortune*, September 6, 2010, p. 148.

21 Ms. Mulcahy's quotes are from Claudia H. Deutsch, "Near the Apex at Xerox and Loving the Hill," *New York Times*, May 13, 2000, p. B2.

22 Paul Allaire's quote is also from Deutsch, p. B2.

23 "It was like being drafted . . ." may be found in "Mulcahy Took a No-Nonsense Approach to Turn Xerox Around," *Stanford GSB News*, December 2004, p. 1.

24 "I spent the first 90 days . . ." is from Claudia H. Deutsch, "At Xerox, the Chief Earns (Grudging) Respect," *New York Times*, June 2, 2002, p. B1.

24 Mulcahy's insistence on commitment is reported in Bill George, "America's Best Leaders: Anne Mulcahy, Xerox CEO," *US News and World Report*, November 19, 2008, p. 33.

24 Ms. Levenson's quote may be found in Claudia H. Deutsch, "Xerox Reports a Profit, but Revenue Is Down 6%," *New York Times*, October 24, 2004, p. B1.

24 "Don't defend yourself . . ." is presented in George, p. 33.

25 The *Money* magazine award is cited in George, p. 33.

25 Mulcahy's Stanford Business School remarks are reported in ibid, *Stanford GBS News*, December 2004, p. 2.

25 Her "to retire at the age of 57" is from her, "Etc. Hard Choices," *Bloomberg Businessweek*, April 26–May 2, 2010, p. 136.

25 Her sentiments regarding Ms. Burns are reported in "The Recession Is Gone, and the CEO Could Be Next," *Bloomberg Businessweek*, February 7–13, 2011, p. 5. See too Ashlee Vance, "At Xerox, a Transition for the Record Books," *New York Times*, May 22, 2009, p. B1, and Mulcahy, "How I Did It . . . Xerox's Former CEO on Why Succession Shouldn't Be a Horse Race," *Harvard Business Review*, October 2010, pp. 47–51.

26 The Korn/Ferry International findings are from Frederik Balfour, with Debra Mao, "The Recession Is Gone, and the CEO Could Be Next," *Bloomberg Businessweek*, February 7–13, 2011, p. 25. See too Schumpeter, "The shackled boss," *The Economist*, January 21, 2012, p. 76.

26 For Spencer Stuart's similar results, see Joan Warner, "Route to the Top," *CEO Magazine*, January/February 2005, p. 22.

26 Booz & Company's conclusions are found in Ken Favaro, Per-Ola Karlsson, and Gary L. Neilson, "CEO Succession 2010: The Four Types of CEOs," *Strategy & Business*, Summer 2011, pp. 2–12.

26 "I loved every minute . . ." is found in her "Etc. Hard Choices," *Bloomberg Businessweek*, April 26–May 2, 2010, p. 136.

26 Her subsequent comments remarks are from "Etc. Hard Choices," p. 136. See too Alicia Clegg, "Choose Tomorrow's Leaders Today," *Financial Times*, November 11, 2010, p. 12.

27 *Fortune*'s Executive Dream Team was first reported in "The Starting Lineup," *Fortune*, September 26, 2011, p. 27.

27 F. Scott Fitzgerald's familiar quote is from his Hollywood novel *The Love of the Last Tycoon*.

27 For more on John Calley's early career, see David Owen, "Return of the Mogul," *The New Yorker*, March 21, 1994, pp. 68–86.

28 His "kids were kings" remarks are from "Biography for John Calley," www.imdb.com.

29 Mike Nichols is quoted in Christy Lemire, "Longtime Studio Chief John Calley Dies at 81," *Seattle Pilot*, September 30, 2011, p. 1.

29 Calley's discussion of Messrs. McQueen and Welles is from Owen, p. 80.

29 John Wareham is quoted in James Krohe Jr., "Breaking Free," *Across the Board*, January/February 2005, p. 34.

29 "When I left Warners . . ." is from Owen, p. 72.

30 His "vegetable" quote is from Stephen Miller, "Film Mogul Retired Early, Got Bored and Came Back," *Wall Street Journal*, September 14, 2011, p. A6. See too Dennis McLellan, "John Calley Dies at 81; Honored Studio Chief and Movie Producer," *Los Angeles Times*, September 14, 2011, p. 1.

30 "I liked the idea . . ." is reported in Owen, p. 73.

30 "Putting rouge on the corpse . . ." is found in Geraldine Fabrikant, "A Strong Debut Helps, as a New Chief Tackles Sony's Movie Problems," *New York Times*, May 26, 1997, p. C1.

30 Mr. Nichols's quote is from "Sony's Mr. Fixit," *The Daily Beast*, October 20, 1996, p. 1.

30 Calley's comments on office redecoration are reported in "A New Leading Man for Sony Pictures," *The Daily Beast*, October 13, 1996, p. 1.

31 His quotes on film-making and its talent pool are from David Ansen, "If Pigs Could Fly," *The Daily Beast*, January 21, 1996, p. 1. Also Owen, p. 73.

31 "It's my life again . . ." is found in Fabrikant, p. C1.

31 The "rolling in feathers" remarks are from Owen, p. 70. See too Brook Barnes, "John Calley, Hollywood Chief, Dies at 81," *New York Times*, September 24, 2011, p. 18.

31 "A terrific experience" quote may be found in "Biography for John Calley," www.imdb.com, p. 1.

32   "I've been lucky . . ." is discussed in McLellan, p. 2.

32   Howard Stringer's quote is from Tim Malloy and Steve Pond, "Longtime Studio Head John Calley Dies at 81," www.thewrap. com. See too Richard Natale, "John Calley, Studio Lion, Dies at 81," *Variety*, September 13, 2011, p. 2.

32   The Henry quote is found in "The Late Great John Calley: Businessman with Soul of Artist, Life Saver," www.indiewire.com.

32   Stringer's remarks are from Richard Natale, p. 2.

32   Michael Ovitz's assessment is reported in Owen, p. 68, and Stephen Miller, "Film Mogul Retired Early, Got Bored and Came Back," *Wall Street Journal*, September 14, 2011, p. A6.

32   For more on the Academy citation, see Lemire, p. 1.

32   Calley's response is found in Brook Barnes, "John Calley, Hollywood Chief, Dies at 81," *New York Times*, September 24, 2011, p. 3.

CHAPTER 3. FOUNDING FATHERS

35   The alleged de Gaulle quote on "indispensable men" is from Steve Lohr, "One Day You're Indispensable, the Next . . . ," *New York Times*, January 18, 2009. See too Steve Rattner, "The 'Great Man' Theory of Business," *Financial Times*, January 20, 2011, p. 21.

35   Steve Jobs's desire to "put a ding in the universe" is reported in "Apple: The Singular Legacy of Steve Jobs," *The Week*, September 9, 2011, p. 18, and "The magician," *The Economist*, October 8, 2011, p. 15.

36   Fidel Castro's quote may be found in Jeffrey Goldberg, "Fidel, Out of His Shell," *The Week*, September 24, 2010, p. 52. See too "A Ghost Reappears," *The Economist*, August 14, 2010, p. 29.

36   The Veijalainen quote is from Alicia Clegg, "Letting Go Is Hard to Do," *Financial Times*, May 6, 2010, p. 12. See also Jeffrey Sonnenfeld, *The Hero's Farewell: What Happens When CEOs Retire* (New York: Oxford University Press, 1988); Noam Wasserman, "The Founder's Dilemma," *Harvard Business Review*, February 2008, pp. 103–109; and Veronica Dagher, "Preparing to Leave," *Wall Street Journal*, April 30, 2012, p. R3.

36 See Schultz and Dori Jones Yang, *Pour Your Heart Into It: How Starbucks Built a Company One Cup at a Time* (New York: Hyperion, 1997), and Schultz, *Onward: How Starbucks Fought for Its Life without Losing Its Soul* (New York: Rodale, 2011).

37 His "destitute" description may be found in Melissa Thompson, "'Starbucks' Howard Schultz on How He Became Coffee King," *Sunday Mirror*, August 5, 2010, p. 1.

37 "I walked . . ." is from Jenny Wiggins, "When the Coffee Goes Wild," Financial Times, December 13–14, 2008, p. 13.

37 "The romance of the Italian coffee bar" is reported, Wiggins, p. 13.

38 Schultz, "I wanted to elevate . . ." is found in "Great Entrepreneur," www.myprimetime.com.

38 "Coffee into gold . . ." is from *Fortune* magazine cover line, August 9, 1993.

38 For more on "building a company with soul," see Tim Talevich, "The Big Four-Oh," *The Costco Connection*, April 2011, p. 30.

39 Schultz's remarks on boredom are found in his *Onward*, p. 16.

40 Professor Deshpande is quoted in Morgen Witzel and Ravi Mattu, "The Perils of a Tarnished Brand," *Financial Times*, June 24, 2010, p. 10.

40 *Wall Street Journal* piece is discussed in his *Onward*, pp. 41–42.

40 "We got swept up . . ." is from Susan Berfield, "Howard Schultz Versus Howard Schultz," *Business Week*, August 17, 2009, p. 31. See too Talevich, p. 31.

40 Schultz's feeling like an outsider is discussed in his *Onward*, p. 17.

40 His association with Michael Dell is reported in his *Onward*, pp. 48–49. See too Claire Cain Miller, "A Changed Starbucks. A Changed C.E.O.," *New York Times*, March 13, 2011, p. 1.

41 His request for commitment is described in Miller, p. 4, and his *Onward*, pp. 57–59.

41 Schultz's triumphant return is from his *Onward*, pp. 42–52. See too David A. Kaplan, "Strong Coffee," *Fortune*, December 12, 2011, p. 101.

42 The New Orleans meetings and Schultz's quotes are found in his "We Had to Own the Mistakes," *Harvard Business Review*, July–August 2010, p. 112.

43 "What leadership means . . . ," see Miller, p. 4. Also Greg Farrell, "Return of the Barista-in-Chief," *Financial Times*, March 22, 2010, p. 14.

43 "No silver bullet . . ." is from his *Onward*, p. 76.

43 Marc Greenberg's quote is reported in *Onward*, p. 326.

43 Schultz's "We have won . . ." may be found in Miller, p. 4.

43 For more on his recent initiatives, see Bruce Horovitz, "Starbucks Remakes Its Future," *USA Today*, October 18, 2010, p. B1.

44 His "little bit of insecurity" is from Melissa Thompson, "'Starbucks' Howard Schultz on How He Became Coffee King," *Sunday Mirror*, August 5, 2010, p. 4.

44 His remarks on the transformation and his legacy are reported in Wiggins, p. 2, and Joe Nocera, "We Can All Become Job Creators, *New York Times*, October 18, 2011, p. 21. See too Julie Jargon, "Starbucks Pushes to Create Jobs," *Wall Street Journal*, October 5, 2011, p. B6, and Brad Heath, "Just Say No to Politicians?," *USA Today*, September 9, 2011, p. B1.

45 For a history of the Kelley family and Outrigger Enterprises, see John W. McDermott, *Kelleys of the Outrigger* (Honolulu: ORAFA Publishing Co., 1990), and Bob Sigall, *The Companies We Keep* (Honolulu: Small Business Hawaii, 2008), pp. 235–237.

46 Frank Haas's quote is from Robbie Dingeman, "Outrigger Hotels Turns 60," *Honolulu Star-Advertiser*, May 13, 2007, p. F1.

47 The Carey quote may be found in "The Honolulu 100," *Honolulu*, November 2005, p. 4.

47 Richard Kelley's quote is from Linda Chiem, "Kelley: His Influence Led to the Growth of Waikiki," *Pacific Business News*, September 16, 2011, p. 37.

48 His remarks on the transition are reported in McDermott, p. 92. See too Russ Lynch, "The Clan Has Thrived in Isles' Tourism Industry," *Honolulu Star-Bulletin*, September 9, 2001, p. B2.

48 "Never got in each other's way" is from McDermott, p. 93.

49 Kelley's role as nonexecutive chair is described in Chiem, p. 37. See too Chiem, "Dr. Richard R. Kelley Helps Outrigger Remain 'in the Family,'" *Pacific Business News*, October 7, 2011, p. B4. See too Jim George, "We All Need to Heed Doc Kelley's Advice," *Pacific Business News*, October 14, 2011, p. 31.

50 Paul Brewbaker's quote is from Dingeman, p. F2.

50 The Carey quote is from Dingeman, p. F2.

50 Chuck Kelley is cited in Chiem, "Dr. Richard A. Kelley . . . ," p. 37.

51 See Randy Pausch and Jeffrey Zaslow, *The Last Lecture* (New York: Hyperion, 2008).

CHAPTER 4. STILL IN THE GAME

53 For more on the Gagliardi story, see Austin Murphy, *The Sweet Season* (New York: Perennial, 2001); Jim Collison, *No-How Coaching* (Herdon, VA: Capital Books, 2001); and David J. Weeres, *Just Call Me John* (St. Cloud, MN: North Star Press, 2010). See too "The Years and Victories Keep Piling Up," *New York Times*, October 15, 2006, p. 9.

55 Gagliardi's lack of a mission statement is cited in Austin Murphy, "Just Don't Call Him Coach," *Sports Illustrated*, November 17, 2003, p. 21. Also Weeres, p. 28; "The Years and Victories Keep Piling Up," p. 9; and Collison, Chapter 3.

55 His thoughts on "retirement" are from Murphy, "Just Don't Call Him Coach," p. 21.

55 "A pretty good life . . ." is from Weeres, p. 1.

56 His early coach experiments are cited in Weeres, pp. 2–4.

56 The sportswriter's quote may be found in Murphy, *The Sweet Season*, p. 103.

56 "I hated to leave . . . ," see Weeres, p. 9.

57 McNally's warning is found in Weeres, p. 10.

57 "Game of mistakes . . ." is from Collison, p. 59. See too "The Years and Victories Keep Piling Up," p. 9, and Weeres, p. 65.

58 "Real gems in the boonies," see Pat Borzi, "Needing a Map to Find a Leader," *New York Times*, December 4, 2010.

58 His comments on student-athletes are found in Collison, p. 36.

58 Paterno's quote is from Thayer Evans, "No Whistles, No Tackling and No End In Sight for St. John's Coach," *New York Times*, September 19, 2009, p. B1.

59 For a discussion of the extended longevity of other Saint John's coaches, see Andy Gardiner, "For Coaches at St. John's, No Greener Pastures," *USA Today*, February 27, 2009, p. 1B.

60 Rev. Backous's quote is from Gardiner, p. 2B. See too Wally Langfellow, "The Legend Lives On: John Gagliardi," *The Minnesota Score*, Winter 2004, p. 1.

61 "We get good kids . . ." is Collison, p. 126, and "The Small Colleges," www.sportsillustrated.asia, September 14, 1970.

61 Gagliardi's "last sacraments" remarks are found in "They Said It," www.sportsillustrated.asia, January 26, 2009. See too Evans, p. B10, and Michelle Kaufman, "The Ageless Wonders: Jack Mckeon and Other Coaches in their 80s," *Miami Herald*, June 30, 2011, p. 1.

61 Joe Gibbs's career is presented in his *Game Plan for Life*, with Jerry B. Jenkins (Carol Stream, IL: Tyndale House Publishers, 2009), and his *Racing to Win*, with Ken Abraham (Colorado Springs, CO: Multnomah Books, 2002).

61 "An examined life" is from his *Game Plan for Life*, p. 19.

62 His early "competitiveness" streak is discussed in his *Game Plan for Life*, p. 15.

63 Nicholas Dawidoff, "Bringing It Big," *The New York Times Magazine*, September 12, 2010, p. 57. See too Erik Spanberg, "NFL's Key Rookies? Men in Headsets," *The Christian Science Monitor*, September 8, 2006, p. 13.

63 "The press was calling . . ." is from Gibbs's *Racing to Win*, pp. 71–72.

63 See Michael Mink, "Bill Walsh's Football Title Rush," *Investor's Business Daily*, February 1, 2007, p. A3. See too his "Holy Macro," *Forbes ASAP*, August 26, 1996, p. 30.

64 Gibbs, *Game Plan for Life*, pp. 227–228.

64 *The Washington Post* report is cited in Gibbs's *Game Plan for Life*, pp. 227–228.

64 Gibbs's remarks on the "money trap" are from his *Game Plan for Life*, chapter 9.

64 "We lost a lot of money" is also from his *Game Plan for Life*, p. 180.

64 "God is the ultimate owner . . . ," see *Game Plan for Life*, pp. 190 and 202.

65 His desire for better work-life balance is discussed in *Game Plan for Life*, p. 21, and *Racing to Win*, p. 246.

65 Joseph Campbell's remarks are variously reported. See, for example, John M. Maher and Dennie Briggs (eds.) *An Open Life*,

Joseph Campbell in Conversation with Michael Toms (New York: Harper Perennial, 1990.)

65 "J. D. suggested . . . ," is from *Game Plan for Life*, p. 209.

65 "We had no idea . . . ," is from *Game Plan for Life*, p. 210.

65 "Our hopes were smashed . . . ," is from *Game Plan for Life*, p. 212. See too his *Racing to Win*, p. 81.

67 Gibbs's desire to coach is found in "Gibbs Deal More Lucrative Than Spurrier's," www.espn.com: NFL, January 7, 2004.

67 David A. Nadler's remarks on "encore" assignments are from his "The CEO's 2nd Act," *Harvard Business Review*, January 2007, p. 66–72.

68 Gibbs's acknowledgment of the changes in coaching are reported in *Game Plan for Life*, p. 24.

68 His comments in the wake of Sean Taylor's death are from Judy Battista, "Redskins' Gibbs Retires After a Trying Season," *New York Times*, January 9, 2008, p. B1, and *Game Plan for Life*, pp. 3, 74–75, and 301.

69 His emotional farewell from coaching is found in Les Carpenter, "Redskins' Gibbs Resigns As Coach," *The Washington Post*, January 9, 2008, p. B1. See too "Gibbs Cites Pull of Family Obligations for Retiring from Redskins," www.espn.com: NFL, January 8, 2008.

69 See Nadler, p. 72. See too "Comeback kings?" *The Economist*, January 10, 2009, pp. 55–56, and Danit Lidor and David M. Ewalt, "Celebrity Second Acts," *Forbes*, April 15, 2006, p. 21.

69 For "greatest sports figure" remark, see Dan Steinberg, "Gibbs Was Great, But Let's Not Forget Baugh and Big Train," *The Washington Post*, November 3, 2011, p. D2.

69 Rabbi Schachtel's quote is from Nick Powdthavee, "We All Want to Be Happy . . . ," *Financial Times*, August 28–29, 2010, p. 1.

69 "God is first . . ." is from Jason La Canfora, "Gibbs' Grandson Has Leukemia," *The Washington Post*, January 24, 2007, p. C1.

CHAPTER 5. FIGHTING BACK

71 The Greek proverb may be found in www.quotationspage.com.

72 See, for example, Randy Roberts, *Joe Louis* (New Haven: Yale University Press, 2010).

72 George Foreman's remarkable career is described in his (with Ken Abraham) *Knockout Entrepreneur* (Nashville: Thomas Nelson, 2009); his *George Foreman's Guide to Life* (New York: Simon & Schuster, 2002); his (with Ken Abraham) *God in My Corner* (Nashville: Thomas Nelson, 2007); his (with Joel Engel) *By George: The Autobiography of George Foreman* (New York: Villard Books, 1995); his (with Barbara Witt) *George Foreman's Big Book of Grilling, Barbecue and Rotisserie* (New York: Simon & Schuster, 2000); and his (with Cherie Calbom) *George Foreman's Knock-Out-the-Fat Barbecue and Grilling Cookbook* (New York: Random House, 1996). See too www.georgeforeman.com.

72 Foreman's description of "the Bloody Fifth" is from *Knockout Entrepreneur*, p. 162. See too his July 11, 2011, interview on "CNBC Titans," www.cnbctitans.com, and "Biography for George Foreman," www.imdb.com.

72 "We couldn't afford . . ." is from his *Knockout Entrepreneur*, pp. 162–163, and his *George Foreman's Guide to Life*, p. xiii.

73 His flag-waving incident is discussed in www.biggeorge.com.

73 His hard edge is described in Jonathan Reynolds "Licensed to Grill," *New York Times*, August 18, 2002, p. 18.

73 His discussion of his heavy spending and philandering may be found in *Knockout Entrepreneur*, pp. 23–24, 32–35, and 86–91. Also "Biography for George Foreman," www.imdb.com.

74 Foreman's quotes after his first defeat are discussed in "Biography for George Foreman," www.imdb.com, and his interview with Dena Ross, "George Foreman's Second Chance," www.beliefnet.com.

74 His economic blunders are outlined in Timothy L. O'Brien, "Fortune's Fools: Why the Rich Go Broke," *New York Times*, September 17, 2006, p. 1, section 3. See too Paul Sullivan, "In Pro Athletes' Finances, A Defensive Line Pays," *New York Times*, March 5, 2011, p. B5, and Arash Markazi, "Q&A with George Foreman," July 16, 2008, www.sportsillustratedcnn.com.

74 See Foreman, *Knockout Entrepreneur*, pp. 117–118.

75 "For all my buddies . . ." is from O'Brien, p. 1.

75 The kinder, gentler George is cited in *Knockout Entrepreneur*, pp. 82–83 and 112–118, and his interview with Ross, "George Foreman's Second Chance."

76 His disappointment after the Briggs fight is cited in *Knockout Entrepreneur*, pp. 7–9.

76 "I immediately looked . . ." is from *Knockout Entrepreneur*, p. 10. See too Nicholas Dawidoff, "When Brilliance Hits a Slump," *Wall Street Journal*, June 13–14, 2009, p. A3.

77 Foreman's insecurities are discussed in O'Brien, p. 1.

77 The Einstein quote may be found in Alice Calaprice, ed., *The Quotable Einstein* (Princeton, NJ: Princeton University Press, 1966).

77 Foreman's comments on "money" are cited in *Knockout Entrepreneur*, p. 12. See too Tim Dahlberg, "For Many Athletes, Retirement Is an Uneasy, Unwanted Change," *Honolulu Star-Bulletin*, July 18, 2008, p. C2.

77 Larry Jones's quote is from Elizabeth Jensen, "TV Land Aims to Tap Into the George Foreman in Everyone," *New York Times*, November 13, 2006, p. B14.

78 The Toole quote is cited in "Jerry Boyd, F. X. Toole," www.mightymix.blogspot.com. See his *Pound for Pound* (New York: Ecco, 2006), and *Rope Burns* (New York: Ecco, 2000).

78 "Keep answering the bell . . ." may be found *Knockout Entrepreneur*, p. 185.

78 The W. C. Heinz remarks are cited in Tim Marchman, "The Bards of Bruising," *Wall Street Journal*, February 19–20, 2011, p. C8.

78 Mike Tyson's life is described in Joe Layden, *The Last Fight* (New York: St. Martin's Griffin, 2007); Daphne Merkin, "I've Learned to Live a Boring Life," *The New York Times Magazine*, March 20, 2011, pp. 24–29; and Pablo S. Torre, "Mike Tyson," *Sports Illustrated*, August 2, 2010, pp. 74–79. Also www.miketyson.com.

78 Gordon Marino, "Finding Calm in Mike Tyson's Pigeon Coop," *Wall Street Journal*, February 26–27, 2011, p. C3, and Merkin, pp. 27–28.

78 The Layden quote is from his *The Last Great Fight*, pp. 30–31.

78 Rooney's assessment is reported in Layden, p. 32.

80 "Violent, primal, cathartic . . ." is discussed in Layden, p. 24.

80 His relative standing with Dempsey et al. is described in Graham Houston, "Which Fights Will Tyson Be Remembered For?" www.sports.espn.go.com/sports/boxing, May 17, 2010.

81 Tyson's self-professed demons are from Jon Saraceno, "Tyson: My Whole Life Has Been a Waste," *USA Today*, June 2, 2005, p. 1B.

81 The Givens quotes may be found in "Tyson and Givens' Divorce Is Official," *AP via New York Times*, www.query.nytimes.com, June 2, 1989.

81 The *Sports Illustrated* quip was also reported in Gary Smith, "The Fight of His Life," October 22, 1990.

82 Merchant's quote is from Layden, p. 200.

82 Matthew Blank is cited in Tim Arango, "Mike Tyson Film Takes a Swing at His Old Image," *New York Times*, May 11, 2008, p. 1.

83 "I want to eat your heart . . ." is reported in www.news.bbc.co.uk/sport1/boxing. See also www.boxing.about.com, March 1988.

83 His "gut you like a fish" is from www.brainyquote.com/quotes/authors/m/mike_tyson_2.html.

83 "My career's been over . . . ," see Layden, p. 255.

83 See Saraceno, p. 1B.

83 His conditioning and hatred of fighting are from Pablo S. Torre, "Mike Tyson," *Sports Illustrated*, August 2, 2010, pp. 74–79.

83 His multiple addictions are discussed in Torre, pp. 74–79; Arango, p. 1, and Saraceno, p. 1B.

84 "He slept with every kind of woman" is from Merkin, p. 29.

84 Tyson's recent transformation is discussed in his interview with Greta Van Susteren, "Mike Tyson: 'I Live a Boring Life I've Learned to Love,'" *On the Record, Fox News*, April 12, 2011; Gordon Marino, "Finding Calm in Mike Tyson's Pigeon Coop," *Wall Street Journal*, February 26–27, 2011, p. C3, and Torre, pp. 74–79.

84 "I'm totally broke . . ." is from O'Brien, op cit., pp. 8–9, and Tim Arango, p. 1. See too "Mike Tyson—Tyson; 'I'm Totally Broke,'" www.contactnews.com, May 7, 2010, and Van Susteren, "Mike Tyson: 'I Live a Boring Life I've Learned to Love'."

84 Tyson's discussion of pigeon racing is from Marino, p. C3.

85 Ms. Oates is quoted in Arango, p. 1.

85 Tyson's current sentiments and thoughts on discipline are from Van Susteren, ibid.

85 "Don't Quit," in expanded version, is presented in "Poems," *O—The Oprah Magazine*, April 2011, p. 173.

85 Tyson's remorse is from his "10 Questions," *Time*, March 14, 2011, p. 68. Also Van Susteren, ibid.

CHAPTER 6. AFTER THE GOLD

87 Chris Evert's "real life" quote is from "Thoughts on the Business of Life," *Forbes*, September 27, 2010, p. 108.

87 Leigh Steinberg's contrarian remarks may be found in Chris Ballard, "What Was He Thinking?" *Sports Illustrated*, February 14, 2011, p. 61. See too Jonathan Zimmerman, "The Dilemma of Retirement," *The Christian Science Monitor*, July 23, 2008, p. 9.

88 Nadia Comaneci's ambitions were described in Charles Schroeder, "After the Games . . . the Laundry," *The New York Times Magazine*, August 2008, p. 72. See too her *Letters to a Young Gymnast* (New York: Basic Books, 2004). Also, Christa Case Bryant, "Living the Olympic Spirit—After Retiring from Sports," *The Christian Science Monitor*, February 7, 2010, p. 27.

88 Steven Ungerleider's quote and the "golden hangover" are discussed in Benedict Carey, "After Glory of a Lifetime, Asking 'What Now?'" *New York Times*, August 18, 2008, p. A1.

88 Heiden's remarks on his early days are from his (with Massimo Testa and DeAnne Musolf) *Faster, Better, Stronger* (New York: HarperCollins, 2008), chapter 1, especially p. 10.

89 His quotes are from his *Faster, Better, Stronger*, p. 180. See too John Gettings, "1980: Heiden's Gold Heist," www.infoplease. com.

91 See Dave Kindred, "The First Man Ever to Turn Ice into Gold," *Washington Post*, February 24, 1980.

91 Heiden's sentiments were reported at "Brainy Quote," www. brainyquote.com.

91 His "nobody" quote is from Larry Schwartz, "Eric Heiden was a reluctant hero," www.espn.go.com.

92 Heiden's remarks regarding "quitting" are from "Brainy Quote," www.brainyquote.com.

93 See Heiden, op cit. Also Marci Alboher, "A Chat with an Olympic Icon, Eric Heiden," *Shifting Careers*, August 19, 2008, p. 1.

93 Heiden's "rewarding" remarks may be found in Dave D'Alessandro, "Eric Heiden Still Humble, 30 Years After Wining Five Olympic Gold medals," *New Jersey Star-Ledger*, February 24, 2010, p. 1.

93 His comments on stubbornness are from Jeré Longman, "Former Speedskating Champion Heiden Is Staying Close to the Ice," *New York Times*, October 1, 2009, p. B4. Also Philip Lee, "A Dose of Tenacity," www.portfolio.com, September 22, 2008.

93 His discussion of the transferability of sports skills to medicine are found in Longman, p. B11. See too Dennis Nishi, "Olympic Training to Become Doctors, Professors," *Wall Street Journal*, February 16, 2010, p. D6.

93 Dara Torres's remarkable career is found in her *Age Is Just a Number*, with Elizabeth Weil (New York: Broadway Books, 2009); Vicki Michaelis, "Better With Age," *USA Today*, July 25–27, 2008, p. 1A. See too Christine Brennan, "40-ish Torres, Chastain Not Calling Time," *USA Today*, April 16, 2009, p. 3C; Elizabeth Weil, "A Survivor of a Certain Age," *The New York Times Magazine*, June 29, 2008, p. 28; and Amy Shipley. "2012 Olympics: Dara Torres pursues speed for the ages, *The Washington Post*, May 25, 2012.

94 For fellow swimmer Janet Evans's comeback at 40, see Janice Lloyd, "Old and Back in the Swim," *USA Today*, August 15, 2011, p. D1, and Karen Crouse, "Back in Fast Lane on New Journey," *New York Times*, February 22, 2012, p. B11.

95 Torres's "menopause" remarks are from Brennan, p. 3C.

95 Her current "enjoyment" is also cited in Brennan, p. 3C, and "What's Driving Dara Torres," *Time*, July 24, 2008, p. 21.

95 Mark Schubert's advice is from Michaelis, p. 1A, and Michaelis, "Torres, 42, Still Rules Pool in 50," *USA Today*, July 10, 2009, p. 2C.

96 Torres's reflection on her teenage success is from *Age Is Just a Number*, pp. 1–3, chapters 4, 5, and 8.

97 Her bulimia issues are also cited in *Age Is Just a Number*, pp. 29–33, and Elizabeth Weil, "A Survivor of a Certain Age," p. 31.

97 Her issue at the 1988 Olympics is from *Age Is Just a Number*, p. 37, and Weil, "A Survivor of a Certain Age," p. 31.

97 Torres's "mission accomplished" remarks are discussed in *Age Is Just a Number*, p 43.

98 Her "emptiness" after the 2000 Olympics is from *Age Is Just a Number*, p. 67.

98 Her workout passions are discussed in Karen Crouse, "Torres Is Getting Older, but Swimming Faster," *New York Times*, November 18, 2007, p. B1. See too Katherine Hobson, "Workout Wisdom for Those Over 40," *U.S. News & World Report*, October 2009, p. 86.

99 Torres's comments on the adjustments required by older athletes are found in Gina Kolata, "Athletes Last Longer Today," *Honolulu Star-Bulletin*, August 14, 2008, p. D5; Lindsey Tannor, "Torres Shows Weekend Athletes That Advanced Age Is No Excuse," *Honolulu Star-Bulletin*, August 8, 2008, p. D2, and Jason Gay, "Revenge of the Sports Geezers," *Wall Street Journal*, May 7, 2012, p. B 14.

99 The description of her rigorous training routine is described in Weil, "A Survivor of a Certain Age," p. 32. See also Torres and Billie Fitzpatrick, *Gold Medal Fitness: A Revolutionary 5-Week Program* (New York: Broadway Books, 2010).

100 Torres's "love" of the 2008 Olympics is from *Age Is Just a Number*, p. 200.

100 Her drug testing regime is discussed in Sharon Robb, "Her Time to Shine," *South Florida Sentinel*, July 9, 2008, p. 2.

101 Coach Bauerle's "without question" assessment is from Karen Rosen, "Passion for Swimming Undying for Torres, 44," *USA Today*, December 6, 2011, p. C12: For her "really over," see Paul Newberry, "Dana Done," *Honolulu Star-Bulletin*, July 3, 2012, p. C1.

CHAPTER 7. BROADCAST NEWS

103 Ken Griffey Jr.'s quote is from Mike Dodd, "Irreplaceable Voices," *USA Today*, April 20, 2011, p. 2C. See too Matthew Futterman, "A Sportscaster's Secret Playbook," *Wall Street Journal*, January 29–30, 2011, p. C11.

104 For more on Vin Scully's career, see Curt Smith, *Pull Up a Chair: The Vin Scully Story* (Washington, DC: Potomac Books, 2009); Rich Wolfe, *Vin Scully: I Saw It On the Radio* (New York: The Lone Wolfe Press, 2009); Tim Dahlberg, "Dodgers' biggest wonder is in the broadcast booth," *Honolulu Star-Advertiser*, June 3, 2012; and Richard Sandomir, "Keeping Scully in Booth Is Dodgers' Easiest Call," *New York Times*, May 10, 2012, p. B 15.

104 Charley Steiner is quoted in Mike Dodd, "Hall of Fame Voices at NLCS," *USA Today*, October 15, 2008, p. 6C. See too Smith, p. 212.

104 Professor Cassuto's quote may be found in his "Baseball and the Business of American Innocence," *The Chronicle Review*, April 8, 2011, p. B14.

105 Scully's quotes and discussion of his youth are from Smith, Chapter 1, and Wolfe, pp. 24–25.

105 "I was walking home . . ." may be found in Tyler Kepner, "Sixty Years in Dodgers' Booth, and Still in Awe," *New York Times*, June 25, 2010, p. B11.

106 Scully's "big break" is discussed in Jerry Crowe, "The Day Vin Scully Came in from the Cold," *Los Angeles Times*, July 27, 2009, p. 27.

106 Red Barber's promise is from Crowe, p. 27.

106 Red Barber's quote is from his and Robert Creamer's *Rhubarb in the Catbird Seat* (Lincoln, NE: University of Nebraska Press, 1968), p. 261. See too Barber, *The Broadcasters* (New York: Dial Press, 1970).

106 Blanche Rickey's quote is from Crowe, p. 27, and Barber and Creamer, p. 262.

107 Scully's description of Red Barber is discussed in Smith, p. 109 and Wolfe, p. 30.

107 "Ladies and gentlemen . . ." is from Kepner, p. B11.

108 Scully's interchange with Mel Allen may be found in Kepner, p. B11.

108 His "uneasy time" is reported in Smith, p. 68.

108 "The Portable Vinny" is also discussed in Smith, p. 69.

108 "I started to feel at home . . ." is from Smith, p. 70.

108 Jim Murray's quote is reported in Smith, p. 66.

109 Scully's rejection of the Yankees' office is cited in Keith Olbermann, "Vin Scully: Voice of the Yankees," http://keitholbermann.mlblogs.com/.

109 Scully's opinion of Mel Allen is from Smith, pp. 95–96.

110 "High fly ball . . ." is reported in "Vin Scully," www.losangeles.dodgers.mld.com.

110 Tom Garfinkel's quote is from Billy Witz, "Enberg Embraces The Echoes of His Past," *New York Times*, August 8, 2010, p. 2.

110 "The nicest residual . . ." is cited in Mike Dodd, "Irreplaceable Voices," *USA Today*, April 20, 2011, p. 6C.

111 Scully's "love" of his job is found in "Season 12," *USA Today*, August 23, 2010. Also Kepner, p. B11.

111 "The roar of the crowd . . ." is from Michael Hiestand, "Keeping Score: Season 62," *USA Today*, August 23, 2010, p. 3C, and Dodd, "Irreplaceable voices," p. 6C.

111 Bob Uecker's life is discussed in Uecker and Mickey Herskowitz, *Catcher In the Wry* (New York: Jove Books, 1982). See too Mark Yost, "Bob Uecker Is Still on the Active Roster," *Wall Street Journal*, March 31, 2011, p. D10. Also Steve Rushin, "Everybody Loves Sportscasters," *Sports Illustrated*, May 23, 2011, p. 12.

112 "To last as long . . ." is from Uecker and Herskowitz, p. 4.

112 Uecker's "fortunate in the minors" quote is cited in Uecker and Herskowitz, p. 16.

112 Chuck Dressen's admonition is from Uecker and Herskowitz, pp. 5 and 25.

112 Uecker's "slumps" quote is from "Bob Uecker Quotes," www.famousquotesindex.com.

113 "The best way to catch . . ." is also reported in "Bob Uecker Quotes," www.baseball-almanac.com.

113 Uecker's sense that his playing days were over is cited in "Bob Uecker Quotes," www.baseball-almanac.com.

113 His comments on fringe athletes are from Uecker and Herskowitz, pp. 51, 71, and 87.

113 Selig's "worst scout" comment is found in Richard Sandomir, "A Master of Timing, Uecker Returns to the Booth," *New York Times*, August 14, 2001, p. B11. Also, Yost, p. D10.

113 Uecker's "yeah I did" response is from Sandomir, p. B11.

114   "I'd take my kids . . ." is cited in "No Hit, All Wit," www.sport-sillustrated.com.

114   "You feel like a part . . ." is from Sandomir, p. B11.

114   Cory Provus's quote may be found in Yost, p. D10.

115   "I'm a baseball guy . . ." is reported in Sandomir, p. B11.

CHAPTER 8. SENIOR STATESMEN

117   William Hogeland, "Our Founding Lame Duck," *New York Times*, February 18, 2008, p. A19. See too Curt Schleier, "Coolidge Knew His Exit Lines," *Investor's Business Daily*, February 20, 2007, p. A4.

118   Ms. Thatcher's comments are reported in Stefan Stern, "Business Leaders Should Exit Gracefully When the Curtain Falls," *Financial Times*, June 13, 2006, p. 8, and Stern, "The Art of the Sweetly Timed Exit," *Financial Times*, August 20, 2004, p. 6.

118   Daniel Henninger, "The Tea Party and Its Demons," *Wall Street Journal*, September 23, 2010, p. A21.

119   Pork-barreller Byrd's "love" of the senate is reported in "The Longest-Serving Senator in American History," *The Week*, July 16, 2010, p. 39.

119   The Disraeli quote may be found in Jason L. Riley, "New York Will Survive Without Bloomberg," *Wall Street Journal*, October 16, 2008, p. A15.

120   Stephen Hess is quoted in Albert R. Hunt, "Political Dynasties Are an American Tradition," *Wall Street Journal*, March 29, 2001, p. A15.

120   For more on Alexis de Tocqueville, see Clell Bryant, "Tocqueville's America," *Smithsonian*, July 2005, pp. 104–107. See also Hugh Brogan, *Alexis de Tocqueville: Prophet of Democracy in the Age of Revolution—A Biography* (New Haven: Yale University Press, 2006).

120   For more on Sen. Coburn's life, see his *Breach of Trust: How Washington Turns Outsiders Into Insiders* (with John Hart), (Nashville: WND Books, 2003). Also, Perry Bacon Jr., "The Senator Fighting Pork," *Time*, May 2, 2006, and George Will, "The Senate's Dr. No," *Washington Post*, February 12, 2006.

121 "You won't fit in . . ." is found in his *Breach of Trust*, p. 8.

121 For Coburn's rebuttal, see David Austin, "Delivering Babies and Legislation: The Anatomy of Sen. Tom Coburn's Maverick Practice of Politics," *Urban Tulsa Weekly*, January 17, 2007.

122 His return to the Senate and accompanying quotes are found in "Nose to Nose, and Glaring, Oklahoma's Senate Race," *The Economist*, October 9, 2004, p. 29.

122 "Politics are hardly ever mentioned . . . ," see Austin, p. 2.

122 His "immoral to spend" is from Perry Bacon Jr., p. 1.

123 "Stupid stuff" is cited in "Times Topics: Tom Coburn," *New York Times*, July 24, 2011, p. 1.

123 Sen. McCaskill is quoted in John King, "Interview with Senator Tom Coburn," *Real Clear Politics*, June 21, 2010, p. 3.

124 Pres. Obama's quote is from Alexander Bolton, "The President Has a Friend on Right Flank," *The Hill*, May 6, 2009, p. 3.

124 Coburn's response is also from Bolton, ibid, p. 3.

124 "I've always considered . . . ," is reported in "Times Topics: Tom Coburn," *New York Times*, July 24, 2011, p. 2. See too his (with John Hart) *The Debt Bomb: A Bold Plan to Stop Washington* (Nashville: Thomas Nelson, 2012), and "Charlie Rose talked to Sendator Tom Cogburn," *Bloombergs Business Week*, May 7–13, 2012, p. 40.

124 See "Required Reading From Senator Coburn," *New York Times*, November 17, 2011, p. A24.

124 Warren Buffett's "real statesman" description is found in Andrew Frye, "Buffett Widens Rift With Republicans by Faulting Tea Party," www.bloomberg.com, August 30, 2011.

125 The *Schindler's List* incident is reported in his *Breach of Trust*, pp. 215–217.

125 For more on the Ensign affair, see Karoun Demirjian, "Sen. Tom Coburn says 'Proud of What I Did in Ensign Case,'" *Las Vegas Sun*, May 26, 2011.

125 Coburn's quote is from Bob Gibbins, "Coburn: Time to Return to Core Values," *Tahlequah Daily Press*, August 30, 2010, p. 1.

126 The "inactive" assessment may be found in Carolyn Lochhead, "Dianne Feinstein and the Senate Age Question," www.SFGate.com, July 6, 2011. See too Richard Borreca, "Political Wisdom Suggests Akaka Should Take Early Retirement," *Honolulu Star-Advertiser*, July 10, 2011, p. F2, and David Shapiro, "U.S. Senate

Hopefuls Too Old to Ever Gain Much Seniority," *Honolulu Star-Advertiser*, March 14, 2012, p. A2.

126   See Bob Jones, "Sorry, Dan, It's Time to Step Aside," *MidWeek*, February 16, 2011, p. 8. Also Richard Borreca, "Political Wisdom Suggests Akaka Should Take Early Retirement," *Honolulu Star-Advertiser*, July 10, 2011, p. F2.

126   Akaka's announcement may be found in Derrick DePledge, "'The Right Time,'" *Honolulu Star-Advertiser*, March 3, 2011, p. A1.

126   "True ambassador . . ." is from DePledge, p. A9.

127   See Michael Keany, "Akaka vs. Case: The Political Showdown of the Year," *Honolulu*, September 2006, p. 62.

128   See "Akaka Re-Election Still Wisest Choice for Isles," *Honolulu-Star Advertiser*, September 3, 2006, p. B2.

128   See Richard Borresa, "Younger generation hasn't shown up yet in isle politics," *Honolulu Star-Advertiser*, June 12, 2012, p. A9.

128   Case's remarks are reported in Kathy Kiely, "Senators Say Age Is No Reason to Quit Running," *USA Today*, August 22, 2006, p. 4A.

128   Sen. Inouye's retort is from Kiely, p. 4A.

129   For the *Time* citation, see Massimo Calabresi and Perry Beacon Jr., "Daniel Akaka: Master of the Minor," *Time*, April 24, 2006, p. 30. See too Keany, p. 64.

130   See Jason Horowitz, "Hawaii Lawmaker Last of Senate's Liberal Lions," reported in *The Japan Times*, October 11, 2010, p. 8. See too "In History of Hawaiian Leaders, Daniel Inouye Stands Alone," www.washingtonpost.com, April 10, 2010, and Jerry Burris, "The Inouye Legacy," *Hawaii Business*, October 2009, pp. 2–27.

130   Sen. Inouye's defense is from Derrick DePledge, "Inouye Warns Akaka of Election-Aid Cuts," *Honolulu Star-Advertiser*, February 26, 2011, p. B3 and Jacy L. Youn, "Tanks a Lot," *Hawaii Business*, February 2005, pp. 24–28.

130   "Akaka Served Isles Honorably," *Honolulu Star-Advertiser*, March 3, 2011, p. A13.

131   Sen. Akaka's quote is found in DePledge, "'The right time,'" ibid, p. A9. See too Dan Boylan, "Potomac Fever Epidemic in Hawaii," *MidWeek*, September 14, 2011, p. 10.

CHAPTER 9. CREATIVE GENIUS

133   For more on the inverted U curve, see Jonah Lehrer, "Fleeting Youth, Fading Creativity," *Wall Street Journal*, February 20–21, 2010, p. W3. See too "The U-Bend of Life," *The Economist*, December 18, 2010, p. 33.

133   Cicero's "On Aging" is discussed in Joseph Epstein, "Nobody Gets Out of Here Alive," *Wall Street Journal*, January 29–30, 2011, p. C5.

134   David Brooks, "The Geezers' Crusade," *New York Times*, February 2, 2010, p. A23.

134   For more on Michael DeBakey, see "Surgery: The Texas Tornado," *Time*, May 28, 1965, p. 1; Lawrence K. Altman, "Michael DeBakey, Rebuilder of Human Hearts, Dies at 99," *New York Times*, July 13, 2008, p. 1; Robert Davis and Steve Sternberg, "Michael DeBakey, 'Best Surgeon Who Ever Lived,'" *USA Today*, July 14, 2008, p. 7D.

134   President Bush's quote may be found in Patricia Sullivan, "Michael DeBakey—Cardiac Surgery Pioneer Who Saved Thousands in His 70-year Career," *The Washington Post*, July 13, 2008, p. 1.

136   "We can't stand by . . ." is from "Surgery: The Texas Tornado," p. 2.

136   DeBakey's quotes on the likely causes of heart disease are reported in "Surgery: The Texas Tornado," p. 2.

138   His thoughts on an artificial heart are from "Surgery: The Texas Tornado," pp. 7–9.

138   "Thank God . . ." is found in Davis and Sternberg, p. 7D. See too Sternberg, "Pioneering Heart Doctor Michael Debakey Dead at 99," *USA Today*, July 15, 2008, p. 1A.

139   Dr. Ochsner is cited in Todd Ackerman and Eric Berger, "DeBakey's Death Is a Heartfelt Loss for Houston, World of Medicine," *Houston Chronicle*, July 13, 2008, p. 2.

140   "The pain was so severe . . ." is found in Sullivan, p. 1.

140   His "gratification" is reported in Lawrence K. Altman, "The Man on the Table Devised the Surgery," *New York Times*, December 25, 2006, p. 21.

140   His turnover is discussed in Cal Fussman, "What I've Learned: Michael DeBakey," http://www.esquire.com/features/whative-learned/michael-debakey-0308.

140   Dr. Nuland's quote is from Ackerman and Berger, p. 1.

140   The Bob Dylan quote is from "Wit & Wisdom," *The Week*, June 3, 2011, p. 19.

141   "A person doesn't have to be a doctor . . ." may be found in Cal Fussman, "What I've Learned: Michael DeBakey," www.esquire.com.

141   For more on multiple lives, see my *Double Lives* (Palo Alto, CA: Davies-Black Publishing, 2002). See too Janet Stites, "MDs With a Cutting-Edge Solution," *Investor's Business Daily*, February 13, 2012, p. A7.

142   Dr. Kuo's career is discussed in Milt Freudenheim, "Adjusting, More M.D.'s Add M.B.A.," *New York Times*, September 6, 2011, p. B1.

142   For more on Dr. Robbins and her quote, see Freudenheim, p. B1.

142   Dr. Bortolazzo is discussed in Joe Drape, "There's a Doctor in the Paddock," *New York Times*, August 17, 2011, p. B13.

142   Dr. Kelley's quote is from Linda Chiem, "Kelley: His Influence Led to the Growth of Waikiki," *Pacific Business News*, September 16, 2011, p. 37.

143   Dr. Prescott's quote is from Freudenheim, p. B1.

144   Dr. Gruber is quoted in Bill Meyers, "Start-Up Fever Rages Through Doctor-Inventor," *USA Today*, January 19, 1999, p. 5B.

144   "There was no other choice . . ." is found in Meyers, p. 5B.

145   Gruber's "time off" remarks are from Amy Alexander, "Going from M.D. to CEO," *Investor's Business Daily*, November 14, 2001, p. A6. See too Pete Barlas, "Doctor Turned Dot-Com Founder Returns, Focuses on Charities," *Investor's Business Daily*, May 15, 2003, p. A6.

145   "An invention doesn't count . . ." is reported in Arlene Weintraub, "The Inventor Who's Making a Business of Charity," *Business Week*, November 1, 2000, p. 23.

145   Gruber's resistance from venture capitalists is described in Meyers, p. 5B. See too Barlas, p. A6. Also Seth Love, "I Gave on the Internet," *Forbes*, October 13, 2003, p. 54.

146 His "turn-downs" is from Anne Fisher, "What's Next? Ever Wonder What You'd Do If You Sold Your Business?" *Fortune*, April 1, 2004, p. 21.

146 "We're trying to build" is found in Mike Allen, "Local Firm Builds Brain Trust Through Acquisitions," *San Diego Business Journal*, December 6, 2004, p. 5.

147 "It appears that Mr. Gruber . . ." is reported in Bruce V. Bigelow, "New CEO Plans Cutbacks to Turn Around Kintera," *San Diego Union-Tribune*, April 19, 2007, p. B1.

147 The LaBarbera quote is from Bigelow, p. B1.

147 Gruber's discussion of Tocagen's goals is from www.tocagen.com.

147 His "best of both worlds" and tribute to Edison may be found in Fisher, p. 21, and Meyers, p. 5B.

CHAPTER 10. THE ENTERTAINER: A SURVIVOR'S GUIDE

149 Jimmy Stewart's advice is cited in Michael Moore, "At the Admiral: Frankie Avalon Is Still the Big Kahuna and He Can Prove It," www.kitsapsun.com, May 28, 2011. See too Eric Felten, "In Hollywood, New Rage Against Age," *Wall Street Journal*, June 25, 2010, p. W11.

149 For more on "television's longest-working actress," see Tom Gliatto, "5 Reasons We Love Betty White, http://www.peoplestylewatch.com/people/stylewatch/package/article/0,,20332854_20338656,00.html.

150 Ms. White's "ridiculous" remarks are from "White's Surprising Renaissance," *The Week*, April 30, 2010, p. 10.

150 Her comments on "retirement" are found in Susan Wloszczyna, "White: This Dame's Still Game," *USA Today*, January 21, 2010, p. 3D, and Bob Minzesheimer, "For Betty White, It's All Happening at the Zoo," *USA Today*, November 29, 2011, p. 1B.

150 For more on Betty White's career, see her *If You Ask Me* (New York: G. P. Putnam & Sons, 2011); her *Here We Go Again* (New York: Scribner, 2011); Tom Sullivan with Betty White, *Together: A Story of Shared Vision* (Nashville: Thomas Nelson, 2008); and

Frank Bruni, "Facing Age with a Saucy Wink," *New York Times*, May 1, 2011, p. B1.

150   The "heaven" quote is from "The Early Betty White: 1947–1973—WFMU Beware of the Blog," www.blog.wfmu.org.

151   See her *Here We Go Again*, p. 99.

151   Her remarks on her two failed marriages are cited in Jeanne Dorin McDowell, "Kristen Bell, Jaime Lee Curtis, and Betty White on Sex, Love, and . . . Staying Hot," *AARP The Magazine*, September 13, 2010, p. 24.

153   Her comments regarding *Golden Palace* are from her *Here We Go Again*, p. 272.

153   Her "the oldest" comments are from Bruni, p. B11.

154   The "incurable workaholic" citation is found in Bruni, p. B11, and Stacy Jenel Smith, "AARP Goes Hollywood with Betty White," *AARP*, May 23, 2011, p. 18.

154   The "Robert Redford" remarks may be found in Wloszczyna, p. 3D.

154   White's friendship with animals is from her *Betty & Friends: My Life at the Zoo* (New York: G. P. Putnam & Sons, 2011). See too Bruni, p. B11.

154   Her advice on success in comedy is found in "White's Surprising Renaissance," p. 10.

154   Her work hours are described in McDowell, p. 24.

155   White's description of her fans are from "Betty White: U.S. Actor, The Museum of Broadcast Communications," www.museum.tv.com.

155   The advantages of old age are discussed in McDowell, p. 24.

155   Woody Allen's "not scared of dying" quote may be found in www.quoteshut.com. See too White's response from *If You Ask Me* (New York: G. P. Putnam & Sons, 2011), p. 258.

155   Ms. White's "just very grateful" is found in Smith, p. 18; her *If You Ask Me*, p. 30; and Marco R. della Cava, "Betty White keeps laughing," *USA Today*, May 20, 2011, p. 1D.

155   For more on Jimmy Dean, see his and Donna Meade Dean's, *Thirty Years of Sausage, Fifty Years of Ham* (New York: Berkley Books, 2004). See too Christine Muhlke, "Jimmy Dean: Singing for His Breakfast," *The New York Times Magazine*, December 26, 2010, p. 18.

156 His famous sausage line is variously discussed. See his and Donna Meade Dean's, *Thirty Years of Sausage*, p. 163, also pp. 180–181. See too Susan Berfield, "Obituary: Jimmy Dean," *Bloomberg Businessweek*, June 21–27, 2010, p. 23.

156 Dean's description of his mother's toughness is present on the dedication page of his and Donna Meade Dean's *Thirty Years of Sausage*. See too Bill Miller, "An Interview with the Dean of Country Music," www.thebillmillershow.com.

156 His "hard workin'" line is from a 1964 interview with *TV Guide* cited in Bruce Weber, "Jimmy Dean, Folksy Singer, Dies at 81," *New York Times*, June 14, 2010, p. 13.

156 His comments on "richness" are discussed in Muhlke, p. 18.

158 Van Morrison's "music is spiritual" quote may be found in www. quoteshut.com.

159 See Fryar Calhoun, "Hi! I'm Jimmy Dean and I'd like you to try my pure pork sausage," *Texas Monthly*, August 1983, p. 121.

159 Dean's "great deal like life" sausage quote is from Muhlke, p. 18, and Weber, p. 13.

160 His comments on "state fairs" may be found in Calhoun, p. 123.

160 Mrs. Dean's remarks are from Muhlke, p. 18.

160 The Mike Douglas incident is discussed in Calhoun, p. 206.

161 Dean's remarks on philanthropy are from Katherine Thomson, "Sausage King Donates $1 Million to Texas College," *Huffington Post*, May 20, 2008.

161 President Kennedy's well-remembered axiom was rendered in the immediate aftermath of the 1962 Bay of Pigs invasion in Cuba.

CHAPTER 11. EXIT LAUGHING

163 For more on Carson's remarkable career, see Laurence Leamer, *King of the Night* (New York: William Morrow, 1989); Fred de Cordova, *Johnny Came Lately* (New York: Simon and Schuster, 1988); Paul Corkery, *Carson: The Unauthorized Biography* (Ketchen, ID: Rand & Co., 1987); Robert Lardine, *Heeeere's Johnny* (New York: Award, 1975); Robert Metz, *The Tonight Show* (Chicago: Playboy Press, 1980); Ronald Smith, *Johnny Carson: An Unauthorized Biography* (New York: St. Martin's Press, 1987);

Stephen Cox, *Here's Johnny!* (Nashville: Cumberland House, 2002); Ed McMahon, *Here's Johnny!* (Nashville: Rutledge Hill Press, 2005); and Ed McMahon with David Fisher, *For Laughing Out Loud: My Life and Good Times* (New York: Warner Books, 1998). See too Alessandra Stanley, "An Inscrutable Alternative to Sleep," *The New York Times*, May 14, 2012, p. C12 and Dorothy Rabinowitz, "Johnny, We Hardly Knew You," *Wall Street Journal*, May 11, 2012, p. D10.

164 Carson's remarks regarding "timing" of his exit is from Leamer, p. 426. Also Cox, pp. 22–23.

164 His "heartfelt good night" is found in Kenneth Tynan, "Fifteen Years of the Salto Mortale," *The New Yorker*, February 20, 1978, p. 47. Also, Leamer, p. 430, and Cox, p. 208.

164 See "Dull Summer Months," *The Washington Post*, December 5, 1993, cited in Bill Zehme, "Johnny Carson: The Man Who Retired," *Esquire*, December 9, 2008, p. 7. Also "Biography for Johnny Carson," www.imdb.com, and Cox, p. 226.

164 Daniel Webster at the signing of the Declaration of Independence, Philadelphia, July 4, 1976.

166 "The hottest item" description is from Ed McMahon with David Fisher, p. 101.

166 McMahon's assessment is from Ed McMahon with David Fisher, p. 101, and Cox, p. 229.

167 Richard Zoglin's "saver" remarks are from his *Comedy at the Edge* (New York: Bloomsburg, 2008), p. 125. Excerpted in *Time*, January 30, 2008.

167 McMahon's remarks may be found in Ed McMahon with David Fisher, p. 165.

167 See Leamer, p. 162. Also Zoglin, p. 143.

167 Jeff Wald's quote is from Zoglin, p. 145.

168 George Burns's assessment is found in Cox, p. ix.

168 Drew Carey's quote is from Robert Bianco, "Heeeere's Johnny, in 50 years of fond memories," *USA Today*, January 6, 2012, p. 8D.

168 Carson's bantering and 1965 skit are described in Adam Bernstein, "For Decades, Comics Ruled Late-Night TV," *The*

Washington Post, January 24, 2005, p. A1. See too McMahon, *Here's Johnny!*, pp. 189–290.

168 The Letterman quote on anchoring is from Andrew Goldman, "Anchor Away," *New York Times Magazine*, April 10, 2011, p. 14.

169 See Leamer, pp. 209–10.

169 Carson's *Playboy* interview occurred in December 1967. See "Biography for Johnny Carson," www.imdb.com.

169 Tynan's "security system" is found on p. 47. See too Leamer, p. 15.

170 Carson's remarks on marriage are cited in "Johnny Carson Quotes," www.brainyquote.com.

170 Leamer, p. 427. Also, Bill Zehme, p. 7.

171 Carson's remarks are from Leamer, p. 426.

171 Jay Leno's "pretenders" is from Leamer, p. 432.

171 Steve Martin's comments may be found in Leamer, p. 432.

171 Bernstein's "second fiddle" quote is from www.leadershipnow.com.

172 Roger Rosenblatt, "The Straight Man," *Modern Maturity*, July–August 1996, p. 20.

172 McMahon "greatest job" assessment is from Richard Severo, "Ed McMahon, Top Second Banana, Dies at 86," *New York Times*, June 24, 2009, p. A13. See too Leamer, p. 145, and Ed MclMahon with David Fisher, p. 133.

172 For more on his career, see his *Here's Ed—or How to Be a Second Banana, from Midway to Midnight* (New York: Putnam, 1976); Ed McMahon with David Fisher, *For Laughing Out Loud*, and Ed McMahon, *Here's Johnny!* (Nashville: Rutledge Hill Press, 2005).

172 His "unique relationship" quote is found in his *Here's Johnny!*, pp. 4 and 26.

173 His desire to broadcast is discussed in *For Laughing Out Loud*, p. 17, and *Here's Johnny!*, p. 12. Also "The Broadcast Pioneers of Philadelphia," www.broadcastpioneers.com.

173 His "great Marine" desires are cited in James E. Wise and Anne Collier Rehill, *Stars in the Corps: Movie Actors in the United States Marines* (Annapolis, MD: Naval Institute Press, 1999), pp. 133–138.

174 McMahon's comments on his "second banana" role are from his *Here's Johnny!*, p. 118; Leamer, pp. 145, 186, and 405, and *For Laughing Out Loud*, p. 126.

174 See David Hinckley, "Ed McMahon Was TV's Everyman," *New York Daily News*, June 23, 2009, p. 1.

174 McMahon's "tight suitcase" remarks are from his *Here's Johnny!*, p. 184, and *For Laughing Out Loud*, p. 180. Also Leamer, p. 412.

175 The mosquito incident and quotes are reported in Leamer, pp. 184–185, and Severo, p. A13.

175 *Here's Johnny!*, p. 83. See too Tom Shales, "As Second Banana, Best of the Bunch," *The Washington Post*, June 24, 2009.

176 The Chanel quote is found in "Wit & Wisdom," *The Week*, May 20, 2011, p. 23.

176 McMahon's problems with retirement are from *For Laughing Out Loud*, chapter 11. See too "Ed McMahon fighting foreclosure on his Beverly Hills home," June 4, 2008, www.news.yahoo.com.

177 His post-broadcasting issues are discussed in *For Laughing Out Loud*, chapter 11. Also, see Edith Honan, "U.S. TV Star Ed McMahon Sued Over Legal Bills," July 30, 2008, www.uk.reuters.com; Ann Brenoff, "Donald Trump to Buy Ed McMahon's House," *Los Angeles Times*, August 14, 2008, p. 12; Steve Gorman, "Ed McMahon Ill With Pneumonia, February 27, 2009, www.uk.reuters.com. See too "Ed McMahon Settles Lawsuit Against Cedars," May 4, 2009, www.tmz.com.

177 The *Larry King Live* remarks are from "Ed McMahon Explains His Mortgage Mess," June 6, 2008, www.articles.cnn.com. See too Severo, p. A13.

177 Don Rickles's assessment may be found in "Ed McMahon Reimbursed by Friends and Colleagues," *New York Daily News*, June 23, 2009, p. 1. See too Anthony Venutolo, "Tonight Show Sidekick Ed Mcmahon Was Everybody's Friend," *The New Jersey Star Ledger*, June 23, 2009, p. 1.

CHAPTER 12. LEAVING ON TOP

180 Galileo's "all truths" quote may be found in www.famousquotesindex.com.

180 Ms. Mulcahy's remarks are from C.J. Prince, "When Bad Things Happen to Good CEOs," *Chief Executive*, October/November 2006, p. 53.

180 Infosys's Murthy is quoted in his "Clear Conscience—Clear Profit," *Wall Street Journal*, September 29, 2006, p. A16.

180 President Pierce's quote is from "Life after the White House," *The Week*, November 21, 2008, p. 15.

181 Neil Diamond's quote may be found in David Sheinin, "At Long Last, Validation," *The Washington Post*, December 4, 2011, p. E4. See too Sandy Cohen, "At 70, Life Is Sweet for Neil Diamond," *Los Angeles Times*, December 23, 2011, p. D23.

181 The Noël Coward quote is found in Joan Conway, "'The Light Reflects My Work,'" *Financial Times*, October 4–5, 2008, p. 11.

181 Alexander Pope is cited in Benedict Carey, "The Fame Motive," *New York Times*, August 22, 2006, p. B2. See too "Thoughts on the Business of Life," *Forbes*, February 3, 2003, p. 132.

182 Professor Sonnenfeld is cited in Carol Hymowitz, "Which CEOs Have the Skills to Survive New Year's Challenges?" *Wall Street Journal*, December 11, 2006, p. B1. See too Stefan Stern, "The Art of the Sweetly Timed Exit," *Financial Times*, August 20, 2004, p. 6.

183 Omidyar's remarks are from Al Franken, "Winning the Rat Race Sure Beats Starving," *USA Today*, May 4, 2002, p. 17A.

183 The Disney quote may be found in Richard Karlgaard, "Seven Lessons of Walt Disney," *Forbes*, December 25, 2006, p. 33.

184 See "Stephen Covey on Recharging Creativity," *USA Weekend*, November 17–19, 2000, p. 19.

184 Scully's description of Red Barber is from Curt Smith, *Pull Up a Chair: The Vin Scully Story* (Washington, DC: Potomac Books, 2010), p. 109.

186 Samuel Johnson's quote on "curiosity" is from www.thinkexist.com.

186 Ken Burns advice may be found in Franken, p. 17A.

187 Steve Jobs's comments on "creativity" are from Jon Swartz and Scott Martin, "'It's the End of an Era' at Apple," *USA Today*, August 25, 2011, p. 2D.

188 See Tamara Erickson, *Retire Retirement* (Boston: Harvard Business School Press, 2008), p. 117.

188 The German proverb may be found in Julian Baggini, "The Last Word," *The Week*, June 4, 2010, p. 44.

188 Keynes famous quote on "the long run" is from various sources; see "John Maynard Keynes," *Economist*, January 5, 2008.

189 Coach Wooden's quote is from www.quoteshut.com. See too "Remembering the Wizard," *Sports Illustrated*, June 14, 2010, p. 32.

190 The Thoreau quote is cited in "Quotes for Dreams," www.motivatingquotes.com/dreams.

191 Marshall Goldsmith's remarks are from his *Succession: Are You Ready?* (Boston: Harvard Business School Press, 2009), p. 106. See too Thomas J. Friel and Robert S. Duboff, "The Last Act of a Great CEO," *Harvard Business Review*, January 2009, pp. 82–89.

191 Ms. Mead's quote is from Richard J.Leider and David A. Shapiro, *Something to Live For* (San Francisco: Berrett-Koehler Publishers, 2008), p. 145.

191 Mother Teresa's admonishment is found in www.quoteshut.com.

191 William Everest Henley's poem "Invictus" appears in *Book of Verses* (London: D. Nutt, 1888). (*Invictus* is Latin for "unconquered.")

191 See Arthur Miller, *Death of a Salesman* (New York: Viking Press, 1949), p. 125.

INDEX

227